The American History Series

SERIES EDITORS
John Hope Franklin, *Duke University*
A. S. Eisenstadt, *Brooklyn College*

R. Kent Newmyer
UNIVERSITY OF CONNECTICUT

The Supreme Court under Marshall and Taney

SECOND EDITION

HARLAN DAVIDSON, INC.
WHEELING, ILLINOIS 60090-6000

Visit us on the World Wide Web at www.harlandavidson.com.

Library of Congress Cataloging-in-Publication Data

Newmyer, R. Kent.
 The Supreme Court under Marshall and Taney / R. Kent Newmyer.—
2nd ed.
   p. cm. — (The American history series)
 Includes bibliographical references and index.
 ISBN-13: 978-0-88295-241-3 (alk. paper)
 ISBN-10: 0-88295-241-2 (alk. paper)
 1. United States. Supreme Court—History. 2. Marshall, John, 1755–1835. 3. Taney, Roger Brooke, 1777–1864. I. Title. II. Series: American history series (Wheeling, Ill.)
 KF8742.N49 2006
 347.73'2609—dc22
                                                  2005025555

Cover illustration: John Marshall presiding over the trial of Aaron Burr. Culver Pictures.

For Rosanne Pelletier

FOREWORD

Every generation writes its own history for the reason that it sees the past in the foreshortened perspective of its own experience. This has surely been true of the writing of American history. The practical aim of our historiography is to give us a more informed sense of where we are going by helping us understand the road we took in getting where we are. As the nature and dimensions of American life are changing, so too are the themes of our historical writing. Today's scholars are hard at work reconsidering every major aspect of the nation's past: its politics, diplomacy, economy, society, recreation, mores and values, as well as status, ethnic, race, sexual, and family relations. The lists of series titles that appear on the inside covers of this book will show at once that our historians are ever broadening the range of their studies.

The aim of this series is to offer our readers a survey of what today's historians are saying about the central themes and aspects of the American past. To do this, we have invited to write for the series only scholars who have made notable contributions to the respective fields in which they are working. Drawing on primary and secondary materials, each volume presents a factual and narrative account of its particular subject, one that affords readers a basis for perceiving its larger dimensions and importance. Conscious that readers respond to the closeness and immediacy of a subject, each of our authors seeks to restore the past as an actual present, to revive it as a living reality. The individuals and groups who figure in the pages of our books ap-

pear as real people who once were looking for survival and fulfill-
ment. Aware that historical subjects are often matters of controversy,
our authors present their own findings and conclusions. Each volume
closes with an extensive critical essay on the writings of the major
authorities on its particular subject.

The books in this series are designed for use in both basic and
advanced courses in American history, on the undergraduate and gradu-
ate levels. Such a series has a particular value these days, when the
format of American history courses is being altered to accommodate
a greater diversity of reading materials. The series offers a number of
distinct advantages. It extends the dimensions of regular course work.
Going well beyond the confines of the textbook, it makes clear that
the study of our past is, more than the student might otherwise understand, at once complex, profound, and absorbing. It presents that past
as a subject of continuing interest and fresh investigation. The work
of experts in their respective fields, the series, moreover, puts at the
disposal of the reader the rich findings of historical inquiry. It invites
the reader to join, in major fields of research, those who are pondering anew the central themes and aspects of our past. And it reminds
the reader that in each successive generation of the ever-changing
American adventure, men and women and children were attempting,
as we are now, to live their lives and to make their way.

John Hope Franklin
A. S. Eisenstadt

CONTENTS

Foreword / VII
Preface and Acknowledgments / XI

CHAPTER ONE: **The Framework of Judicial Statesmanship** / 1
Limitations on Judicial Lawmaking / 6
The Potential of Judicial Statesmanship / 10
The Court and The Men and Women on It / 16

CHAPTER TWO: **John Marshall and the Consolidation of National Power** / 18
The Struggle for Judicial Power: Marbury *v.* Madison / 22
Consolidating National Power / 39
A Philosophy of National Power / 52

CHAPTER THREE: **Capitalism and the Marshall Court: Judicial Review in Action** / 55
The Marshall Court, State Power, and Agrarian Capitalism / 59
The Court and the Rise of the American Business Corporation / 70
Retreat under Fire / 79

CHAPTER FOUR: **The Taney Court: Democracy Captures the Citadel** / 89
King Andrew's Court / 92
Corporations and The Court: The New Look / 94

The Taney Court and The Commerce Clause / 101
Continuity Versus Change: The Haunting Presence of John Marshall / 108
The Case for Judicial Statesmanship / 113

CHAPTER FIVE: **The Court's Time of Troubles: Slavery, Sectionalism, and War** / 118

The Court and Slavery / 122
The Fugitive Slave Question / 123
Slavery in the Territories / 127
Enter Dred Scott / 131
Pitfalls of Judicial Discretion / 138
The War Years: The Court Survives / 142

CHAPTER SIX: **The Legacy of the Supreme Court under Marshall and Taney** / 146

Bibliographical Essay / 153
Glossary of Legal Terms / 170
The Supreme Court, 1801–1864 / 172
Index of Cases / 176
Index / 179
Illustrations follow page 88

PREFACE AND ACKNOWLEDGMENTS

In preparing the second edition of *The Supreme Court under Marshall and Taney,* I have consulted what I believe to be the best and most relevant scholarship on the antebellum Court. As a glance at the bibliography will indicate, I have also continued to rely on many of the outstanding books and articles that guided me in writing the first edition. Recent scholarship has led me to modify and refine my earlier account on a number of important points. I am pleased to say, however, that the new material has not compelled me to change the basic format of the book or modify its conceptual premise, which is that the unique contributions of the Marshall and Taney courts, when taken together, laid the foundation for the modern institution. Understanding the Court during its formative period will, I hope, provide some useful insights into its continued (and hotly debated) involvement in shaping American society.

There is nothing like writing a synthetic work to remind one of the collective and cumulative nature of historical scholarship. I am grateful to fellow historians, past and present, whose labors have made mine easier. In preparing this new edition, I would also like to thank Andrew J. Davidson for his enthusiastic and knowledgeable support. Thanks also to Lucy Herz, the production manager, for her generous assistance; to Elizabeth Demers for her excellent copy editing; to Claudia Siler, proofreader, and to Pat Rimmer, indexer. I am especially indebted to my wife, Rosanne Pelletier for her encouragement and for her keen editorial eye.

CHAPTER ONE

The Framework of Judicial Statesmanship

[The Supreme Court will] "not obtain the energy, weight and dignity which are essential to its affording due support to the National Government, nor acquire the public confidence and respect which, as the last resort of the justice of the nation, it should possess."

Chief Justice John Jay (1801)

We are under a Constitution, but the Constitution is what the judges say it is. . . .

Chief Justice Charles Evans Hughes (1907)

The Supreme Court under Chief Justices Marshall and Taney, from 1801 to 1864, spanned the formative years of the republic. During this period the American people cast off the vestiges of colonial status and laid the political and economic foundation of the modern nation-state. The Court played a significant role in this enterprise of nation-building, although it was not always victorious. For example, President Jackson's refusal to enforce the Marshall Court's Cherokee Indian decisions effectively nullified them. The Union victory in the

1

Civil War repudiated the Taney Court's *Dred Scott* decision, later over-turned by the Thirteenth and Fourteenth Amendments. Indisputably, however, the Court became an essential cog in the machinery of democratic government. Its decisions, and those of the individual justices on circuit, touched the lives of Americans in numerous and complicated ways. In the course of shaping policy, the antebellum court also defined its own powers and laid down lasting ground rules for judicial governance. John Jay's gloomy prophecy was wrong. By mid-century the justices had become the authoritative interpreters of the Constitution. The outlines of the modern Court were clearly visible.

To understand the Court's remarkable rise to power we must logically begin with a general view of judicial authority—its sources, limitations, and potential. And the first thing one encounters is ambiguity and conflict, for the fact is the American people have never been, nor indeed are they now, entirely comfortable with the Court. A quasi-aristocratic institution, whose members are appointed for life and who are not answerable directly to the people, troubles the democratic conscience. Popular suspicion is further increased by the fact that the Constitution does not explicitly grant the Court the right of judicial review—the power to negate federal and state statutes and state judicial decisions that conflict with the Constitution. The silence of the framers on such a vital point has invited some critics of the Court to deny its authority altogether. Some historians too (most prominently Edward Corwin and William Crosskey) have argued that judicial review was not intended by the framers but was instead the audacious creation of John Marshall in *Marbury* v. *Madison* in 1803.

Even the doubters, however, must concede that the Court as set forth in 1787 was no ordinary court of law. Unlike the English high courts, which developed as adjuncts to the King's household, the Constitution in Article III puts the federal judiciary with "one Supreme Court" at its head on a separate and equal footing with Congress and the executive. Life tenure for federal judges, also granted by Article III, further enhances judicial independence—not just from the political branches but from the people themselves. Yet the Court's authority, like that of the elective branches, emanates from the American people acting in their sovereign capacity in the Constitutional Convention and state ratifying conventions. The Constitution gives the Court a generous grant of power—one "altogether unprecedented in a free country," as one contemporary critic observed. Article III, which deals with the federal judiciary, divides jurisdiction into two broad categories. The first, based on subject matter, extends to all cases in law and equity arising under the Constitution, federal laws and treaties, and to all admiralty and maritime cases. The second category, based on the nature of the parties in litigation, includes controversies between citizen and citizen (provided they were from different states), between a state and a citizen of another state, between state and state, and state and nation. Cases in both categories of jurisdiction come before the Court only on appeal from the lower federal courts and from the highest courts of the states. Only cases "affecting ambassadors, other public ministers and consuls" come directly to the Court under its original jurisdiction.

The Court's power of judicial review lies at the very basis of this expansive grant of authority. The framers did not mention judicial review explicitly or define its scope, but the Constitution itself indicates that they intended some form of "judicial control," to use Charles Beard's general phrase. Article III, as noted, gives the Court final appellate authority over all cases in which the interpretation of federal law is at issue. Article VI declares that the "Constitution, and the laws of the United States which shall be made in pursuance thereof, and all treaties made, or which shall be made under the authority of the United States, shall be the supreme law of the land."

In effect, Article VI creates a hierarchy of law that the Court is bound to recognize in deciding cases. Only federal statutes "made in pursuance" of the Constitution are valid; those that are not, if the facts of the case turn on the question, are bound to be held null and void. In only two cases before the Civil War—*Marbury* v. *Madison* (1803) and *Dred Scott* v. *Sandford* (1857)—did the Court declare an act of Congress unconstitutional. But it should be noted that the Court can lay down constitutional law when it upholds statutes as well as when it voids them, providing of course that it gives a reasoned justification for its action. Indeed, as Alexander Bickel shows in his subtle discussion of the Court's powers in *The Least Dangerous Branch* (1963), the Court often bestows legitimacy on federal statutes simply by refusing to consider their constitutionality.

As it turned out, the most hotly contested issue during the ante-bellum period was not judicial review over acts of Congress, but the Court's power to review the constitutionality of state statutes and state court decisions. Ironically, the framers were fairly clear on the matter. Article VI explicitly bound "the judges in every state" to uphold the supreme law of the land, "anything in the constitution or laws of any State to the contrary notwithstanding." One could argue (although to do so defies the clear logic of Article VI) that this provision left the power to interpret federal law in the hands of state courts. However, a Congress that contained forty-four members who had taken part in either the Philadelphia Convention or one of the state ratifying conventions, clarified the matter by passing Section 25 of the Judiciary Act of 1789. Section 25 gave the Court the power to reverse or affirm judgments, brought by writ of error from state courts, that were adverse to the validity of an act of Congress. If the Supreme Court reversed a state decision adverse to the act of Congress, it struck down the state statute upheld by the state court. If the Supreme Court affirmed a state court decision that invalidated a congressional act, the Court, in fact, declared that act unconstitutional. In either case the Supreme Court claimed the final word in settling disputes between national law and state law.

Judicial review emanates not only from Articles III and VI, but indeed from the fundamental (and radical) idea of a written constitution itself. A written document embodying only general principles requires interpretation by its very nature, and interpretation has historically been the province of courts of law. A written document that proclaims itself the supreme law of the land also tapped into the eighteenth-century tradition of higher law—the belief in eternal, unchanging principles of right, knowable to humankind and binding human actions. Since the seventeenth century, the colonists had struggled to give institutional expression to this ancient doctrine in their legal codes and instruments of government. The Supremacy Clause of the Constitution was the climax of this long quest. By merging the ancient tradition of higher law with the radical new idea of a written constitution, the framers struck a blow for the legitimacy of the new government—and for the rule of law. Shaped by legal-minded pragmatists who feared anarchy as much as tyranny, the founders created, in the apt words of William Vans Murray, a government "of definition and not of trust and discretion." And one thing the framers did not trust was unbridled democracy. They believed that judicial review was a republican remedy for the democratic ills of republican government.

If a written constitution pointed towards judicial review, so did American experience with the English common law. As early as 1610, Sir Edward Coke, chief justice of the King's Bench, invalidated an Act of Parliament authorizing the College of Physicians to issue licenses to practice medicine, implying that the judicial courts were guardians of the supreme law. Coke's embryonic notion of judicial review in Dr. Bonham's case gave way in Great Britain to the supremacy of Parliament (a story told in Jack Sosin, *Aristocracy of the Long Robe,* 1989). Coke's idea, however, found fertile soil during the American Revolution when the newly independent states adopted written constitutions. On numerous occasions before 1787, American state courts invalidated legislative acts that were in violation of state constitutions, although the power to do so was nowhere explicitly granted. The delegates at Philadelphia (thirty-four of whom were lawyers) were aware of these precedents and could hardly have missed the appropriateness of judicial review to the work at hand. They also understood (as H. Jefferson Powell shows in his "The Original Understanding of Original Intent," *Harvard Law Review,* 1985) that the common-law rules of statutory interpretation that developed over the centuries aided the judges in their interpretative duties.

If the framers intended judicial review, as most scholars concede they did, they most certainly did not say what it meant. Moreover, the debate over meaning, which began in the state ratifying conventions, continues to the present day. Questions abound. When was the power of judicial review to be used? What were its limits? Were the Court's decisions final and binding on the other branches of government? And, how could they be enforced if Congress and the president opposed them? And what about the states? Article VI specifies that state judges follow the supreme law of the land, even in defiance of state law. But who will enforce the Court's decisions if states refuse to obey them, as they have on numerous occasions? Not the Courts, since as Hamilton observed in *Federalist* 78, "it has no influence over either the sword or the purse; no direction either of the strength or the wealth of the society. . . ." The president has the duty and the power to enforce the Court's decisions, but what if he chooses not to do so, as when Andrew Jackson refused to back the Marshall Court's rulings in the Cherokee cases?

And what of the American people themselves? Their representatives created the Court when they created and ratified the Constitution. In effect, the sovereign people speaking in their most deliberate and rational moment agreed to limit themselves. But would future generations understand the difference between the sovereign people speaking in solemn convention, and the people speaking through their regularly elected representatives? More to the point, would the people tolerate the anti-majoritarian power of judicial review once they embraced party-based democracy, as they did in the early nineteenth century? The answer to that question depends to some extent on the wisdom and informed judgment of the American people. Even more important, it depends on the ability of the Supreme Court to make itself indispensable by ruling wisely. In any case, the people will judge the judges. When they do so, it is important that they understand the peculiar limitations and special potential of judicial government, as well as its unique qualities of statesmanship.

Limitations on Judicial Lawmaking

Critics since Thomas Jefferson have complained that the Court's powers are political in nature—that is to say, the justices make policy for the people without being answerable to them. The Court's anti-majoritarian problem is a real one, and (as Alexander Bickel makes clear in his *The Least Dangerous Branch: The Supreme Court at the Bar of Politics*, 1962), it is also complicated. For one thing the will of the people, for various reasons, is not perfectly reflected in the political branches of government. For another, the Court is not necessarily at war with American democracy or at fundamental odds with the democratic process; indeed, it is essential to it. Moreover, if the Court makes law when deciding cases, as critics charge, it generally does so institutionally and intellectually in ways that differ from the political branches.

To begin with, the Court is limited by the "case controversy" nature of its work. The "most significant and least comprehended limitation" on judicial power, said Justice Robert Jackson, is that it proceeds solely on the basis of litigation. When the Constitutional Convention refused to bestow a general veto power on the judiciary by making it part of a council of revision, and when it defined judicial power in terms of "cases" and "controversies," it left no doubt about the matter. That the Court can speak only when confronted by "real, earnest, and vital controversies" between parties is a substantial restriction. Since issues come before the Court only when initiated by a party to a controversy, the Court has limited control over the timing of its decisions. The Court's rulings are also limited by the facts of the case since they define the scope of the Court's ruling—"the extent of its sway," to quote Justice Frankfurter. The Judiciary Act of 1925, which gives the Court wide discretion in the selection of the cases it hears through the certiorari procedure, permits the modern Court to circumvent the case-controversy limitation. But the Marshall and Taney courts had little control over their dockets, and most of the cases the Court heard contained little real potential for shaping either law or policy.

The Court's work is conditioned not only by the nature of the cases before it but by the lawyers who argue them. Lawyers are the connecting link between citizens and the state. Their briefs and oral arguments bring the facts of the case and the relevant principles of law before the judges. It follows that the skill and learning of lawyers shape the Court's law. And so also do the lawyers' social-professional connections. Equality before the law depends on equal access to legal counsel—and access has not been equal. This is not to say that poor people have never been represented. In various state jurisdictions before the Civil War, even slaves occasionally had their day in court. Dred Scott's suit for freedom altered the course of American history. Still, the fact remains that those with wealth, education, and social standing have ready access to lawyers, and thus have special access to the courts of law, including the Supreme Court. Institutions like the American Civil Liberties Union (ACLU) and the National Association for the Advancement of Colored People (NAACP) have given the poor and anonymous a new voice. But in the days of Marshall and Taney, women and blacks were not permitted to practice law, and interest-group litigation was still limited to privileged groups like the New England Mississippi Land Company or the privately controlled Second Bank of the United States. The Bank retained the exclusive services of many of the great lawyers of the age including William Wirt, the Attorney General of the United States.

The democratization of the bar in the late antebellum period did not diminish the law-making role of elite lawyers. It is a striking fact that most of the great questions of public law affecting the life of the young nation were framed for the Court by lawyers acting for private individuals and groups. Even in leading constitutional cases, the government was generally not represented, although government lawyers could bring suits to enforce national law and could appear before the Court when the United States was a party of record. But during most of the period, the Attorney General's office—the government's legal arm—was a narrowly conceived one-man operation. Until 1853, attorney generals maintained a private practice and appeared for private litigants in such leading cases as *Dartmouth College* v. *Woodward* (1819), *Cohens* v. *Virginia* (1821), *Brown* v. *Maryland* (1827), and *Luther* v. *Borden* (1849). Counsel for the government appeared in none of the great commerce clause cases of the period, although this litigation played a key role in shaping the constitutional structure of the federal system. A department of justice was not created until 1870, and not until 1937 did the government gain the general right to become a party in suits where the constitutionality of an act of Congress was questioned. Lawyers could, of course, serve the public welfare while serving private interests, but there was no assurance that they would.

The common-law character of the judicial process also limits and defines the Court's policymaking discretion. Of course, constitutional law is not the common law and the Supreme Court is not a common-law tribunal. But because the early Court had not yet developed its own institutional tradition and because the justices were all trained in the common law, they adopted large portions of its methodological and philosophical premises. These self-imposed rules derived from the common law made for consistency and worked to restrain the judge's natural inclination to read his own policy preferences into law. Nowhere was this more apparent than in the common-law principle of stare decisis, which obliges judges to follow settled precedents when the facts permit. This rule did not eliminate judicial discretion. In the early years of the republic, especially during the tenure of Chief Justice Marshall, there were few public law precedents to follow. The Taney Court had less opportunity to set precedents, but often found itself adjusting those made by the Marshall Court to fit the new democratic age. Nevertheless, stare decisis, like the other common-law rules of interpretation adopted by the Court, served to check the law-making discretion of the justices. If the Court makes law, it most often does so retail and not wholesale, as Justice Frankfurter aptly noted.

Still, because the justices are human, they sometimes succumb to the temptation to legislate rather than adjudicate. Blatant law-making, however, is risky because the Constitution makes the Court vulnerable to the political branches and ultimately to public opinion. It is true that the justices owe no formal allegiance to the presidents who appoint them. But it is also true that chief executives since George Washington have used the power of appointment to influence the Court's decisions, sometimes in crassly opportunistic ways. The Court also relies on the executive branch to enforce its decisions. Since many of the Court's decisions in the antebellum period impinged on the authority of the states, the need for executive backing was absolutely essential. Even with executive support the effect of the Court's decisions was often delayed or dissipated in various ways: by outright resistance, by diversionary legal tactics, or simply by misunderstanding the Court's ruling. The latter problem was acute in the time of Marshall and Taney because the Supreme Court Reports were not widely circulated and because communications between the Court, the state courts, and the lower federal courts was slow and cumbersome.

The Court is also limited by its dependence on Congress. The House of Representatives can impeach judges, and the Senate can try them for treason, bribery, high crimes, or misdemeanors. In certain instances, legislators can have the last word simply by legislating around the Court's decisions or by initiating amendments to undo them. Since Article III leaves the size of the Court up to Congress, that body can influence or impede the Court's work by enlarging or reducing its numbers, or by threatening to do so. Most important, a large portion of the Court's jurisdiction is at the mercy of Congress. With the exception of the constitutional grant of original jurisdiction—limited to cases "affecting ambassadors, other public ministers and consuls and those in which a state shall be a party"—all cases come to the Court by way of appellate jurisdiction "with such exceptions and under such regulations as the Congress shall make." For the most part Congress has used its authority wisely—and often with the guidance of the justices themselves. On numerous occasions, however, the Court has been reined in by congressional efforts to truncate its jurisdiction.

The Court's dependence on the political branches serves as an ever-present reminder to the justices to restrain themselves. Even more fundamentally, so does its reliance on the goodwill of the American people. Rarely does the Court defer explicitly to public opinion (which may be fortunate, since the American people have historically been surprisingly uninformed about the workings of the Constitution). Still the Court cannot ignore the fact that, as De Tocqueville observed, it "would be impotent against popular neglect or contempt of the law." Moreover, as Bruce Ackerman demonstrates, there are various ways the people can influence the Court and its law. If they are sufficiently aroused—as they were for example in 1828 and in 1968—they can elect a president who can use his power of appointment to change the Court's composition and its direction. The people also shape the law—and thus limit the Court's lawmaking capacity—in a more profound way than by opposing it: they live and work independently both of legislators and the law they make. As Willard Hurst shows (*Law and the Conditions of Freedom in the Nineteenth-Century United States*, 1956), law is only the framework within which human activity takes place. It is no substitute for human creativity. However sagacious the Court might be, it can neither make a people great, nor save a people bent on destruction.

The Potential of Judicial Statesmanship

The Court may be circumscribed by its legal character, but it is not weak in the potential of statesmanship. Indeed, the Court's "great and stately jurisdiction" calls for statesman-like judging. Judicial interpretation always involves discretion, since the generality of law can never encompass the particularity of life. This is especially true with constitutional interpretation. The framers of the Constitution intended their work to govern a growing republic, so they created only a skeletal framework of government—an anatomical rather than a physiological structure, as Justice Frankfurter observed. Often they compromised, or deliberately obfuscated, important issues in order to assure ratification. Sometimes the framers were unintentionally confusing. Where the document was general, obscure, or silent, the Court has spoken.

Not everything, of course, was unsettled, but in the crucial areas, there was considerable play in the joints. Neither the text of the Constitution nor the debates of the framers or ratifiers, for example, clearly defined the powers granted to Congress "to regulate commerce," or to make all laws which shall be "necessary and proper" for the execution of the enumerated powers. As the nation grimly discovered while grappling with the question of slavery in the decades leading to the Civil War, the power of Congress to "make all needful rules and regulations" respecting territories was subject to various conflicting interpretations. So was Article I, Section 10, which prohibited the states from "impairing the obligation of contracts," and also the Tenth Amendment, which reserved to the states those powers not delegated to the United States. Such vital subjects as corporations, railroads, and banks, were not even mentioned. Political parties—which became essential to the operation of the Constitution—were not contemplated by the founders, who equated party with faction. Obliged to make the Constitution relevant to the changing needs of the people and faced with the vagaries of the text the justices, in Justice Holmes's famous words, fell back on "the felt necessities of the time, the prevalent moral and political theories, [and] intuitions of public policy. . . ."

The Court makes its mark most obviously when it interprets the Constitution, but it also governs in less dramatic ways. The interpretation of federal statutes, for example, has always been a substantial part of the Court's work. Congressional legislation is complex and frequently ambiguous; the Court necessarily joins in the legislative process when it fills in the gaps. Cases coming under its admiralty and maritime jurisdiction, especially in the first quarter of the nineteenth century, permitted the Court to consult the ancient and elaborate body of maritime law for rules to guide American commerce. Related questions of international law governing war, peace, and neutrality gave the justices unusually wide latitude in shaping law.

Common-law questions also consumed a large portion of judicial energy in the early years—and continued to do so even after the Marshall Court ruled in 1812 that there was no federal criminal common law. Every state (except Louisiana, whose legal tradition was French) built its jurisprudence on a common-law foundation, which meant that the Court encountered common-law questions in cases coming before it under diversity of citizenship jurisdiction. Settling these disputes gave the justices a chance to clarify American private law. For some, like Justice Joseph Story, it was an opportunity rarely missed.

Listing these avenues of judicial creativity is not to suggest that the business of interpreting federal law was open-ended, or that the judges were free to follow their whims or their ideological prejudices. Congressional statutes frequently allowed little interpretive leeway. And even when statutes were imprecise and the Constitution ambiguous, bold judicial improvisation was discouraged. In construing statutes, for example, the Court could consult legislative history and/or supplementary legislation to eliminate uncertainty. As for the Constitution, many of its phrases were clarified by congressional and executive action or informed by common-law usage and rules of interpretation. And, once constitutional or statutory questions were clarified by decision, interpretive latitude was at least partially restricted by stare decisis.

Still, none of these restraints eliminate that element of judicial discretion so essential to judicial statesmanship. Issues of national law, arising in a unique federal system, were frequently not amenable to common-law construction. The Court need not defer to the constitutional interpretations of the other branches. Moreover, stare decisis does not entirely curtail interpretive latitude. Indeed, throughout the Marshall period the Court made precedents instead of following them. Moreover, as the Taney Court demonstrated, the decisions of the Marshall Court often left the door open for doctrinal adjustment. Previous decisions could even be circumvented or overruled, although doing so ran the risk of jeopardizing the Court's legitimacy. While the framers' intent and the history of the period provided the Court with interpretive guidelines, neither were definitive in the matter of interpretation. Some contemporaries, John Marshall included, believed that intent was expressed mainly in the text of the Constitution; others like James Madison turned to the ratification debates. There were other problems, too. The deliberations of the Philadelphia Convention were secret; the delegates had pledged themselves to silence and generally kept their word. The "official" *Journal of the Convention* was not published until 1819, and it was so spare as to afford little notion of what had actually occurred. Robert Yates's account, published in 1821, did little more to lift the veil. Madison's *Notes of the Debates* was not published until 1840, after many of the formative constitutional decisions (based, ironically, on intent) had been made. As the scholarship of James Hutson shows, even Madison's account left much in doubt. Moreover, the *Federalist* by Hamilton, Madison, and Jay—published in 1788 and widely read—was a pro-ratification tract rather than an impartial exposition of intent.

As a guide to interpretation, history was also notoriously permissive. It was especially vague on the fundamental question of whether the Constitution was a source of power or an instrument of limitation. The Revolutionary heritage pointed to the latter. Having waged a war against the unlimited authority of Parliament and the King, Americans and their representatives at Philadelphia had no intention of conceding the same powers to Congress and the president. At the same time, the Constitution was clearly designed to correct the debilitating lack of national power in the Articles of Confederation by enlarging, among other things, congressional authority over taxation and interstate commerce, and by making national law binding directly on American citizens. Historians have done much to clarify the multiple meanings of the document (one outstanding example being Jack Rakove's *Original Meanings*, 1996). Contemporaries, however, were more inclined to read the Constitution through spectacles of self-interest. States' rights theorists since Jefferson have seen the Constitution as a limitation on government, while nationalists perceived it as an instrument of power. The choice of interpretation soon became a matter of party division and, inevitably, of divisions among the justices themselves.

Style (the manner in which the justices wrote their opinions) was another important source of judicial statesmanship and judicial reputation. Judicial review does not simply mean saying yes or no to the parties in litigation. Unlike trial courts, whose primary purpose is settling the case at hand, the Supreme Court clarifies national law by supplying a "reasoned justification" for its decisions. In the process, the justices provide guidelines for the lower federal courts to follow and for the lawyers who argue federal cases. Judicial opinions also have the potential to educate the public about the Constitution. Indeed, as Charles Evans Hughes explained, for all practical purposes (at least until the American people themselves object), the judges' interpretation of the Constitution *is* the Constitution. To accomplish all these things, judicial opinions must, at the very least, be legally persuasive and clearly written. Great opinions embody important principles in memorable language that not only educates but inspires. Judges like John Marshall in the nineteenth century or Benjamin Cardozo in the twentieth who master the idiom of the law are the ones history remembers.

Clearly the Supreme Court is armed with enormous power. No one would argue that this power has always been used wisely—witness for example *Dred Scott*, the Court's great "self-inflicted wound." On the other hand, few would deny that the structure of the Court and its mode of operation are uniquely suited for the chore at hand. Never composed of less than six justices (nine since 1837, except for a short period during the Civil War), the Court is neither too small to preclude an enlightening clash of opinion nor too large to stifle debate or prevent agreement. Its internal rules permit, indeed demand, careful independent research and creative individual reasoning. The science of jurisprudence, bound up in the time-honored tradition of the Court, supplies the intellectual rules of the game. The responsibility of meting out justice to real people restrains careless speculation. Secrecy of conference invites open and candid deliberations, just as the publication of signed opinions encourages responsibility and excellence of craftsmanship. By giving minority justices a voice—and a chance to pioneer new law—dissents and concurrences work to keep the majority on its toes. Probably no other institution of government is better designed to speak to the rationality and morality of the American people.

The Court thus transcends many of the institutional restraints placed on it by the Constitution, including those imposed by the separation of powers. As James Madison explained in *Federalist* 51, when each of the branches performs its own function—indeed when the officeholders of each branch selfishly defend their own turf—each checks the other. Judicial review itself rests on the functional distinction established by the separation of powers. This does not mean, however, that the Court is necessarily at odds with the political branches. National government operates just as much through the mutual cooperation of the separate branches as it does through their mutual suspicions and jealousies. Although it rarely makes the headlines, the Court has generally worked in harmony with its coordinate branches. Not infrequently it takes interpretive clues from them (as Marshall did in *McCulloch* v. *Maryland* for example). Sometimes—as in *McCulloch*—the Court has expanded rather than limited the powers of Congress. When the Court supports the elected representatives in Congress and the executive branch it becomes part of the democratic process, and further enhances its own legitimacy.

The Court can also transcend the separation of powers limitation when it vocalizes the dominant values of the American public. Admittedly, there is much to put the Court and the people at odds, namely the Court's nonelective membership, its secrecy, its unfamiliar mode of operation, and its frequently obscure language. When the Court strikes down an act of Congress it defeats the will of the people, at least temporarily. For all this, however, there is a possible affinity between the people and the Court that amplifies its authority. More than the legislative and executive branches, the Court brings the power and moral authority of the government to bear directly, and often dramatically, on individuals and groups. Of all the branches, it is most closely identified with the Constitution; thus popular reverence for that sacred document accrues vicariously to the Court (as President Roosevelt discovered in 1937 when his Court-packing scheme failed). Most important, however, in adjudicating the problems of the nation, the Court may speak for, not against, the majority. When it chooses to represent the popular will, or when it takes for the foundation of its law the highest ideals of the people, the Court adds to its symbolic capital—and its ability to heal its own self-inflicted wounds.

The Court and the Men and Women on It

The Court is an institution and as such its structure, functions, and power may be analyzed abstractly. But the Court itself is not an abstraction. As Justice Frankfurter noted, "individuals, with all their diversities of endowment, experience, and outlook, determine its actions." Since humanity cannot be kept from the hallowed temple, it behooves us to ask what human qualities are in demand there, what qualities make judicial statesmen of justices.

A justice must have a mastery of the law and a deep knowledge of the workings of society. The narrow, often selfish, interests of parties before the Court must be understood in relation to history, must be projected into the future, and measured against the general welfare of the nation. That understanding, translated into legal precept, must then be brought coherently and clearly, and eloquently if possible, to the printed page. It is work for thinkers and—as Justices Holmes, Cardozo, and Frankfurter demonstrate—for the historian, philosopher, prophet, and poet. A great judge must be all these without ceasing to be a judge, that is to say, without ceasing to strive for the ideal of law—the regular, rational, and impartial administration of justice.

Few justices have possessed these high qualifications in sufficient degree to be called judicial statesmen. Even the great justices have rarely possessed all of them or have applied them with perfect consistency. And each justice has had to grapple with his or her own limitations. Thomas Reed Powell makes the point well:

> . . . Judges may have passions and prejudices as do men of lesser breed without the law. Judges argue from undisclosed assumptions, as may you and I. . . . They form their judgments after the varying fashions in which you and I form ours. They have hands, organs, dimensions, senses, affections, passions. They are warmed and cooled by the same summer and winter and by the same ideas as a layman is.

From the unavoidable intrusion of this humanity into the business of judging comes the final qualification for greatness. Oliver Wendell Holmes expressed it succinctly: Asked by a friend what his secret was, he replied simply, "Long ago I decided that I was not God." From this admission might come, as it did in Holmes' case, a skepticism about absolutes, a self-imposed judicial restraint, and a realization that the Court frequently governs best when it governs least.

Although individuals make up the Court, the student of history eventually must return to a consideration of the Court as an institution, to its collective nature. In truth, the whole is greater than the sum of its parts. Thanks in large part to the genius of Chief Justice Marshall, the opinion of the Court is the product of the private interchange of ideas among the several justices rather than the opinions of the individual justices. It almost always embodies ideas from previous conferences, from earlier opinions, indeed, from the entire historical experience of the Court. Excessive individuality, moreover, is softened by institutional responsibilities and checked by a sense of tradition and collective destiny. Brilliance of mind and artistry of expression are called forth by circumstance, to be sure. But even the greatest of the justices lean on the body of the whole Court and the ancient tradition of the law.

The complexity of judicial creativity and the difficulty of the Court's task should caution the historian against harsh judgments or anachronistic interpretations. Forewarned, then, and with a notion of what it can and cannot do, let us consider how the Court under Marshall and Taney grappled with the problems of the American people in the first sixty-four years of the nineteenth century—and how in the process they laid the foundation of the modern court.

CHAPTER TWO

John Marshall and the Consolidation of National Power

But we think the sound construction of the Constitution must allow to the national legislature that discretion, with respect to the means by which the powers it confers are to be carried into execution, which will enable that body to perform the high duties assigned to it, in the manner most beneficial to the people.

John Marshall (1819)

From Independence to the Treaty of Ghent in 1815, the overriding question in American history was whether the new nation—besieged by hostile governments without and by sectional and partisan divisions within—had sufficient power to survive. After Ghent, the question was whether the nation had enough power to achieve greatness. Though the Supreme Court under John Chief Justice Marshall (1801–1835) was as much concerned with this crucial issue as Congress and the president, it seemed most unlikely in 1801 that the Court could seriously affect the course of history.

This is not to suggest that Supreme Court history began with John Marshall. The multi-volume *Documentary History of the Supreme Court, 1789–1800* (1985–), edited by Maeva Marcus, has as-

18

sembled a vast amount of new material on the 1790s, which demonstrates conclusively that the Court was a working institution when Marshall took over the reins in 1801. For all of its progress, however, little had happened during the Court's first twelve years to contradict Hamilton's observation of 1788 "that the judiciary is beyond comparison the weakest of the three departments of power," or to allay Chief Justice Jay's fear that the Court's weakness was permanent. President Adams's appointment of John Marshall as chief justice—supported unenthusiastically even by the Federalists—did little to brighten the outlook.

Yet within ten years the Marshall Court had enlarged its authority well beyond what Hamilton or Jay could have imagined. By 1825 it had placed the powers of Congress on a broad and permanent constitutional footing. Not only did the Court enlarge national authority, but its decisions taken as a whole embodied a bold economic strategy for national greatness (the subject of Chapter Three).

The gulf between promise and accomplishment presents the first interpretive problem about the Marshall Court. And, as it usually does, contemporary discussion has established the framework for scholarly debate. The Democratic Republican party led by Thomas Jefferson, victorious in the election of 1800, was the first to weigh in, accusing Marshall of running roughshod over his weak-willed colleagues in order to make the Court an instrument of national consolidation. The Federalists, out of power in the political branches, looked to Marshall and the Court to save the republic from the rising tide of states' rights democracy. And the more the Jeffersonians inveighed against Marshall, the more heroic he became in the eyes of conservative nationalists.

Federalist hopes and Jeffersonian fears combined to create the myth of Marshall as a chief justice who completely dominated his court and used it to shape the nation. He was a natural for the heroic role. Few Americans embodied so well the values of the eighteenth and nineteenth centuries. An aristocrat by birth and political philosophy (in an age when gentlemen still ruled), he was a democrat in manner (when democracy was on the rise). Whether outracing his comrades in rare moments of leisure at Valley Forge, pitching quoits with Richmond cronies, tempting Justice Joseph Story away from his Puritan habits with a bit of Madeira, or guiding the Court in conference, his democratic demeanor, openness, humor, and natural grace made him one of the most widely revered public figures of his age. He was not a legal scholar like his colleague Story, and some historians (like David Currie), noting the result-oriented pragmatism of many of Marshall's opinions, have wondered whether he was a truly great lawyer. Some like Andrew McLaughlin have even suggested that he was a great justice because he was not a great lawyer. Unquestionably, however, he was blessed with a superbly incisive mind, an ability to listen, and a quick and often eloquent pen. At the time of his appointment he had risen to the top of Virginia's highly competitive and talented bar.

Marshall had also compiled an impressive record of service to state and nation—as a combat infantry officer during the Revolution, as a member of the Virginia House of Burgesses, as a delegate from Richmond and Henrico County to the state ratifying convention in 1788, as special ambassador to France during the XYZ negotiations in 1797, as a Congressman (at Washington's behest), and, briefly, as Secretary of State under John Adams. His knowledge of the law and devotion to the republic were beyond question. *The North American Review* (January 1836) summed up his thirty-four years as Chief Justice aptly when it observed that "one could hardly help thinking that the office was made for the man, or the man for the office."

The process of hero-worship, begun in earnest by Joseph Story in the 1830s, flourished at the end of the nineteenth century with Allan Magruder's worshipful biography in 1890 and with James Bradley Thayer's more balanced short study in 1901, and gained momentum with the centennial celebration of Marshall's ascent to the Court. The climax came with Albert Beveridge's *The Life of John Marshall*, 4 vols. (1916–1919) and Charles Warren's *The Supreme Court in United States History,* 2 vols. (1922). With prodigious documentation Beveridge unabashedly celebrated the victory of light (conservative nationalism) over darkness (Jeffersonian states' rights agrarianism). And, by sheer force of emphasis and pervasive romanticism, his biography made Marshall synonymous with the Court, depicting him as the epic hero of American nationalism. Warren's history (still one of the outstanding works on the Court) was more scholarly, more balanced, and more generous in spreading the glory to include Marshall's colleagues, but showed the same preference for conservative nationalism. In failing to analyze and explain the greatness he described, Warren leaves the impression that the Marshall Court and John Marshall were destined to be on the winning side of American history.

Recent historiography, for the most part, has not gainsaid the genius of the chief justice or the lasting achievements of his Court, but it has been both less worshipful and more analytical. In the spirit of Legal Realism of the 1930s, modern students question the formalist approach to law that removed the Court and justices from the political process, that denied judicial discretion, and that obscured meaningful historical alternatives involved in adjudication. Put simply, modern students assume the burden of putting the Marshall Court back into history, measuring its accomplishments against the potential of the historical moment. Such was the message of James Bradley Thayer's *John Marshall* (1901) and Oliver Wendell Holmes's heretical pronouncement the same year, namely that Marshall presented "a strategic point in the campaign, of history, and part of his greatness consists in his being there."

Marshall's Court and his constitutional jurisprudence, as he came painfully to understand, were not always victorious. His vision of the nation and the modern nation-state are light years apart. The reassessment—one might say the contextualization—of Marshall and the Marshall Court is taking place on various levels. Three hefty volumes on the Marshall Court in the *Oliver Wendell Holmes Devise History of the Supreme Court* series (1971–) explore the Court in unmatched detail: the decisions, the justices, the lawyers who argued, and the entire apparatus and working conditions of the Court. The definitive edition of *The Papers of John Marshall* (1974–) has made possible several new biographical studies: for example, two longer works by R. Kent Newmyer and Jean Edward Smith and two shorter studies by Herbert Johnson and Charles Hobson. Close study of the opinions themselves, their internal logic, rhetoric, and structure, also continues to yield new insights (as for example, the monographs of Robert Lowry Clinton and Sylvia Snowiss on *Marbury* v. *Madison,* and Maurice Baxter's study of the great commerce clause case of *Gibbons* v. *Ogden*). The bicentennial celebration of *Marbury* has generated numerous conferences and workshops and dozens of articles exploring every aspect of that famous decision.

This new scholarship has uncovered previously unnoticed political and economic premises as well as nuances and uncertainties of doctrine that belie the notion of a Marshall-dominated Court handing down pure law. Judicial biography is also contributing to a more sophisticated view of the Court by showing the variety of experience and complexity of motives behind decision making, and the sometimes imperceptible boundary between judicial bias and the search for objective legal principles. Several historians have called attention to the collective nature of the Marshall Court. Studies like Donald Roper's pioneering article in 1965 on the non-monolithic nature of the Marshall Court, along with Donald Morgan's *Justice William Johnson* (1954) and R. Kent Newmyer's *Justice Joseph Story* (1985) make it clear that Marshall shared authority with some very able colleagues, who left their own imprint on the Court's work. The jurisprudence of the Marshall Court, it now seems clear, was much more the product of compromise and accommodation than was once thought. The chief justice was a great leader of the Court, not because he imposed his will on it, but because he institutionalized collective decisionmaking that drew on the diverse talents of his colleagues.

All of this is to say that historians have begun to recover the multifaceted complexity of the early Court's history. Case studies and legal doctrine continue to be important, to be sure (witness for example David P. Currie's lucid treatment of case law during the Court's first hundred years). Increasingly, however, constitutional law (and private law too) is being treated as a dimension of American culture. G. Edward White's volume on the Marshall Court, for example, puts the Court in the context of republican ideology. The Court also played a pivotal role in the post-1815 "market revolution," a point emphasized in Newmyer's biography of Marshall.

The Struggle for Judicial Power: *Marbury* v. *Madison*

A full understanding of the Court must be sought in its symbiotic relationship with the rest of American history. The "campaign of history," to follow Holmes's interpretive lead, in which Marshall and his colleagues were engaged, concerned the issue of national union—and here they found abundant opportunity for creative action. It is clear in retrospect that ingredients for success were not lacking. Nationalist statesmen could count on the deep patriotism of one generation of Americans who had waged a successful national revolution, and of a second whose zeal was replenished by another war with the same enemy. Moreover, the nationalist impulse of the Revolution had been captured and institutionalized by the Federal Constitution. No serious scholar, with the possible exception of William Crosskey, has argued that the new government was monolithically national; all agree that it was the product of a compromise between localists and centrists. But it is hard to read the document closely and in comparison to the Articles of Confederation without sensing that a transformative shift had taken place—at least on paper.

Radical though it might have been, it was also rooted in practical wisdom and built from native materials, including three of its most fundamental concepts: federalism, the separation of powers, and as Jennifer Nedelsky shows, a deep respect for private property. Constitutional government was also bolstered by an inherited tradition of popular respect for legal order that had survived the upheaval of the Revolution. Both the moral authority of President Washington and a dozen successful years of nationhood gave momentum to the young republic. The security provided by three thousand miles of ocean, plus the prospect of prosperity rooted in an enterprising people and a rich continent, were additional advantages that few emerging nations possessed.

True nationhood, however, was as much potential as it was fact; even the federal Union, as the Civil War demonstrated, was not guaranteed. Indeed, many of the factors favoring nationalism contained the seeds of states' rights, beginning with the Revolution itself. If independence created the need for the Constitution, it also (as Gordon Wood shows in his *Radicalism of the American Revolution*, 1995) unleashed the social and political forces that could undercut the very foundations of the established social order on which the Constitution rested. Provincialism, with its indifference to national welfare and suspicion of national power, was also unleashed by independence. Given the diverse nature of the northern and southern states and the new West, the pursuit of economic happiness could just as easily divide the nation as unite it. The same is true of continental expansion, as the talk of New England separatism in the 1780s suggests.

Buffeted by these centrifugal forces, it was far from certain whether the nation could last. Conceivably it might do so on terms other than those laid down at the Philadelphia Convention. More likely though, if national union was not attained with the Constitution of 1787, it would not be attained at all. The future of the republic, then, rested on the capacity of that document to contain and accommodate the forces of political, economic, and intellectual change, and harness them to the national purpose. A crucial question—and a great unknown in 1801—was how and by whom the Constitution would be interpreted.

The new chief justice understood full well what was at stake, as did the new president. The two Virginians had already taken measure of one another and neither liked what they saw. Jefferson, convinced that the Marshall Court was a Federalist battering ram, vowed to "eradicate the spirit of Marshallism." Marshall, who had been appointed to keep Jefferson's party from vitiating the new Constitution, promised not to "disappoint his friends."

To succeed he would have to consolidate the interpretive authority of the Court. Fortunately, he did not have to start from scratch. As the scholarship of Julius Goebel, Jr., William Casto, and others has shown, the Jay and Ellsworth Courts had begun to build constructively on the generous grant of power in Article III. The early Court was aided, too, by the Judiciary Act of 1789 and the Process Acts of the early 1790s, which successfully established the structure and procedure of the federal judiciary, including the Supreme Court. With the help of Congress and the support of President Washington (who looked on the Court "as the Key-stone of our political fabric"), the Court began to consolidate its position as a separate and independent branch of the government. For example, when Congress passed an act in 1792 requiring the justices on circuit to pass on the validity of certain pensioners' claims stemming from the Revolution, the justices objected strenuously on the grounds that such duties were not "properly judicial." Justices James Wilson and John Blair, on circuit in Pennsylvania, went a step further by boldly refusing to obey the act and informing President Washington that it was unconstitutional.

A year later the Court struck another blow for judicial independence, this time against executive encroachment, when it refused to render certain advisory opinions requested by the president. Most important, the justices established precedents for judicial review, first while riding circuit when they voided several state statutes in conflict with the Constitution, and then en banc in *Ware* v. *Hylton* (1796), when they voided a Virginia law confiscating Tory property as a violation of the Treaty of 1783. Finally, in *Hylton* v. *United States* (1796), the Court considered whether a Virginia statute taxing carriages violated the Constitution itself, specifically Article I, Section 3, which required direct taxes to be "apportioned among the several states." Although the justices upheld the act, the case confirmed the widely held belief that the Court had the authority to strike down acts of Congress in violation of the Constitution.

In the process of defining its own authority, the Jay and Ellsworth Courts came out resolutely in support of the conservative nationalist policies of the Washington and Adams Federalists. As Casto shows, this was neither surprising nor accidental, since Washington and Adams appointed justices who resisted state efforts to diminish national authority. In fact, almost all of the Court's important decisions in the 1790s cut into state sovereignty—and none more forcefully than *Chisholm* v. *Georgia* (1793), where the Court held that a state could be sued against its will in a federal court by a private citizen of another state. (The decision was never enforced because of the Eleventh Amendment, which prohibited such suits, and because of the outright resistance of Georgia.) The Court's interpretation of international law and neutral rights and its recognition of a federal criminal common law (that is, a body of federal crimes not specified by statute) added further to national authority and also to the growing distrust of the Court by the states' rights party of Thomas Jefferson. These policies and the axioms of interpretation used to justify them—the contract clause of the Constitution, the doctrine of natural law limitations on legislative power, and the notion of the Court as the constitutional voice of the sovereign people—were all part of the historical legacy passed down to the Marshall Court.

Looking at the accomplishments of the first decade and focusing only on the text of the Court's opinions, one might conclude that judicial authority was solidly established when Marshall took over. In the larger context of the first decade, however, it was clear that such was not the case. The Court claimed the power of judicial review, to be sure, but the Virginia and Kentucky Resolutions of 1798 (written by Madison and Jefferson respectively) insisted that the sovereign states, not the Court, had the power to settle constitutional disputes. Congress got in the act, too, and in fact Congress, not the Court, was at the center of constitutional development during the first dozen years of the new government. It was Congress, in the Judiciary Act of 1789, that established the entire system of federal courts. The first ten amendments to the Constitution—the famous Bill of Rights—was the work of Congress. The first debate over implied powers (concerning the constitutionality of Hamilton's proposed national bank) took place in Congress and in the president's cabinet. The first debate over the president's treaty-making authority took place in the House of Representatives (during the debate over the Jay Treaty in 1795). The Eleventh Amendment, which overturned the Court's decision in *Chisholm,* was initiated by the states and passed by Congress on its way to ratification in 1798. Other constitutional issues—the president's removal power, for example, and questions about the meaning of the First Amendment raised by the Alien and Sedition Acts—were settled by legislative action, not judicial decision. This is not to say that the Court's powers of judicial review in the 1790s were inconsequential, but rather that the Court had no monopoly on constitutional interpretation, and no claims to finality. Separation of powers was obviously a work in progress.

Nothing was settled, least of all the Court's prestige—as a look at its slender docket reveals. The Court had been open for business for a year and a half before deciding a case. By 1801 it had decided only sixty-some cases—averaging less than one case of real significance each year. As the rapid turnover in membership and the difficulty of finding talented replacements indicated, aspiring statesmen did not see the Court as the place to make their mark. Twelve men had served there prior to 1801. Five, including two chief justices, had resigned, and five others, including John Marshall, had declined appointments. By 1800, the Court was adrift. Most if not all of the truly outstanding jurists—James Wilson, James Iredell, Oliver Ellsworth—were gone. Those remaining were a mixed lot: William Paterson was perhaps the ablest all around; Samuel Chase was brilliant, but his ability was frequently negated by political intemperance; Marshall's close friend Bushrod Washington was more than able; William Cushing, very able when well, was frequently ill; and Alfred Moore was all but invisible, writing only one opinion during his five-year tenure. Significantly, none of Marshall's first colleagues possessed qualities of leadership that might have caused them to challenge him.

On top of its other woes, the Court found itself involved on the losing side in the bitter political battles of the day. The Democratic-Republicans, having gained the presidency and both houses of Congress in the election of 1800, were in a position to humble the Court. By their own reckoning, they had ample justification for doing so. The Court's conservative nationalist jurisprudence put it at odds with the states' rights democracy of the emerging Jeffersonian Republicans. Chief Justices Jay and Ellsworth both had served as special foreign emissaries for the Federalist Party during their tenures—a fact Republicans interpreted as another mark of judicial partisanship. The enthusiasm with which Federalist judges enforced the Sedition Act of 1798 against Republican critics also aroused bitter resentment, as did their refusal to consider the Act's constitutionality. The anti-Jeffersonian political harangues that Justice Chase delivered from the bench brought these feelings to a boil. Finally, there was the Judiciary Act of 1801. If a formal declaration of war between the Marshall Court and the new administration was necessary, this was it. Passed by the lame-duck Federalist Congress, the Act enlarged the jurisdiction of the federal courts at the expense of state judiciaries, created sixteen new circuit judgeships for Federalists, and reduced the Supreme Court from six members to five so that President Jefferson would not be able to fill the next vacancy. The gauntlet was down.

The question facing the new chief justice in 1801 was not so much whether his Court would build on the accomplishments of the first decade, as whether it would be permanently humbled by "the revolution of 1800," as Jefferson called his election. One thing was clear: immediate action was imperative lest judicial weakness become an institutional habit. The Court had few offensive weapons in its arsenal. Its vulnerability to the aroused Republican forces, moreover, made dramatic action inadvisable.

Marshall escaped this dilemma by quietly reforming—indeed transforming—the internal working procedures of the Court. Relying on the unifying effect of Republican threats, the Federalist sympathies of his colleagues, and his own charisma, Marshall persuaded his associates to abandon seriatim opinions for a single majority opinion written by one justice. That justice most often was John Marshall. From 1801 to 1805, he wrote twenty-four of the Court's twenty-six opinions; the other two were cases on which he did not sit because they had come up from his own circuit. During this period there were no dissents and only one separate opinion. Up to 1810, Marshall had written 147 of 171 opinions, including all the important ones. The appointment of stronger minds to the Court was soon to reduce Marshall's dominance. But what remained unchanged was the fact that the Court now spoke with one voice. Until it did, it could not claim to be the authoritative interpreter of the Constitution.

But unity alone was not enough. What the Court needed was a victory—and this seemed most unlikely. During Marshall's first two years, the Court had decided only seven cases and there had not been a significant one since 1798. Moreover, the Republican juggernaut had begun to roll. In 1802, in the midst of ominous anti-Court rhetoric, the Judiciary Act of 1801 was repealed, returning the judiciary to the system of 1789. On the heels of the repeal came another bill establishing new terms for the Court—in effect adjourning it for fourteen months (from December 1801 to February 1803). During this time, the Republicans sharpened their impeachment weapons and talked of wholesale slaughter.

There was the possibility, of course, that the Court might take the offensive itself and invalidate the Judicial Repeal Act of 1802 (on the grounds that eliminating the new circuit courts created by the Act of 1801 violated the life tenure provisions of the newly appointed circuit judges). Ultra-Federalists, including Marshall's colleague Justice Chase, imprudently urged it to do so. But fortunately for the Court, John Marshall was more intrigued with the unemployment problem of William Marbury. Back in February 1801, the Federalists had passed a bill authorizing President Adams to create as many justices of the peace for the District of Columbia as he thought expedient. Forty-two offices were created and, at the last minute, filled with trustworthy Federalists. When Secretary of State Madison assumed his new duties on March 5, he found the commissions duly signed, sealed, and ready for delivery. President Jefferson ordered his friend Madison not to deliver the commissions, though he later commissioned thirty justices of the peace, including twenty-three of those nominated by Adams. During the December 1801 term, Marbury and three other dispossessed officials requested a writ of mandamus from the Court ordering Madison to show cause why he should not be compelled to deliver their commissions.

Marbury v. *Madison* (1803) clearly was not one of those cases born great. If it promised anything, it was disaster, for the facts seemed to lead the Court to a fateful confrontation with Republican power. Should the Court issue the writ and Madison and Jefferson ignore it, judicial power would be humbled. If the Court refused to issue the writ, the Republicans—and the executive department, for it was also a struggle between departments—would win by default.

Marshall, following the new procedure, spoke on behalf of the unanimous Court. His most famous opinion was compelling in its apparent simplicity, its rhetoric, and its tone of absolute assuredness. The key questions (which Marshall borrowed from attorney Charles Lee's argument) and the Court's answers amounted to one paragraph: Had Marbury a right to his commission? If so, did the law afford him a remedy? If it did, was the remedy a mandamus issued by the Court? Affirmative replies to the first two questions seemingly painted the Court into a corner. A negative reply to the third, justified by Marshall's unique reasoning, however, not only allowed it to escape humiliation but turned retreat into victory. The Court cannot issue a writ of mandamus, declared the Chief Justice, because the power to do so (granted in Section 13 of the Judiciary Act of 1789) was an unconstitutional enlargement of original jurisdiction—a subject defined by the Constitution itself in Article III, and thus not subject to congressional authority. And *Marbury* was an original jurisdiction case. Accordingly, the Court had no choice, Marshall declared, but to void Section 13 as an unconstitutional exercise of congressional power. William Marbury had lost his job, and the Supreme Court consolidated its authority to review acts of Congress by striking one down.

Behind the facade of simplicity was some legal maneuvering that must have caused Jefferson to wonder whether the judicial branch really was a good place to bury his old enemy. Marshall's first move was to reverse the regular order of Lee's questions (warning him there would be "some departure in form" from the points stated in argument). Had he considered the jurisdictional issue first, he could have disposed of the case without ruling on Section 13. The case was brought directly to the Court under its original jurisdiction, and original jurisdiction as defined by Article III was limited to cases "affecting ambassadors, other public ministers and consuls, and those in which a State shall be a party." Being none of these, Marbury had no standing to sue.

Instead of treating the jurisdictional issue first, however, Marshall addressed the questions dealing with Marbury's legal rights and remedies. And these questions led directly to the president's decision to withhold the commissions (a decision he apparently grounded on the assumption that they were not legally binding until they had been delivered). Citing common-law principles for authority, Marshall ruled that the commissions were legal once they had been signed by President Adams.

In short, Marbury was not asking the Court to create a right but to protect one that already existed—and protecting private rights, as Marshall pointed out, was the defining duty of courts of law from time immemorial. In the course of explaining all this, Marshall not so subtly reminded Jefferson that even the president of the United States was not above the law. It was a lecture Jefferson would not forget—or forgive—and one Marshall surely would not have dared give to Washington or Adams.

After the lecture, striking down Section 13 seemed almost anticlimactic. It did matter of course that the Court voided an act of Congress on constitutional grounds since it was the first time it had done so. What mattered most, however, was Marshall's reasoned justification for judicial review. The substance of his argument generally followed Hamilton's *Federalist* 78, which Marshall had read in preparation for his defense of judicial review in the Virginia ratifying convention. The justification was simple and "long and well established." The "original and supreme will" of the sovereign people created the written Constitution, which is the supreme and paramount law of the land. That Constitution made the Court a *legal* institution and as such imposed on it the burden of explaining what that law was. All else followed. If the legislature passed an act in conflict with the supreme law of the Constitution, the Court, in deciding a case properly before it, had no choice but to uphold the Constitution and void the act. The duty was imposed on the Court by the sovereign people themselves; not to perform it would be "immoral." In the midst of such obvious truths, the central question of whether Section 13 was really in conflict with the Constitution was all but forgotten—at least until the Jeffersonians came to understand the real meaning of judicial review (which they did when they read Marshall's opinion in *McCulloch* v. *Maryland* in 1819).

Marbury is the Court's best known opinion—the one universally taught in law schools and college courses, and the one most frequently cited by the Court itself when it needs to bolster its authority. It is also one of the most controversial, and most of the controversy (echoing arguments from Marshall's own time) centers on whether his opinion should be taken seriously as law or whether it was merely (perhaps even cynically) politics masquerading as law.

Scholars who consider the opinion to be political point to the indisputable fact that Marshall salvaged victory from defeat—and that he did so by a strategy so effective that it must have been calculated. For example, his opinion made judicial review seem both unavoidable and innocuous. As it applied to original jurisdiction cases, Section 13 was of small overall importance. In any case, it was a judicial matter (which even Jefferson conceded was within the proper ambit of judicial review). Indeed, voiding it appeared to be an act of judicial self-denial—especially when six days later *Stuart* v. *Laird* sustained the constitutionality of the Republican Repeal Act of 1802. Marshall's emphasis on the doctrine of limited national government, moreover, reminded the Jeffersonian opposition that judicial review was congenial with their own small government philosophy. Indeed, the brunt of the Republican attack on the decision in 1803 was not against the principle of judicial review but against Marshall's brusque censure of the president—further evidence to some that Marshall was a master manipulator. Finally, adding further to this image was the argument (developed most fully by Edward Corwin and repeated over the years by other scholars) that Marshall need not have voided Section 13 at all, but did so cynically in order to reach the question of judicial review. Rather than void that section, the argument goes, the chief justice might simply have ruled that the mandamus provision of that section was not an unconstitutional enlargement of original jurisdiction but merely a power incident to it.

While it is pointless to deny the political dimensions of the case, there are sound reasons for avoiding the harsh judgment of Corwin and company—starting with the fact that Marshall did not create the political situation that threatened his Court. Neither did he manipulate the case in order to create judicial review—for the simple reason that judicial review was already widely accepted by parties of all persuasions in 1803. And what about Corwin's contention that Section 13 did not really enlarge original jurisdiction—and therefore did not have to be voided? While not implausible, it ignores the fact that Charles Lee argued strenuously that Section 13 authorized Congress to expand original jurisdiction—and that Congress had in fact done so. In responding to arguments of counsel, Marshall did what judges in the common-law tradition regularly did. Moreover, he laid to rest an interpretation of original jurisdiction that was in clear violation of the framers' intent.

Nor should the impact of Marshall's decision on the doctrine itself be overestimated. It is true that *Marbury* was the first time the Court actually voided an act of Congress on constitutional grounds, and Marshall's justification combined with that fact gave some traction to the doctrine that it never had before. But Marshall never claimed finality for the Court's decisions, never claimed that they were binding on the other branches, and never broached the question of enforcement. One thing he certainly did not do (despite voiding an act of Congress) was to pit himself or the Court against the general powers of Congress (which he championed throughout his career). Not until *Dred Scott* in 1857 did the Court strike down another act of Congress. Saying "no" to Congress in 1803, however, gave authority to the Court when it said "yes"—which it subsequently did with great regularity. Ironically, it was when the Court *upheld* the authority of Congress in *McCulloch* v. *Maryland* (1819) that the full meaning of judicial review became apparent.

Marshall's mandamus decision may not have changed the course of constitutional history, as the myth makers insisted, but it was nevertheless a constructive "coup" (a word used by both Beveridge and Corwin). For the first time the Supreme Court, speaking in a single voice, struck down an act of Congress and, primarily because of Marshall's strategic good sense, made good its claim.

The greatness of *Marbury*, in short, was not that it advanced the doctrine of judicial review but rather that it consolidated a beachhead in hostile territory—one from which further advances could be made. Marshall's goal was survival rather than aggrandizement. By saying no more than history would allow and by knowing what *not* to say, he kept Republican moderates on his side, isolating the radicals who wanted to destroy the Court. The timing was crucial. Had the Court waited longer to assert its authority, its weakness might have become habitual.

All this is to argue that *Marbury* was not an act of judicial aggression (as is often said) but rather a holding action that bought the Court time. It was also the opening battle of a long war of survival with Jefferson. And because of the impending impeachment campaign against Federalist judges, it was uncertain in 1803, and for two years thereafter, whether the mandamus opinion was a victory hymn or a swan song. Republicans had threatened removals since the late 1790s, and now they meant to act. Federal District Judge John Pickering, who unwisely mixed alcohol with his Federalism, was the first to go. In 1805, Justice Samuel Chase was impeached for misconduct in the sedition trial of James Callender as well as in the treason trial of John Fries, and for his anti-Jefferson political harangues to grand juries in Delaware and Baltimore. It was a decisive moment, for as John Quincy Adams noted, the whole Court, "from the first establishment of the national Judiciary," was on trial.

Chase's acquittal (helped by a brilliant defense team and inept Republican management) rested finally on the recognition that he was guilty not of "treason, bribery, or other high crimes and misdemeanors" (the constitutional grounds for removal), but of political intemperance. The Senate's acquittal in effect validated the Court's mandamus opinion, since it virtually eliminated impeachment ("a mere scarecrow of a thing," concluded Jefferson in disgust) as a means of controlling the Court. The Republicans, it should be added, salvaged a small victory by teaching the judges to subdue their political passions and improve their judicial manners.

Chase's good fortune, however, did not lift the Republican siege. Two years later, in the treason trial of Aaron Burr, the Jeffersonians and the judiciary (or rather, President Jefferson and Chief Justice Marshall) faced off again. Burr's refusal to concede the presidency to Jefferson in the disputed election of 1800, and his subsequent flirtation with Federalist secession intrigues in New York, turned Jefferson bitterly against him. All this prepared the president to believe that Burr's mysterious expedition down the Ohio River in 1806 was for the treasonable purpose of separating the Southwest from the Union. Indeed, even before Burr was indicted, Jefferson pronounced him guilty (before a special session of Congress). During the trial in Richmond, presided over by John Marshall sitting on circuit, Jefferson micro-managed the prosecution in order to assure a conviction.

Marshall, on the other hand, while technically scrupulous in his legal rulings at the trial, could not disguise his contempt for the president. Over the strenuous protest of government counsel, he released Burr on bail and, during the pretrial hearings, appeared at a dinner given in honor of the defendant by his chief counsel. He allowed (some said encouraged) statements by counsel that were derogatory to Jefferson. (Eyewitness Nathaniel Saltonstall reported that Burr's lawyer Luther Martin "don't stick very closely to the question before the Court but likes better to rub the Executive.") And most audaciously, Marshall, at the request of defense counsel, issued a subpoena duces tecum to the president requesting him to forward relevant documents, or else appear in person. Jefferson delivered the papers, but did not appear; nor did Marshall think he would. Both men made a telling point about the powers of their respective offices.

Obscured though it was by political theater, the crucial aspect of Burr's trial was its effect on the American law of treason—and on determining whether the judiciary or the executive would decide what that law was. Article III, Section 3, of the Constitution defined treason as "levying war" against the United States or "adhering to their enemies, giving them aid and comfort," and required either "confession in open court" or "the testimony of two witnesses to the same overt act" as grounds for conviction. The prosecution's charge that Burr's procurement of men at Blennerhassett's Island was treasonous raised two fundamental and related questions: First, what was the meaning of "levying war"? And second, were all parties involved in treason principals, as in English treason law? Since Burr had not been present at the assemblage of men, both issues were highly relevant.

Marshall read the Constitution strictly on both questions. Levying war meant an overt act of creating war and "must be proved by an open deed." And, procuring or advising treason was not itself treason, for the Constitution did not recognize the common-law doctrine of constructive treason. In any case, procurement would have to be proven by two witnesses to the overt act. Both holdings assured Burr's acquittal, since no levy of war had been proven and since no witnesses to the overt act of procurement could be produced. The chief justice was as pleased with the political implications of his decision as Jefferson was dismayed by them. That he twisted the law for political ends, as the Republicans and some historians have charged, however, does not make sense, as Robert K. Faulkner ("John Marshall and the Burr Trial," September 1966) and R. Kent Newmyer (in his biography of Marshall) demonstrate. Marshall's strict reading of the Constitution and firm position on evidence put the American law of treason beyond the easy grasp of political expediency, as the framers of the Constitution had intended.

The clash between the president and the chief justice should not obscure the fact that the Court and the Republicans had come to share enough ground for a rapprochement. There had, in fact, always been a theoretical affinity between judicial power and the Republican policy of limited government. And the moderate Republicans' acceptance of judicial review in 1803, as Richard Ellis's *Jeffersonian Crisis* shows, suggests that they recognized this. Even Marshall's opinion in the *Burr* trial was congenial to Jeffersonian doctrine, since it struck a blow for individual liberty against governmental power.

The shift in the positions of the two parties after 1800 also paved the way for reconciliation. Having lost power in Washington, the Federalists turned from nationalism to states' rights. On the other hand, the Jeffersonian Republicans, faced with the responsibilities of governing, and challenged by the militant sectionalism of the Federalists, became the party of nationalism. Their resolute nationalist policies, particularly the Embargo of 1807 and the War of 1812, brought open resistance (even talk of secession) from New England Federalists. It became painfully clear to the Republicans that national authority depended heavily on the federal courts. By 1809, with Jefferson's retirement and three Republicans on the bench (William Johnson, 1804; Henry Brockholst Livingston, 1806; and Thomas Todd, 1807), the stage was set for a new period of temporary reconciliation.

United States v. *Peters* (1809) signaled the change. Since 1779, the state of Pennsylvania had resisted a decree of the Committee on Appeals of the Continental Congress, which reversed a prize decision of the state admiralty court. When in 1803 federal district Judge Richard Peters affirmed the Committee's decision, the Republican-controlled legislature threatened to resist the decision by force. By 1808, when the Supreme Court was asked for a writ of mandamus compelling Peters to execute his decision, the cause had assumed ominous implications for the nation. The successful assertion by a state legislature of its right to interpret federal law—accompanied by threats of violent resistance—would encourage New England in its overt opposition to the Embargo and would, as Hall's *Law Journal* put it, send the Constitution "to the trunkmaker as a Damn'd Paper, Black as the ink that's on it: senseless bauble!"

Marshall quashed both possibilities in a forceful opinion upholding the power of the nation to enforce its laws by the "instrumentality of its own tribunals." When the Pennsylvania legislature petitioned President Madison for redress, he firmly refused; when Governor Snyder threatened to call out the militia, Madison made it clear that such a move would be met by national authority. The fact that a moderate states' rights Republican president—widely regarded as "the father of the Constitution"—should back a nationalist decision of a Court led by a moderate Federalist chief justice, was a much-needed affirmation of judicial authority.

The *Peters* case, as it turned out, was only a reprieve in the states' rights assault on the Marshall Court. Seven years later, in the famous case of *Martin* v. *Hunter's Lessee*, the battle resumed in earnest. The *Martin* case, which pitted the legal establishment of Virginia against the Court (and against the person of the chief justice) originated during the American Revolution when Virginia passed an act confiscating Tory lands within the state and subsequently sold those lands to private citizens. Other citizens claimed the same lands by titles that ran back to the original Tory owners, and for thirty-odd years they contested the validity of the state confiscation act. The Supreme Court voided that act in *Fairfax's Devisee* v. *Hunter's Lessee* (1813), on the ground that it conflicted with the Treaty of 1794 with England. After consulting with Jefferson and Monroe, the Virginia Court of Appeals not only refused to obey the Court's decision, but also denied the constitutionality of Section 25 of the Judiciary Act under which the case had been heard. It was this refusal and denial that came, on another writ of error, before the Supreme Court in the *Martin* case.

Speaking for a unanimous Court (minus the chief justice, who recused himself because of his personal interest in the disputed lands), Republican appointee Joseph Story chastised the Republican state of Virginia for following the states' rights course of Federalist Massachusetts, his own native state. Fusing together law, logic, and policy, he made a case for appellate jurisdiction that was "unanswerable and conclusive," as Chancellor James Kent later put it. Because some constitutional questions (over which the Court had Article III jurisdiction), could be heard in the first instance by state courts, it was imperative, declared Story, that those state court decisions be reviewable by the Supreme Court. Section 25 provided for this essential process of review; to repudiate that section would curtail the powers granted to the Court by the Constitution. It is a "doubtful course," Story continued, to argue that the Supreme Court should not have the final power of review because that power might be abused. "From the very nature of things, the absolute right of decision, in the last resort, must rest somewhere. . . ."

Before and after this powerful assertion, Story delivered obiter dicta that carried judicial nationalism even further. Operating on the now familiar premise that it was not the states but the whole people who created the Constitution, Story arrived at the threshold of implied powers—the doctrine that became the constitutional hallmark of the "golden age." And before he was finished, he set a new precedent for judicial aggressiveness by informing Congress that it was constitutionally obliged to maintain the final review power of the

Court. ("What would be thought of a judgment of the Court of King's Bench," declared the shocked *United States Magazine and Democratic Review* twenty-two years later, "that should lecture Parliament on what it must enact!") In 1816 it was neither Congress nor the president who objected, but the states' rights theorists of Virginia, who soon launched the first comprehensive anti-Court movement in American history. Story's opinion stood—and still stands—as an unanswerable defense of the Court's appellate jurisdiction—which as Charles Warren observed, is the "keystone of the whole arch of Federal judicial power."

John Jay, who was still alive in 1816, might well have retracted his gloomy pronouncement of 1801, that the Court lacked and would never acquire "energy, weight, and dignity." For in the first decade and a half of Marshall's tenure, it was the Court—and not Congress, or the president, or the states—that presented itself as the most authoritative interpreter of the Constitution. The record was impressive. Over bitter opposition, the Court had confirmed its power to review state acts and to pass final judgment on federal questions coming from state courts. It had turned the implications in the Constitution concerning judicial review of congressional acts into solid precedent. And in the process of acquiring power, the Court developed techniques for using it: the united bench delivering a single opinion, the convenient device of obiter dicta, and the educative possibilities of judicial opinions among others. Melding the techniques and interpretive guidelines of the common law with constitutional text, the judges had begun to fashion a distinctive new tradition of American public law. Finally, the Court, through its chief justice, had begun to justify itself to American democracy. Marshall insisted, whenever he got the chance, that when the Court spoke, it did so in the people's name and from an allegedly certain Constitution that left reasonable room for interpretation but none for judicial partiality.

The Court's claim of being the repository of constitutional truth looked stronger when compared to the difficulties the states and other branches of the national government had in interpreting the Constitution. State efforts (those of Virginia and Kentucky in 1798 and 1799 and those of Pennsylvania in 1809) faltered because of their anarchic implications and their lack of support from other states. Presidential limitations in the area of constitutional interpretation were apparent in the purchase of the Louisiana Territory in 1803. Here, Jefferson was forced to set aside his theory of limited government to do what expediency required. A constitutional system that could not embrace the responsibilities of governing and that had to be suspended at the dictates of expediency was no system at all. The long-range advantages of judicial over executive interpretation were further apparent in the Burr treason trial. Congress also failed as a forum for rational and conclusive constitutional debate. Indeed, while the Court was bringing order in its own house, the national legislature descended into factional anarchy. When a semblance of order was finally restored in the 1820s with the reestablishment of the two-party system, it was an order based on constituent politics that functioned by cajolement and compromise. The imperative of congressional parties, it turned out, was often to dodge constitutional issues rather than to resolve them.

Neither the states, nor the president, nor the Congress surrendered their right to interpret the Constitution and all continued to influence constitutional law. But it was the Supreme Court that emerged from the struggles of the early nineteenth century as best qualified to speak authoritatively. Authority—and this is where John Marshall made his mark—followed demonstrated ability.

The foundation of judicial government had been laid, and, history permitting, the Court was ready to build on it.

Consolidating National Power

The War of 1812—fought for ends which had been largely achieved by diplomacy, concluded by a treaty that settled nothing that was unsettled, and devoid of military glory except for a battle won after the war ended—hardly seemed the occasion for a resurgence of nationalism. Yet the war dissolved the miasma of apprehension that had hung over the republic since independence. In 1815, for the first time in its history, the United States was simultaneously at peace with Europe and with itself. France, beaten and weak, was no threat; Britain, also exhausted, was already calculating the advantages of free trade, a policy that would bind it to the United States in mutual self-interest. Separatist tendencies—the monopoly of no one section or party—and partisan feelings seemed to disappear as the fortunes of the Federalists ebbed. The diverse economic energies of the agrarian South, the commercial North, and the burgeoning West appeared to be the foundation blocks of a self-sustaining national economy, rather than forces of disunity. With the ardor of the Revolution restored, with confidence in the well-wishes of a "superintending providence," the young nation cast a disdainful glance back at Europe and set out for the Pacific, certain of finding utopia on the way.

As contemporary statesmen well knew, they needed to build an enduring and powerful nation by capitalizing on this historic moment. There is no country, said Madison in his Annual Message of 1815, "where nature invites more the art of man to complete her own work for his accommodation and benefit." "Art" took the form of a national bank, a protective tariff, and federally sponsored internal improvements. National mercantilism would bind together diverse sections in mutual advantage and ensure that national unity would accompany continental expansion. The question was whether the Constitution, incorporating eighteenth-century notions of limited government, could yield sufficient power to accommodate nineteenth-century aspirations. And, more to the point, could those political and economic groups attached to the idea of limited government be assured that economic nationalism and constitutional union were advantageous?

The Court had not yet grappled with the constitutional issues raised by national mercantilism. What it had said in its important prewar decisions had, in fact, inclined toward the Jeffersonian doctrine of constitutional limitations. Yet given the fact that the justices were members of the national government, there was reason to believe that they would favor a nationalist construction of the Constitution. And if institutional self-interest did not incline them to favor nationalism, it at least freed them from selfish prejudice against it. The justices had also imbibed the strong national sentiments generated during the Revolutionary War—Marshall, the veteran of Valley Forge, more than the rest. All of them, Federalists and Republicans alike, had seen national greatness go begging for want of unity and power. Not surprisingly, the Court set out to make the Constitution support the "great national interests," to use Justice Story's words, "which shall bind us in an indissoluble chain."

McCulloch v. *Maryland* (1819) was an ideal place to begin. The case focused on the Second Bank of the United States and through it, touched on the great political and economic issues of the day. Chartered by Congress in 1816, the Bank was part of the American mercantilist system; its job was to aid the government in fiscal operations and provide a national system of credit and a uniform national currency. But instead of restraining state banks (supposedly one of its duties), the Bank, under its first president, competed against them in speculation and the reckless extension of credit. In 1818, the Bank saved itself from the impending crash by calling in its loans but, in doing so, brought down a number of overextended state banks, especially in the South and West. On the assumption that the Bank caused the panic (and because of pressure from jealous state banks), seven states passed laws restraining the Bank's operations. In Maryland the retaliation took the form of a tax on the notes of all banks—including the Baltimore branch of the Bank of the United States—not chartered by the state.

The Bank's appeal of the state court decision that upheld the Maryland tax brought two vital constitutional questions before the Supreme Court: Had Congress the power to charter a bank? If so, did Maryland have the right to tax its operations within the state? On the Court's answers rested not only the fate of the Bank but the whole system of national mercantilism. And more. For the first time, the Court had to determine the scope of congressional powers and their relation to the powers of the states. The responsibility was "awful," said Marshall—but it is hard to believe he really minded it.

Speaking for a unanimous Court, Marshall opened with the humble disclaimer that the Court was only doing what it had to do— fair warning that something important was in the offing. Then, quietly dropping his humility, he turned to the radical assertions of state sovereignty pressed on the Court by counsel for Maryland. In answering them, he set forth (with the aid of William Pinkney's brilliant argument at the bar) the "great principle" of national supremacy on which his opinion—and the entire edifice of constitutional nationalism—would rest. "In America," Marshall conceded, "the powers of sovereignty are divided between the government of the Union, and those of the States. They are each sovereign, with respect to the objects committed to it, and neither sovereign with respect to the objects committed to the other."

In one important respect, however, national sovereignty is supreme over state sovereignty. Though the national government is limited, within its sphere of powers it is supreme over the states. This did not mean that Marshall disregarded states' rights; in many areas, including control over slavery, they were controlling. But it is also true that *McCulloch* made national supremacy the informing spirit of the Constitution and the guiding principle of its interpretation. The government of the United States occupies the high ground in the American federal system because—and here Marshall the conservative sounded the democratic theme—"It is the government of all; all its powers are delegated by all; it represents all, and acts for all." Marshall sincerely believed in divided sovereignty, but he also believed that the American people and not the states created the Constitution.

So much for constitutional theory. The key question still remained: Was the incorporation of the Bank by Congress (a power not specifically mentioned among the enumerated powers in Article I, Section 8) within the protective perimeter of national supremacy? Emphatically yes, said Marshall, and in support of his view he called on history, law, policy—and Alexander Hamilton. The constitutionality of incorporation had been debated exhaustively and affirmed in 1791 by Congress (in regard to the First Bank of the United States); for twenty years, before its charter was allowed to lapse in 1811, its existence had been accepted by both parties. Marshall admitted that prescription could not justify a usurpation of power, but he felt it proved there had been none. Regarding the absence of the right of incorporation among the enumerated powers, he argued that if every power necessary to a government had to be listed, the Constitution would become a legal code, the prolixity of which "could scarcely be embraced by the human mind." And in words Felix Frankfurter thought the most important ever uttered by an American judge, Marshall emphasized, "We must never forget that it is a constitution we are expounding."

This famous sentence has been cited over the years in support of "the living constitution," but in fact Marshall did not believe that the

Constitution was an open-ended invitation to judicial interpretation
and reinterpretation. Rather he believed that the framers entrusted the
people's representatives in Congress with power to match the "exigencies of the nation." "A government, instructed with such ample
powers, on the due execution of which the happiness and prosperity
of the nation so vitally depends, must be entrusted with ample means
for their execution." The document itself supports this extension of
congressional powers beyond those enumerated, Marshall added.
Implied powers are nowhere forbidden. The word "expressly" was
deliberately stricken from the Tenth Amendment by the Constitutional
Convention, thus avoiding an explicit limitation on congressional authority. But above all, following the specific enumeration of powers
in Article I, Section 8, the Constitution gave Congress the power to
pass "all laws which shall be necessary and proper for carrying into
execution the foregoing powers."

The scope of congressional power, in Marshall's "original intent" reading came to hang on the meaning of "necessary." Counsel
for Maryland agreed with Thomas Jefferson that the word meant to
exclude from Congress the choice of means and bound it strictly to
the exercise of specified powers. Marshall took the Hamiltonian view
that it was a grant of "additional power," one that left Congress discretion in the choice of means to execute "those great powers on which
the welfare of the nation essentially depends." Common usage and
constitutional syntax, he asserted, supported his position. But most
conclusive was the fact that to hold otherwise would leave the Constitution a "splendid bawble." His argument left it instead—in his own
famous words—a constitution "intended to endure for ages to come,
and consequently, to be adapted to the various *crises* of human affairs."

With a strong assist from Hamilton (whose memorandum to
Washington on the constitutionality of the First Bank of the United
States he followed closely), the chief justice pulled the various strands
of his argument together, stating the constitutional rule governing the
interpretation of the enumerated powers in Article I, Section 8: "Let
the end be legitimate, let it be within the scope of the constitution,
and all means which are appropriate, which are plainly adapted to
that end, which are not prohibited, but consist with the letter and spirit

of the constitution, are constitutional," By this rule the Bank (barely mentioned before) was constitutional. The act of incorporation was not prohibited and was an obvious means for achieving the great ends of national government, most importantly the power "to lay and collect taxes" and "borrow money on the credit of the United States." The Bank was a means to these ends, and therefore, it was constitutional and "part of the supreme law of the land."

Marshall's doctrine of implied powers, bold though it was, rested on the specific text of the Constitution. In addressing the question of Maryland's right to tax the Bank, he had no textual foundation on which to rely. The Constitution, he conceded, had, "no express provision" for limiting the states' crucial power to tax. But, by piling inference on inference, he made up this deficiency. Start, he said, with the principle already expounded that the Constitution and laws made in pursuance of it are supreme. Admit that the creation of a bank by implication is among those constitutional and supreme laws. Concede further that "a power to create implies a power to preserve" and, further still, that "the power to tax involves the power to destroy . . . and render useless the power to create." Acknowledge finally that "there is a plain repugnance, in conferring on one government a power to control the constitutional measures of another, which other, with respect to those very measures, is declared to be supreme over that which exerts the control," and you have the answer. Without bothering to consider whether the Maryland tax did in fact threaten the Bank with destruction (which it did not), Marshall found it unconstitutional.

Marshall then translated this specific instance into a general rule, harmonized it with his earlier principle, and arrived at a guideline defining the limits of state power: "States have no power, by taxation or otherwise, to retard, impede, burden, or in any manner control, the operations of the constitutional laws enacted by Congress to carry into execution the powers vested in the general government."

Marshall's opinion—or rather his state paper—was a bold exercise in judicial lawmaking. The government of limited and enumerated powers became, without benefit of amendment, the government of expansive powers. Marshall reconciled state and national sovereignty within the federal system by using as his touchstones both the idea of national supremacy and its corollary—that states are chronic aggressors against national authority. Approaching the Constitution with the expectation that it must supply what the nation needs, Marshall sounded what became a dominant theme in American constitutional law.

These principles were not mere legal generalities, but practical responses to pressing questions. For those who believe Marshall's nationalism was unnecessarily expansive, it should be noted that he was responding to Maryland's lawyers who, in the spirit of the Virginia and Kentucky Resolutions, argued that the national government was a mere agent of the sovereign states. Marshall was also conscious of the acquisition of vast new territory in the Adams-Onís Treaty of 1819. As he observed in his opinion, the Republic now extended "from the St. Croix to the Gulf of Mexico, from the Atlantic to the Pacific." Federal internal improvements were required to bind the nation together, and Congress, armed with implied powers, was empowered to authorize them should the elected representatives of the American people choose to do so.

In effect, *McCulloch* authorized Congress to enact a national economic plan commensurate with the post-1815 surge of nationalist sentiment. At the same time, Marshall's ruling on state taxing power restrained the states from interfering. On the latter point, the chief justice was rarely so categorical—or less convincing. First, he avoided the difficult question of degree: whether and at what point Maryland's tax actually threatened the operations of the Bank. Instead he assumed without proving, that state taxation per se would destroy the Bank; and second, that the Bank, though it was controlled by private capital, was an agency of the federal government and thus immune from state taxation. This simplistic doctrine of tax immunity (extended to include state immunity against federal taxation in *Weston* v. *Charleston*, 1829) did not do justice to the complexity of the problem. After resulting in much confusion, the reciprocal tax immunity doctrine was abandoned by the Court in the early twentieth century.

As in *Marbury* v. *Madison*, the genius of the *McCulloch* opinion lay not in its originality but in its timing, practicability, clarity, and eloquence. It was not original. Hamilton had fully and powerfully stated the doctrine of implied powers in his cabinet memorandum of 1791. Congress verified the doctrine by twice chartering a national bank and by providing financial support for a system of internal improvements. The Court itself had intimated implied powers as early as *United States* v. *Fisher* (1805), and Story boldly expanded the principle in *Martin* v. *Hunter's Lessee* (1816). Disparagement of state power was another common nationalist theme, as a reading of the *Federalist* makes clear. And the notion of a supreme Constitution based on popular sovereignty had been judicial stock-in-trade since the Jay-Ellsworth Courts. Even Marshall's famous statement that the Constitution was meant to endure for all ages was a widely shared assumption. Marshall did not create these nationalist principles. What he did do was seize them at the moment when they were most relevant to American needs and congenial to the American mind, and (aided by the rhetoric of Alexander Hamilton and the argument of William Pinkney) he translated them gracefully and logically into the law of the Constitution. Basing his interpretation of the law on the needs and spirit of the age, Marshall gave them a permanent place in the lexicon of constitutional truths. Hamilton himself was unable to do as much.

In 1819, however, the verdict of history was not yet in. Marshall's constitutional nationalism had not pleased the whole nation. The Northeast generally found the Court's nationalism congenial to its economic aspirations and rallied behind *McCulloch*. Southern states, on the other hand, countered with their own view of the Constitution, one that looked increasingly like the old Articles of Confederation. Three weeks before the *McCulloch* decision, a bitter, searching debate on slavery and the nature of the Union was set off by the Tallmadge amendment prohibiting slavery in the new state of Missouri. And even as Marshall was reading the Court's opinion, the first shock waves of the Panic of 1819 reverberated. If the "era of good feelings" had ever existed, it had ended. The forthcoming depression reminded southerners of the special policy needs of slave-based agrarianism; they concluded that much more was exacted from them by the Bank, the protective tariff, and internal improvements than was given. Driven to a new awareness of their vulnerability by the Missouri Debates, the slaveholding states began to think of themselves as the slaveholding South. Their fear—and it governed politics and law for the remainder of the antebellum period—was that the Marshall Court's nationalism had put them at the mercy of an ever-increasing, and perhaps anti-slave, northern majority.

Driven by perceived by self-interest, the southern states rallied around the states' rights constitutional theory, which in the wake of

McCulloch became more formal and comprehensive, as well as more militant. The South would finally settle on John C. Calhoun's theory of nullification and secession as their best protection. But Virginia led the way by launching a virulent verbal attack on the "damnable heretical" usurpation of the Marshall Court. Judge Spencer Roane of the Virginia Court of Appeals, spurred on by Jefferson, began the assault with a series of articles repudiating the *McCulloch* opinion in the powerful *Richmond Enquirer*. John Taylor of Caroline County followed with a full refutation of the doctrines of Hamilton and Marshall (and he equated the two) in *Construction Construed and Constitution Vindicated* (1820). While the battle of words raged, Virginia's legislature met, condemned the Court, and instructed congressional delegates to set in motion constitutional amendments that would humble it.

In the case of *Cohens* v. *Virginia* (1821), the Court ran headlong into these aroused champions of states' rights, and Marshall made the most of the opportunity to put down the Court's critics and reaffirm its appellate authority under Section 25. The Cohen brothers were convicted in the borough court of Norfolk, Virginia, for selling lottery tickets in violation of state law. On the grounds that they had acted under a congressional law authorizing lotteries in the District of Columbia, they appealed directly to the Supreme Court on a writ of error. The first and most important question before the Court was whether it could maintain jurisdiction under Section 25 of the Judiciary Act.

But behind this legal issue, said Marshall, there lay questions "of great magnitude" concerning the nature of the Union and of the position of the Supreme Court in the federal system. The chief justice did not exaggerate. The issue was not just the meaning of the Eleventh Amendment which prohibited suits by individuals against the states. In refuting the Court's right to review state court decisions on federal law, counsel for Virginia, with the support of the Virginia legislature, also argued that state courts, not the Supreme Court, have the final word on the meaning of the Constitution. In attacking Section 25, Virginia asked the Court to say grace at its own funeral.

The chief justice's refutation of the states' rights contentions of Virginia was "one of the strongest and most enduring strands of that mighty cable woven by him to hold the American people together as a united and imperishable Nation," thought Albert Beveridge. And it rested on two premises: that the Constitution made a nation and that state jealousy perpetually threatened to unmake it. That nation is supreme, the objects for which it was created are supreme, and the departments of the federal government, while functioning to attain those objects, are supreme. The judicial department is no exception. Article III designates national law (i.e., questions where the rights of litigants depend on the construction of the Constitution or federal laws) as the Court's province, and in this area there can be no division—as Virginia maintained—between state and federal judiciaries. Appellate jurisdiction over state courts was a constitutional imperative when federal questions were involved, as established by Section 25 and by *Martin* v. *Hunter's Lessee*. The Eleventh Amendment, Marshall continued, was intended solely to prevent suits by individuals against states without their consent and it could not be used either to take questions of federal law from the purview of federal courts or "to maintain the sovereignty of a state from the degradation supposed to attend a compulsory appearance before the tribunal of the nation." Moreover, since Virginia had initiated the case against the Cohens and not the other way around, the Eleventh Amendment did not apply.

After this impassioned lecture on the Court's duty to maintain national law, Marshall ruled for Virginia on the ground that the lottery statute was not a national law, since it applied only to the District of Columbia and was not intended to authorize the sale of tickets in Virginia. Far from placating Virginia, this technical victory caused the state to double its efforts against the Court. Spearheaded by Virginia theorists and backed by the prestige of Thomas Jefferson, the attack on the Court soon spread to other states in the South and West.

Nowhere was Court-hatred more defiant than in the new state of Ohio. In direct opposition to the *McCulloch* ruling, that state levied a tax on the Bank of the United States and, in open contravention of a circuit court injunction, collected it and refused to return the money. In January 1821, Ohio outlawed the Bank entirely. The Bank turned to the Court for the enforcement of its rights, reviving the old questions of its constitutionality and its immunity from state taxation and raising the new one of whether the Bank would be given legal remedies sufficient to maintain its constitutional ground.

Drawing on *McCulloch* and *Cohens*, Marshall (with Justice Johnson in dissent) reaffirmed the Bank's constitutionality, voided the Ohio law, and gave the nation a new lecture on constitutional nationalism. By upholding the charter provision giving the Bank access to the federal courts, Marshall added substantially to the Bank's arsenal of legal weapons against state opposition. He further diminished the Eleventh Amendment (a process he had started in the *Cohens* case) by holding that it did not bar the Bank's suit against Osborn, since the name of the state of Ohio did not appear on the record. Much more important than this interpretation of the Eleventh Amendment, which in fact was abandoned in *Ex parte Ayers*, 123 U.S. 443 (1887), was Marshall's ruling that agents of the state are personally liable for damages inflicted while implementing an unconstitutional statute.

But it was New York rather than Ohio and steamboats rather than banks, that provided Marshall with an opportunity to lay the last great foundation block of congressional authority. *Gibbons v. Ogden* (1824) originated in a series of acts dating back to 1787. The New York legislature had granted to the Fulton-Livingston steamboat interest the exclusive right of steam navigation on state waters, including the adjoining coastal waters and the Hudson River between New York and New Jersey. There had been several efforts to break the monopoly, but these were defeated in the state courts. The last challenge came from Thomas Gibbons, who had started a competing steamboat line. Gibbons was enjoined by Aaron Ogden, who sailed under license from the Livingston monopoly, and in 1820, the New York Court of Errors sustained the injunction. Gibbons then took his case to the Supreme Court. He argued against the monopoly on the grounds that the New York act which had given the company its exclusive rights conflicted with the federal Coasting License Act of 1793 and with the commerce clause in Article I, Section 8.

For the first time in its history, the Court had a chance to clarify the meaning of the commerce clause and to coordinate federal and state power in this area. The immediate economic issue was hardly less important than the constitutional one. By the time the case was argued, three states had passed retaliatory statutes against New York and several others had begun the practice of granting steamboat monopolies. Such practices threatened to fractionalize national commerce and retard the use of new transportation technology—the steamboat in 1824, perhaps the railroad six years later.

In his opinion, Marshall began by speaking deferentially of the state court whose decision he was about to reverse; he then turned to the meaning of the commerce clause, and by extension to the meaning of all the enumerated powers in Article I, Section 8. The "well-settled rule" for their interpretation, asserted Marshall (though in fact the question had not previously come before the Court), was to construe the enumerated powers "by the language of the instrument which confers them, taken in connection with the purposes for which they were conferred." The powers granted in Article I, Section 8, were plainly stated: they were intended for the "general advantage" of the American people. The inexorable conclusion, therefore, was that "the sovereignty of Congress, though limited to specified objects, is plenary as to those objects."

Marshall vitalized enumerated powers in the *Gibbons* case in the same way in which he went beyond them to reach implied powers in *McCulloch*—by interpreting the Constitution according to the potent doctrine of national supremacy. Commerce was not, as counsel for the state insisted, a mere "interchange of commodities." Rather, declared Marshall, it includes "every species of commercial intercourse" among the states. And "among" means "intermingled with," which in turn means that the power of Congress over commerce does not stop at state boundaries but "may be introduced into the interior." Like other powers vested in Congress, the "power to regulate" is "complete in itself, may be exercised to its utmost extent, and acknowledges no limitations other than are prescribed in the Constitution." The "sole restraints" against an abuse of this power, Marshall added (with an uncharacteristic nod to popular democracy), are the "wisdom and discretion of Congress" and ultimately the power of the vote.

Three possibilities were open to the Court in ruling on state authority in the area of interstate commerce. The first, urged by Webster and closest to Marshall's conception of national power, was that the grant of power to Congress automatically and totally prohibited state legislatures from touching upon interstate commerce—at least its "higher branches." Less drastic was the proposition permitting states to legislate in areas of interstate commerce until Congress legislated on the same subject, at which time the state acts would give way. The third alternative, a refinement of the second, allowed state regulations of interstate commerce to exist concurrently with those of Congress unless there was a direct and substantial conflict between the two, in which case the state act would give way. Extreme nationalists liked the first solution, and states' righters, for want of something better, might be persuaded to take the third.

Marshall's opinion (explicated lucidly in White's *The Marshall Court* [1988] and Maurice Baxter's *The Steamboat Monopoly* [1972]) was an intricate blend of decisiveness and calculated vagueness that occupied solid nationalist ground, placated both extremes, and left the Court room to make future adjustments. He accepted the third alternative—the one least offensive to the states—but in applying it added the nationalistic substance of the second. This he did by a broad reading of the federal Coasting License Act of 1793, under which Gibbons was licensed. Though the act merely required federal licensing of vessels engaged in the coastal trade, Marshall held that it was a national guarantee against state interference in interstate commerce. He then found the New York monopoly statute in conflict with this act and voided it. In his argument, however, Marshall hinted that the grant to Congress of commerce power in Article 1, Section 8 was itself sufficient to void the state act even without an actual conflict.

The practical consequences of *Gibbons* were as profound as the legal footwork was dazzling. The opinion disrupted an unpopular monopoly (thus negating democratic criticism), prevented state fragmentation of commerce, established a national market for commercial activity, and kept the states from impeding new technology. Doctrinally the result was resolutely nationalist: interstate commerce was defined so broadly that, in the twentieth century, it was able to embrace the revolution in communications and transportation and also provide constitutional support for national welfare legislation. Just by legislating, Congress could claim the whole field of interstate commerce from the states at any time. And, if the interpretation of the Licensing Act was any precedent, a little legislation would go a long way. By implication, this broad approach to the commerce power would apply to the other enumerated powers as well.

In *Brown* v. *Maryland* (1827) the nationalizing potential of the *Gibbons* ruling was made explicit. A Maryland tax law requiring importers of out-of-state goods and other wholesale vendors to take out a state license was the point at issue. Marshall's majority opinion, over the strong dissent of Justice Thompson, struck down the law as a violation of the constitutional prohibition of state duties on imports, even those coming from sister states (an interpretation not warranted by the Constitution and later reversed by the Court). Marshall also voided the law as a violation by Maryland of Congress's power to regulate interstate commerce, despite the fact that Congress had not legislated on the subject. The implication here (building on the hint in *Gibbons*) was that the commerce power was foreclosed to the states just because it had been given to Congress. Leaving that possibility dangling, Marshall went on to state the rule for demarcating state and national commerce powers: as long as imported goods remained in the "original package," they could not be taxed by the states.

A Philosophy of National Power

Perhaps at no time in its history was the Court so close to transcending the policy-making limitations of the judicial process as in the six years from 1819 through 1824. This was largely due to a happy combination of circumstances following the War of 1812. Congress, the executive, and the Court were inspired to come into accord by the formative possibilities of the age, and they were supported by a popular and progressive national sentiment. Indeed, Congress paved the way for implied powers by acting on them. But neither Congress nor the executive was consistent enough in its practice or comprehensive enough in its articulation to replace the Court as the authoritative interpreter of the Constitution.

The absence of a well-defined party organization also left a vacuum that permitted, if it did not invite, judicial activism. In addition, the series of related, comprehensive questions confronting the Court encouraged, even necessitated, an expansive exegesis that went far beyond the usual policy-making limits of case-controversy. In exploiting this potential, the Court was not circumscribed by precedents and, for the same reason, its work was precedent-making. Fortunately for the authority of its pronouncements, the Court did not have to originate de novo constitutional principles to fit the age. With the help of a brilliant bar led by William Pinkney, William Wirt, and Daniel

Webster, it could and did draw on the nationalist political tradition rooted in the Revolution, potentially embodied in the Constitution, expounded by Hamilton, reflected in the policies of Washington and Adams and the dominant wing of the National Republican Party. It seems fair to say, as James Madison did in 1830, that the Marshall Court's nationalist interpretation of the Constitution was "sustained by the predominant sense of the Nation."

John Marshall did not originate constitutional nationalism. Neither did he have to teach it to his colleagues (not even that assiduous Jeffersonian William Johnson, as Morgan's biography makes clear). More than historical legend admits, the Court's nationalist decisions during the "golden years" were collective efforts. As Marshall himself insisted in his debate with Roane in 1819, "the opinion which is to be delivered as the opinion of the court is previously submitted to the consideration of all the judges; and if any part of the reasoning be disapproved, it must be so modified as to receive the approbation of all, before it can be delivered as the opinion of all."

Yet it made a difference that John Marshall was there—and not, say, Spencer Roane as Jefferson wanted, or even Joseph Story—for his genius fitted the age. His command of constitutional law and his gift for logical analysis made him the intellectual leader of the Court, while his patience, gentle demeanor, and sense of fairness enabled him, as primus inter pares, to keep his colleagues on task. Though his opinions emerged from the deliberations of his colleagues, they were also, in the words of Benjamin Cardozo, molded "in the fire of his own intense convictions."

John Marshall represented the Court in its greatest national moments. His separate opinions, taken collectively, as Joseph Story took them in his *Commentaries on the Constitution* (1833), amount to a treatise on constitutional nationalism. Each opinion performed a special function in his exposition; all had nationalism and moral didacticism in common. He relied on repetition and anticipation. Thus, while expounding implied powers in *McCulloch*, Marshall explored the principle of national supremacy that would vitalize the enumerated powers in *Gibbons*. In the *Cohens* opinion, he replied to criticism of the *McCulloch* ruling and reasserted the axioms set forth by Story in *Martin* v. *Hunter's Lessee*. At the same time, he anticipated the *Gib-*

bons decision by alluding to the supremacy of granted powers and to the idea of commerce as a national activity. *Brown* v. *Maryland* explored the theory set forth in the *Gibbons* decision—that the regulation of commerce belongs exclusively to Congress—and added the commerce clause to implied powers as a judicial weapon against state taxation of national business. Each decision turned on judicial discretion and strengthened judicial authority, yet perpetuated the myth of judicial modesty. None precluded flexibility of interpretation by future courts. At the same time, the whole production bristled with Augustan rhetoric and moral imperatives: the nationalist doctrines which the chief justice liked were "part of our history," "self-evident" and "universally understood," doctrines which "the good sense of the public has pronounced," "the people have declared," and "America has chosen." The Court, Marshall insisted, had only to heed and then pronounce these verities of American experience.

Marshall's protestations of judicial passivity should not obscure the important shift in constitutional law wrought by his Court. In the first place, he envisaged a Constitution sufficiently flexible to keep abreast of historical change—one that could evolve through judicial interpretation as well as by formal amendment, as the framers had planned. This was the real meaning of judicial review—the meaning that was not fully understood at Philadelphia. By the Court's power of interpretation, the compromises, deliberate obscurities, and convenient silences of the Constitution, as well as the unresolved tension between national and state power, fell into the background. Gone was the earlier image of the Constitution as an "accommodating system," as a "work of compromise," in Justice William Paterson's words. Marshall's vision of the "spirit and true meaning of the Constitution" tidied up the clutter of history. Through a clear and certain and supreme Constitution, the American people had spoken. Union was hypostatized into Nation; the government of limited authority, so much a part of colonial and revolutionary constitutionalism, became a government of sufficient power. The Constitution via the Marshall Court became the symbol of that Nation and the source of its vitality—a living, dynamic organism, based, as Nathan Dane had hoped in 1789, "on open manly principles."

CHAPTER THREE

Capitalism and the Marshall Court: Judicial Review in Action

Scarcely any political question arises in the United States that is not resolved, sooner or later, into a judicial question.

Alexis de Tocqueville (1835)

In shaping constitutional law to meet the economic needs of the growing nation, the Marshall Court implicitly recognized that the possession of constitutional power is inseparable from its use. The justices, however, did not acknowledge that they might be making economic policy when they decided constitutional cases, and they did not justify their decisions by referring to the results they were intended to produce. Rather they insisted—and indeed probably believed—that they were following the intent of the framers (this without asking whether the framers themselves might have had an economic agenda). Critics like Thomas Jefferson and John Taylor of Caroline County, and astute observers like Alexis de Tocqueville, however, were quick to see that constitutional law and economics were intimately connected. And late nineteenth-century students of the Marshall Court—spurred on by the policymaking excesses of the Waite Court—rediscovered what the early critics knew: that "official" explanations of decision-making, such as "the intent of the framers" or the eternal verities of natural law discovered through legal science, often obscured more than they explained. Taught by Darwinian science to be skeptical of absolutes, respectful of facts, and appreciative of organic change, they concluded that law, through the fallible person of the judge, was rooted not in logic but as O. W. Holmes, Jr., wrote in his *Common Law* (1881), in "experience" and in "intuitions of public policy."

When historians attuned to the new history looked at the Court as James Bradley Thayer did in his pioneering classic, "The Origin and Scope of the American Doctrine of Constitutional Law" (1893), they discovered its policymaking attributes. When they looked closer as Corwin did in "The Basic Doctrine of American Constitutional Law" (1914), they recognized that the policy made by the antebellum Court was largely economic. What was not—and still is not—clear was how the function of economic policymaking fit into the overall scheme of judicial government. At one extreme, the socialist historian Gustavus Myers (*History of the Supreme Court* [1912]) accused the justices of conspiring with an exploitative capitalist elite against the democratic portion of the people. Louis Boudin (in *Government by Judiciary* [1932]) made the same charge twenty years later with more scholarship and less ideology. Both Myers and Boudin assumed that the justices made policy at will with scant regard for the legal rules of the game. On the other hand, in *The Supreme Court in United States History* (1926), the work that set the dominant tone for much subsequent historiography, Charles Warren acknowledged the economic influence of the Marshall Court but considered it less important than the Court's formal role as interpreter and protector of the Constitution. He made no effort to explain the relationship between law and economics.

That relationship still puzzles students of the early Court. On the one hand, it was too close to be accidental and too extensive to be dismissed as a mere by-product of the search for legal verities. On the other hand, there is little evidence that the justices cynically manipulated the law to reach predetermined economic ends. There is even less evidence of a conscious conspiracy between the justices and economic interest groups. An account is needed that would explain the substantial, inseparable, deliberate, yet nonconspiratorial relationship between American capitalism and the Marshall and Taney Courts.

During the 1930s, when the Court's economic bias was much in view, a more sophisticated explanation of constitutional law and economics began to emerge. Max Lerner's "The Supreme Court and American Capitalism" (1933), for example, was a notable early effort to abandon the conspiracy view of the Court for a broader cultural approach to judicial history. Following Lerner's essay, and likewise drawing insight from the economic battles of the New Deal Court, came three distinguished works: Carl Swisher's 1935 biography, *Roger B. Taney* (in fact a history of the Taney Court), treated the economic basis of judicial statesmanship frankly; Frankfurter's *The Commerce Clause under Marshall, Taney, and Waite* (1937); and Benjamin Wright's *Contract Clause of the Constitution* (1938), revealed the extent to which two key clauses of the Constitution, with constructive interpretation by the Court, shaped economic history. Two more recent books (C. P. Magrath on *Fletcher* v. *Peck* [1966] and Stanley Kutler on the *Charles River Bridge* case [1971]) best illustrate the role that economic interest groups played in the work of the Court. A socioeconomic history of the Court that weaves these various strands of scholarship into a comprehensive whole remains to be written, but Hurst's previously mentioned *Law and the Conditions of Freedom in the Nineteenth-Century United States* (1956) provides a conceptual basis on which such a work could rest, as does Charles G. Seller's *Market Revolution* and Jennifer J. Nedelsky's *Private Property and the Limits of American Constitutionalism* (1990). R. Kent Newmyer treats the Marshall Court's role in the market revolution in *John Marshall and the Heroic Age of the Supreme Court* (2001).

To explain the legal-economic nexus in the Marshall and Taney period, then, one might begin with Max Lerner's observation—extrapolated from Holmes, refined by Corwin, and conceptualized by Hurst—"Between our business enterprise and our judicial power there is the unity of an aggressive and cohesive cultural pattern." The cultural proposition uniting law and economics (and much else in the nineteenth century) was the conviction that the individual was the raison d'être of civil society and the agent of economic progress. And the vitalizing force behind creative individuals and the measure of social status was private property. Property, Chancellor Kent declared in the tradition of Locke, Blackstone, and Madison, was "inherent in the human breast." It was provided by God to lift men from sloth and stimulate them to display "the various and exalted powers of the human mind." (Or, as Francis Lieber put it, "Man yearns to see his individuality represented and reflected in the acts of his exertions—in property.") This impulse, continued Kent, "pervades the foundations of social improvement" and is the wellspring of civilization and the vehicle for national greatness. National advancement, both functionally and ideologically, was inseparable from the dynamics of economic individualism. If progress depended on the creative individual, as Kent, Marshall, and Story among others believed, it followed that government should foster the release of individual energy; the heritage of colonial mercantilism supported this conclusion.

For those who assumed the responsibility of making government serve national progress by promoting economic individualism, however, there were serious complications. Contrary to the opinion of some historians (Louis Hartz's *Liberal Tradition in America,* for example), agreement on Lockean premises and the morality of individual enterprise did not produce a social, economic, or cultural consensus. The rich and varied economic landscape of the nineteenth century encouraged some to pursue utopia through agriculture, others through shipping or manufacturing. Still others turned to selling, to finance, or to the professions. Overarching these groups were further divisions: rich-poor, free-slave, established-aspiring, creditor-debtor, corporate-individual.

According to its own lights and in proportion to its strength, each group competed for nature's bounties and for the government's assistance in exploiting them. By the early nineteenth century, if not before, self-interest forged these diverse groups into two amorphous but increasingly self-conscious regional and cultural coalitions: "the agrarian-minded" southern and western states and "the commercial-minded" middle states and New England, to use the apt phraseology of Lee Benson. Neither had a monopoly on devotion to national union. Each increasingly viewed itself as the best hope of American civilization and each demanded that the Court sanction its own version of the Constitution. From the framing and ratification of the document onward, the definition of constitutional power was inseparable from considerations of economic policy. In shaping economic history as well as constitutional law, the Court could cement—or disrupt—the Union and shape national character.

Responding to the demands of the most energetic economic interests—those who had the best lawyers and the most to gain from the law—the Court worked to unleash the consolidating forces of interstate commerce by forging a national market wherein property would be secure and goods and credit could flow freely across state lines. The preference came naturally, following the cultural imperatives of the age. And the justices no less than other men of the age—perhaps more so, since they came from the socially and educationally advantaged class (see John Schmidhauser, "The Justices of the Supreme Court: A Collective Portrait" [1959])—imbibed the heady draught of capitalism. As practicing lawyers, many of them (and John Marshall more than most) had associated with the dynamic sector of the business community. As judges, they came easily to the conclusion that what helped the venturesome entrepreneur also helped the general welfare, and they worked consistently to translate nineteenth-century notions of economic man into legal rules that maximized economic activity.

It followed logically that when the Court had to choose among the economic interests competing for favor, the most broad-based and dynamic of these received priority. The Court attended, therefore, more to agrarian capitalism than subsistence agriculture, more to corporate business operating across state lines than to domestic producers operating in local markets, more to the rich than to the poor, and more to the freeman than to the slave. And when confronted with the conflicting demands of agrarian capitalism based on states' rights, on one hand, and national, commercial (read "dynamic") capitalism, on the other, the Marshall Court gave preference to the latter as the more essential to economic progress and national union. Whether the Court's preference actually strengthened the Union—or weakened it by exacerbating southern sectionalism—is an open question.

The Marshall Court, State Power, and Agrarian Capitalism

There were few aspects of the Court's work that did not provide an occasion for buttressing the forces of capitalism. Even the consolidation of its own power held potential advantages for the business community. As the highest legal authority in the land, the Court could, as

The North American Review assured its readers in 1828, put national law on a "steady and regular foundation." It was exactly this body of certain and uniform law, free from local and state idiosyncrasies, that expanding business needed. (As Daniel Webster advised Justice Story: "It is a great object to settle the concerns of the community; so that one may know what to depend on.")

Viewed in this light, even the routine cases constituting most of the Court's work—such as those concerned with revenue bonds, salvage, maritime insurance, land titles, liens, bills and notes, agency, patents, and corporate law—were means of facilitating and nationalizing economic activity. Much of this important work was done at the circuit court level, where the travelling judges sat in their respective circuits with federal district judges. It should be remembered, too, that as much as ninety percent or more of judicial labors at the Supreme Court level dealt with common-law questions which were mostly economic in nature. It is not surprising, as Sylvia Snowiss, Charles Hobson and others have shown, that constitutional law in the age of Marshall was infused with common-law rules.

The great nationalist decisions of the Marshall Court also originated in economic conflict and contributed to the expansion of national capitalism. *McCulloch,* decided in favor of the largest corporation and most powerful monopoly in the country, underwrote a national system of internal improvements. If Congress had followed the Court's lead, the system would have revolutionized national commerce. The *Gibbons* decision not only prohibited states from interfering with interstate commerce but also gave Congress the constitutional authority to pass other laws promoting an "economic E Pluribus Unum," to cite Webster's argument in the case.

The Marshall Court's most direct and effective contribution to the emerging national market, however, was not enlarging congressional power but limiting state power. Indeed, the Court's expansion of congressional authority in cases like *Gibbons* and *McCulloch* seemed at times to be aimed at curtailing state action rather than generating national legislation. In any case, the Court did not disguise its preference for interstate capitalism and its skepticism of state-based legislative democracy. To appreciate its preferences, it is necessary to understand the extensive political and economic competition between the states and national government in the antebellum period—the clash, that is to say, between state and national mercantilism. State government (as the scholarship of Louis Hartz and Oscar and Mary Handlin among others has shown) was the main source of legislative activity and administrative innovation. And more so than Congress, state legislatures assumed most of the responsibility for encouraging enterprise. They responded with an amazing range of laws that included grants of incorporation, preferential tax policies, direct state investment (when the private sector lagged), and even outright state ownership. State regulation of wages, prices, and quality of goods and services rested on the assumption that private economic activity served the public good. Whatever its justification, however, state intervention in the economy could and did inconvenience powerful segments of the business community—by regulating private property, by passing debtor-relief laws, and by favoring local over national business interests. In addition, states' rights philosophy became the refuge for groups that feared the intrusion of outside market forces—those who lacked access to national power and therefore opposed its exercise for the benefit of others.

Given this fact, and given the assumption that government should serve economic enterprise, it was inevitable that the states and the nation would clash over economic policy. This struggle has constituted a basic theme in American history from the Articles of Confederation to World War II, and with the resurgence of modern conservatism, to the present day. State mercantilism was supported by a tradition rooted in colonial history, by its capacity to accommodate a variety of local interests, and by its advantageous association with popular democracy. On the other hand, the most innovative entrepreneurs—those who favored new technology and the new corporate form of business organization—along with those in society caught up in dreams of national glory, turned to the national government to promote their interests and keep the states from interfering with them. In the period following the War of 1812, they increasingly turned to the Marshall Court where they got a sympathetic hearing.

It soon became evident that the Court favored national mercantilism. In consolidating its own power, it had come down hard both on state legislatures and state courts. As previously noted, the Court's decisions expanding national power invariably restricted state mercantilism. *McCulloch* v. *Maryland* boldly encroached on the state power to tax and gave preferential treatment to a national corporation competing against state institutions. The *Gibbons* decision undid state promotional activity on behalf of state-based enterprise and gave Congress the authority to overrule state legislation in the area of interstate commerce. *Brown* v. *Maryland* added a further judicial barrier to state taxation and economic regulation (to the great satisfaction of Baltimore's commercial community).

Expanding congressional and judicial authority in order to limit state power was a hallmark of Marshall Court jurisprudence. But Article I, Section 10 of the Constitution gave the justices a more direct check on state power by prohibiting the states from emitting "bills of credit," passing ex post facto laws, and, most important of all, from "impairing the obligation of contract." The Court also relied on the quasi-legal doctrine of vested rights—a combination of John Locke, natural rights, and common-law concepts—that protected private property from legislative regulation even without specific reference to the Constitution. The Court had used Article I, Section 10, and the vested rights doctrine against the states before 1801, but had explored neither fully. The Marshall Court forged this inheritance into what Edward Corwin called, in his article of the same name, "the basic doctrine of American constitutional law."

It was no surprise that the Court began formulating this "basic doctrine" in support of agrarian capitalism. From the colonial period on, American law encouraged those involved in conquering the continent and acquiring land. It was assumed that the Supreme Court would continue this legal benevolence. The land speculators among the framers, and there were many, made sure that land disputes would be decided by the Supreme Court rather than the Senate. As Peter Magrath's fine study of *Fletcher* v. *Peck* (1810) makes clear, their faith was well placed. The case originated in 1795 when the Georgia legislature granted thirty-five million acres, the so-called Yazoo lands, to four private land companies at the bargain price of less than one and one-half cents per acre. It was soon discovered that all but one of the legislators voting for the bill had been bribed and that many other officials—including two United States senators, the district attorney for the state, a judge of the Superior Court of Georgia, a federal district judge, and Justice James Wilson of the Supreme Court—were implicated in the fraud. The guilty legislators were straightway returned to private life. In 1796, the new legislature repealed the original grant and voided all property rights attached to it. And to emphasize the point, the legislature publicly burned the original act and expunged all traces of it from state records.

While the repeal was in progress, however, the land companies sold portions of their grant to third parties—one being a well-organized interest group called the New England Mississippi Company, which purchased eleven million acres. John Peck of Boston, a director of this company, sold a small portion of his 600,000-acre investment to Robert Fletcher of New Hampshire. Fletcher then sued Peck in the federal circuit court in Massachusetts for breach of warranty of title, i.e., for selling him land which he did not rightfully possess. As Magrath proves beyond doubt, both the initial transaction and the suit were feigned to circumvent the Eleventh Amendment and bring the constitutionality of the Georgia repeal before the Supreme Court. This became obvious when Fletcher appealed the circuit court decision, despite the fact that it completely validated his title to the Yazoo land.

The complex issues in the case called for a response to a basic problem in nineteenth-century political economy. In repealing the grant the state legislature had performed its mercantilist duty. To deny it this power in the face of an obvious fraud would scuttle the public welfare and invite special interests to invade state legislatures—a practice for which they hardly needed encouragement. However, giving state legislatures an unlimited right to revoke previous grants could jeopardize confidence in all public grants and the private contracts based upon them; this, in turn, would discourage investment and thwart creative enterprise. A middle course would be to designate the Supreme Court as the judge of what grants should be voided. But to do so, Marshall realized, would plunge the Court into a tangled jungle of legislative interest-group politics with no clear legal path to follow.

Marshall's opinion for the majority wisely extricated the Court from the business of standing in judgment on the legislative process, while at the same time advancing the interests of large land speculators. His legal reasoning was boldly creative, to say the least. By focusing only on the question of the private contract between Fletcher and Peck (by a literal interpretation of the pleadings, in other words), the chief justice was able to declare that the only question before the Court was one of "title." That point established, he went on to reason that "It would be indecent in the extreme, upon a private contract between two individuals, to enter into an inquiry respecting the corruption of the sovereign power of a State." Legislative motive was not an area in which the Court was willing or equipped to adjudicate, a position that subsequent Courts have frequently affirmed. On the other hand, the question of whether a state legislature could "annihilate" a bona fide contract between two private citizens and "destroy the presumption of property thus held" was an issue the Court could answer. That the people of Georgia had been defrauded of several million acres of public land was no business of the Court but a matter between them and their agents. What the legislature could have done other than what it did—that is, to elect a new legislature and repeal the corrupt grant—Marshall did not say.

In denying Georgia the right to void a private contract, the chief justice turned to the clause in Article I, Section 10, of the Constitution that prohibited the states from impairing "the obligation of contract." But there were some embarrassing problems. Very little had been said about the contract clause either at the Constitutional Convention or in the state ratifying conventions. What had been said linked it and the other provisions in Section 10 to the problem of state currency regulation. As to the meaning of "contract," the general opinion of those who had any opinion at all (as B. F. Wright's *Contract Clause of the Constitution* [1938] shows) was that it applied to private contracts between A and B but not to public ones between the state and private parties (as was the case with Georgia's grant to the land companies). Opposed to this restrictive view were scattered private statements, before and after 1787, asserting that "contract" embraced public charters and grants. The most powerful of these was Hamilton's private legal brief of 1796 arguing that the Georgia rescinding act (the one before the Court) came within the prohibition imposed by the contract clause. The circuit court's decision in *Vanhorne's Lessee* v. *Dorrance* (1795), which used the contract clause along with vested rights to void a legislative act taking private property, was the closest thing to legal precedent available.

Sensing the weakness of relying entirely on the contract clause, Marshall approached the subject cautiously through the doctrine of vested rights, which he had broached before in his mandamus opinion. "It may well be doubted whether the nature of society and of government does not prescribe some limits to the legislative power . . . ," Marshall observed. And, without citing any precedent or referring to the Philadelphia Convention or the state ratifying conventions, he went on to declare that the original grant by the Georgia legislature was a contract within the meaning of Section 10 and that the rescinding act was an unconstitutional impairment of it.

The closest Marshall came to a justification of this holding was his assertion that it was not precluded by the words of the clause and that the "sentiment" of the framers was in favor of protecting property from state "passions." To prop up his assertions (or perhaps to divert attention from them), Marshall declared that the ex post facto provision in Section 10 would also have voided the act—conveniently forgetting that *Calder* v. *Bull* (1798) had limited the ex post facto clause to criminal matters. Apparently, he still had some doubts about the contract clause, for when he finally returned to it in his opinion, he linked the clause firmly to vested rights, voiding the Georgia rescinding act "either by general principles which are common to our free institutions, or by the particular provisions of the Constitution of the United States." Justice Johnson, preferring not to rely on those "particular provisions," based his concurrence entirely on vested rights.

The Yazoo opinion readied the contract clause for use as a constitutional weapon against state interference with property rights, expanded the meaning of property to include the right to acquire as well as possess, and advertised the judicial process to future capitalists as an instrument of economic policymaking.

Whether the decision fulfilled Madison's expectations in *Federalist* 44, that the contract clause would "inspire a general prudence and industry, and give a regular course to the business of society," is less certain. Perhaps it did establish a "regular course." State grants were contracts with the Court's imprimatur upon them. The state and its people were forewarned that they would be stuck with bad bargains, and individuals who did business with the state knew where they stood. But whether the struggle for legislative favors that the opinion encouraged furthered "prudence and industry" is highly doubtful. In any case, the opinion was in good nineteenth-century style. It was revealing that Jefferson's appointee and friend William Johnson should make this point. Property once granted to a man, he wrote, "becomes intimately blended with his existence, as essentially as the blood that circulates through his system." So the very "reason and nature of things" prohibited the state from revoking such a grant.

New Jersey v. *Wilson* (1812) was the first in a long series of contract decisions that came in the wake of the *Fletcher* opinion. In 1758, the colonial government of New Jersey had granted tax exemption to certain lands belonging to the Delaware Indians who, as a quid pro quo, had surrendered other land claims to the colony. In 1801, the Delawares sold their New Jersey lands and moved on to New York; in 1804, the state repealed the tax exemption. The purchasers of the Indian lands claimed these tax privileges, arguing that the state repeal violated the contract made with the Indians and was void under the contract clause. In his opinion, Marshall ignored the importance to the state of its power to tax land as well as the unique nature of the tax exemption in question; if he had dealt with these matters, the burden of proof would have been on the speculators. Since the state had not required a surrender of tax exemption as a condition in permitting the Indians to sell, Marshall ruled, the favored position became attached to the land and was passed on with the sale. The excessive zeal of the Court in promoting land speculation should not be obscured by the fact that New Jersey disregarded the decision and continued to collect taxes for some sixty years.

In a series of decisions following the New Jersey case, the Court managed, simultaneously, to assert the supremacy of national law, stabilize land titles, and consolidate the interests of large speculators. In *Fairfax's Devisee* v. *Hunter's Lessee* (1813), Justice Story for the Court used the Treaty of 1794 to void a Virginia statute confiscating Tory lands during the Revolution. He also upheld the right, contested by Virginia, of an alien to inherit land. Besides supporting national law, the decision validated the claims of speculators to nearly 300,000 acres of rich land in the Northern Neck of Virginia. Marshall recused himself because he was one of the main speculators, although it is hard to imagine that he was not consulted by his colleagues.

In *Terrett* v. *Taylor* (1815), Virginia took another blow from Justice Story, who was becoming as infamous in that state as Marshall. The colony of Virginia had granted lands for the support of the Episcopal Church, but after the disestablishment of religion, the state repealed these grants. Fearing that the divestiture acts of 1798 and 1801 would "uproot the very foundations of almost all the land titles in Virginia," Story fused the contract clause and natural rights doctrine to strike them down, noting sonorously that the Court was "standing upon the principles of natural justice, upon the fundamental laws of every free government, upon the spirit and letter of the constitution of the United States. . . ."

Green v. *Biddle* (1823) climaxed a series of decisions in which expansive interpretations of the contract clause advanced the interest of large land speculators. Better than any, it laid bare the undemocratic consequences of the Court's preferences. The case arose from a 1791 agreement between Virginia and Kentucky (at the time of the latter's separation from Virginia) in which Kentucky promised not to invalidate titles to land held under Virginia law. Kentucky pioneers— and most of the legal profession as well—did not understand the intricacies and uncertainties of Virginia land law or appreciate the virtues of absentee ownership. Assuming that they held valid titles, these Kentuckians took up land and labored to improve it, only to find in many instances that they owned neither the land nor their improvements. Without money or connections, they were prey for unscrupulous speculators and lawyers. Kentucky attempted to ease the plight of these settlers with a series of laws providing, among other things, that no claimant under Virginia title could take land until he had reimbursed the original settler for improvements made on it. The questions in *Green* v. *Biddle* were whether the 1791 agreement between Virginia and Kentucky was a contract within the meaning of the Constitution, and if so, whether the Kentucky claimant laws violated it.

The case had been argued three times, and, by 1823, it had become a rallying point for states' rights and anti-Court forces in the South and West. The Court was sensitive to their opposition but not deterred, even though three justices were absent. Justice Washington's opinion, joined by Story and Duvall with Johnson concurring, invalidated the Kentucky laws on the ground that they violated the original agreement between the states and thus the contract clause of the Constitution—this despite the fact that there had been no talk in or out of the Constitutional Convention about the contract clause being extended to agreements between sovereign states. Nor was the Court deterred by the fact that the Virginia land law that it upheld was notoriously irrational, inefficient, and unjust. To the great pleasure of Jefferson (and at his urging), Justice Johnson revived his democratic sentiments and entered a strongly worded separate opinion, which was, in all but name, a dissent.

The Court (as Paul Gate's "Tenants of the Log Cabin" [1962] demonstrates) did not have the last word, however. The squatters were not persuaded by protestations of judicial sincerity and they refused to obey the decision. (We are answerable, declared Justice Washington, "to God, our consciences, and our country.") The state supported the protesters, in part because the decision was rendered by a minority of three (since three justices were absent and one dissented). Kentucky went on to pass more effective claimant laws, and then joined with other disaffected states in a concerted move to curb the Court's power. One anti-Court resolution provided that a two-thirds majority of the Court was necessary to void any state or federal law. The Court responded by adopting an informal rule that a clear majority of the whole court was required to settle constitutional cases.

A series of lesser known cases that also helped wealthy landowners ran parallel to and complemented the contract clause decisions. *Huidekoper's Lessee* v. *Douglass* (1805) led the way. Pennsylvania had passed a law in 1792 prohibiting land speculation and absentee ownership by making title contingent on occupancy. (The law was directed particularly against the Holland Land Company, which claimed several hundred thousand acres of state land.) Reversing the decision of the state supreme court, Marshall interpreted the ambiguously worded statute out of existence. He validated the Holland Land Company claims by holding that the grantee by warrant had title even if he did not occupy the land, providing he tried to do so and was prevented by enemies of the country, i.e., American Indians. Twenty-five years later the conservative *American Quarterly Review* praised the Court for rising up "in its power and independence" to put the pretentious

"Squatters" in their place. Another quarter century later the Taney Court, which had presumably made peace with American democracy, resuscitated *Huidekoper's Lessee* to confirm the titles of large speculators to choice lands in California.

In the meantime the Adams-Onís Treaty of 1819 provided some fertile opportunities for the big investors. Under that treaty, the United States agreed to recognize land grants made by the King of Spain prior to January 24, 1818. While ratification was pending, however, a spate of hastily manufactured and fraudulent grants was made to American adventurers by Spanish officials. To validate their precarious titles, these speculators turned to the federal courts. The Court accommodated them in a series of decisions (*United States* v. *Arredondo*, 1832, for example) by applying the principle and spirit of *Fletcher* v. *Peck* and refusing to look behind the face of the grant for fraud. "He who would controvert a grant executed by the lawful authority," as the Court put it in the *Clarke* case in 1834, ". . . takes upon himself the burden of showing . . . that the transaction is tainted with fraud." Armed with this presumption of legality, speculators made good their claims to several million acres from the Louisiana Purchase and the Florida and Mexican cession territories.

The Supreme Court, it seems fair to say, lived up to its advance billing as a friend of those seeking capital gains in the land market. But in view of nature's plenitude and the prevailing assumption that the law would help those who helped themselves, the preferences of the Court were understandable—if not inevitable. No doubt the judges honestly believed that what helped Superintendent of Finance Robert Morris, President Washington, Justice Wilson, the Reverend Manasseh Cutler, Senator Daniel Webster, and General John C. Fremont (to mention a few prominent land investors) also helped the common people. John Marshall, who was a sizeable speculator himself, left no doubt about the matter. What the multitudes who cleared the land and fought both nature and the Indians thought about this trickle-down theory can only be surmised. Two things are certain. First, the plain folks who settled the continent just kept coming—with or without the assistance of the law. Second, enterprise in land whetted appetites, provided the financial base, and set the style for more dynamic forms of economic activity.

The Court and the Rise
of the American Business Corporation

No development during the antebellum period was more significant in shaping the economic history of the country than the rise of the business corporation. Not that the corporation was an American original. As early as the sixteenth century, the corporation had assumed its essential character, i.e., an association of private individuals for the accomplishment of private goals. As a societal organization, like the trade and professional guilds or religious orders, it had even deeper roots. The corporate device was well known in both England and the colonies in the seventeenth and eighteenth centuries, but it was employed almost exclusively as an instrument of political organization. Its application to business, and particularly to productive enterprise, was rare. In fact, throughout the eighteenth century hardly more than a dozen business corporations were chartered in England and, up through the Revolution, even fewer in the colonies. Yet it was mainly as an instrument of economic activity that the corporation made its mark on American history. The adaptation of the politically oriented corporate heritage to the economic exigencies of the American people was a major creative accomplishment of antebellum law—one in which the Supreme Court played an important role.

The combination of individual and associational features in the corporation made it ideally suited to nineteenth-century American ideas and needs. As de Tocqueville observed, the associational impulse pervaded the age. Americans applied associations of every degree ("moral, serious, futile, general or restricted, enormous or diminutive") to projects of every description (political, religious, educational, and economic). Far from contradicting the individualism of the age, the associational drive was a logical extension of it. If the individual was the agent of progress and individual accomplishment the measure of morality, it was only natural that individuals should join together for the more efficient accomplishment of their private goals. And nowhere was the collective impulse more appropriate than in the exploitation of nature.

Obviously, Americans made the connection. In 1780, the business corporation was almost unknown; by the end of the century,

American states had chartered 310 corporations. To be sure, most of these were connected with turnpikes, bridges, and canals, but eight were in productive enterprises. Between 1800 and 1817, 1,794 more corporations were chartered, with a large proportionate increase of those engaged in production. By 1830, the New England states alone had established 1,900 corporations, 600 of which were devoted to manufacturing and mining. Individual enterprises, copartnerships, and unincorporated joint stock companies continued to outnumber corporations. But before the end of the Taney period, the corporation had proven that it was the most viable, dynamic form of business organization.

There were other reasons—besides its congeniality to the individual-associational impulse—that the corporation was the primary vehicle for the economic revolution. Like these other devices, the corporation permitted the accumulation of capital from a broad base, which was especially important in a country without consolidated class wealth. It also permitted the efficient and centralized management of capital. What made the corporation uniquely attractive to America, however, was that it was an ideal instrument by which government could perform its obligation to aid private enterprise. Given the individualism of the age, it was only logical for government to promote enterprise by aiding these associations. Indeed, as de Tocqueville brilliantly perceived, this was the only way a democratic government could act. To work through an aristocratic class was impossible since there was none. To bestow privileges on select individuals violated egalitarian principles. It was impracticable for government to assume large-scale economic enterprise, given the embryonic state of administrative techniques—not to mention the potential threat to democracy that might ensue from too much government. The charter thus gave legal recognition to an association of private individuals and armed them with a portion of sovereign power and privilege—a solution that satisfied both expediency and ideology.

The corporation, then, was a creation of the law. However, it needed a body of legal principles to define and to guide it before it could serve American economic needs. For this, American lawmakers turned to the inherited body of corporate law, as well as related principles from other legal fields. But the inheritance was only partly applicable to American circumstances. The corporate form had to fit into the federal system and the democratic polity. And further, this basically political device had to be transformed into an economic instrument that would serve the peculiar individual-oriented pattern of American economic life. It was this collision of legal tradition with the "pressure of new interests," as Roscoe Pound observed in *The Formative Era of American Law* (1938), that provided the basis for a remarkable period of legal creativity. American lawmakers fused these elements into the most sophisticated body of corporation law in the Western world. (The legal story is told in E. M. Dodd's indispensable *American Business Corporations until 1860* [1954].)

The Supreme Court was only one of several lawmaking agencies engaged in formulating corporate law. The legislative charter—granted at first by special acts for each corporation and, increasingly in the 1830s, by general statutes of incorporation—bestowed legal life on private associations, gave them power and rights, and imposed duties and obligations. With the exception of the twice chartered Bank of the United States, state legislatures, rather than Congress, granted these charters. Exactly how these new legal entities would function became apparent only in practice, and the job of filling in the interstices of statute law with essential detail fell to the state and federal courts.

State judiciaries led the way in this creative enterprise. Beginning around the turn of the nineteenth century, an ever-increasing body of state decisional law—on such matters as the internal governance of the corporation, the transfer and sale of corporate shares, the nature of corporate contracts and property rights, the liability of corporate agents, the liability of shareholders for corporate debts, and the liability of the corporation itself for torts—made the corporation a workable business instrument. State courts also contributed to public corporation law by determining the relations of the corporation to legislative power. Among other things, they settled the doctrine of eminent domain and provided devices—the prerogative writs of mandamus and ultra vires—that could be used against a corporation exceeding or abusing its charter grant.

Through its diversity of citizenship jurisdiction and its broad powers in both law and equity, the Supreme Court was able to join with state courts in shaping the private law of corporations. Sometimes, as in Justice Story's opinion holding corporations liable for contracts made by their agents (*Bank of Columbia* v. *Patterson's Administrator* [1813]), the Supreme Court showed the way. Sometimes it built onto doctrines broached first in state courts, such as Story's distinction between public and private corporations (in *Terrett* v. *Taylor* [1815] and his concurrence in the *Dartmouth College* case [1819]); or his holding in *Wood* v. *Dummer* (1824), that the capital stock of a corporation was a trust fund for its creditors; or with the series of Supreme Court decisions defining the legal responsibilities of corporate agents. At other times, regarding tort liability of corporations for example, the Court (*Fowle* v. *Common Council of Alexandria* [1830]) merely recognized doctrines formulated in state courts. Occasionally the Supreme Court encroached on the jurisdiction of state courts to make its points. But most often it built on the creative efforts of state judges like John Bannister Gibson of Pennsylvania, Lemuel Shaw of Massachusetts, and Chancellor James Kent of New York.

The Court left its primary mark on corporate development as the interpreter of the Constitution and arbiter of federal power by defining the legal status of the corporation; by facilitating its operation across states lines; and by limiting state control over corporate charters. In thus defining the corporation's private rights and public responsibilities, the justices were influenced by inherited legal principles (largely of a common-law nature), by state law, and by nineteenth-century notions of politics, economics, and morality. In making corporate law, the Court gradually fused these ingredients into an authoritative ideology—if not a philosophy, then at least workable ground rules for corporate enterprise.

The decisive question was whether the corporation would derive its legal character from the individuals who comprised it, or from the public authority that created it. If the former, then the rights of private property could be attached to the corporation and cloak its operations. If the latter, government control over the corporation as a predominantly public instrument would be implicit. In *Head* v. *Providence Insurance Co.* (1804), the Court grappled with this issue for the first time. Marshall's legal definition of the corporation clearly emphasized its public character and implied legislative dominance over it. The corporation, he declared, "is the mere creature of the act to which it owes its existence," and "all its powers" and the manner in which they may be used are determined by this act.

This definition corresponded historically to the mercantilist view of the corporation as an instrument for the accomplishment of public goals. Such a definition continued to make sense as long as corporate enterprise was predominantly engaged in public service—i.e., turnpikes, canals, hospitals, and the like. With the increased use of corporations in private economic enterprise, however, this quasi-public conception seemed less tenable. The Court began to shift its view of the corporation accordingly.

In *Bank of the United States* v. *Deveaux* (1809), which dealt with a corporation's right to sue in federal courts, the Court began the process of adjustment. The jurisdictional issue raised the question of corporate character again. As an abstract legal creature, the corporation was unknown to the Constitution or the Judiciary Act of 1789 and must, Marshall admitted, "be excluded from the courts of the Union." Only if the Court could look beyond the legal entity to the individuals involved could a jurisdictional accommodation be made. Marshall proceeded to turn this contingency into law. The corporation is, he repeated, an invisible, artificial creation of the law. But a corporation is also the individuals who comprise it. And although the citizenship of these members cannot make the corporation a citizen within the law, common sense and the common law make it clear, said Marshall, that these individuals do have legal rights which attach to the aggregate. The right to sue is one of them. Accordingly, either a federal or state corporation may sue in federal courts under the diversity of citizenship clause providing its members are citizens of a state other than that of the party being sued.

The practice of determining jurisdiction by looking at the individuals behind the corporate name later proved unworkable and had to be abandoned, but its implications were large. For if the individual and private nature of the corporation might be emphasized for jurisdictional purposes, why not for the purpose of bestowing other private legal rights, such as the protection of corporate property from legislative interference? In *Terrett* v. *Taylor* (1815), Story separated the public and private aspects of corporate character, dealt with implicitly in earlier cases, into two separate categories—public corporations and private corporations. This was a distinction not yet established in American law. The functional difference between the two categories had to do with legislative control over them. The charters of public corporations, conceded Story, might be modified "under proper limitations," but, according to his definition, this category included only "counties, towns, and cities." The property rights of private corporations—all the rest—were protected by both natural rights and constitutional law. The stage was now set for including the privileges granted by the government in charters under those property rights which could not be abridged by subsequent legislation. The drama, starring John Marshall with Joseph Story and Daniel Webster in supporting roles, was entitled *Dartmouth College v. Woodward* (1819).

The College case seemed unpromising material for the cause of capitalism. The issue was whether the New Hampshire legislature could amend Dartmouth's charter (granted by George III in 1769) by increasing the number of trustees and making them appointees of the governor. This change was intended to transform the college into a state-controlled university. In the state superior court, Judge Richardson rejected arguments asserting that the legislature's act violated vested rights, the New Hampshire Constitution, and the contract clause of the United States Constitution. Instead, he ruled that the college was a public corporation and therefore subject to state regulation in the public interest. The constitutional issue in the case (whether the contract clause prohibited states from altering corporate charters) came before the Supreme Court on a writ of error.

Marshall had promised "cautious circumspection" in dealing with such important matters, and in many respects his opinion was rooted in the English common law governing private corporations. In other respects, however—and most certainly in its consequences—his opinion was audaciously creative. Marshall's argument rested on his factual holding that Dartmouth College was a "private eleemosynary institution" and therefore a private corporation. A charter to such a corporation is really a contract within the protection of the contract clause of the Constitution, and, therefore, the New Hampshire act amending the charter must be void. In concluding that private ("eleemosynary") and public ("civil") corporations ("institutions") differed in their subordination to legislative control, Marshall relied on Story's distinction between public and private corporations in *Terrett* v. *Taylor*. And Story, supported in turn by Bushrod Washington, spelled out the technicalities and implication of the distinction in a separate concurring opinion. But even with all this scholarly firepower, the fact remained that the immunity of "private" corporations from legislative control had no solid foundation in Anglo-American law, and Marshall himself implied as much when he admitted Parliament's unlimited power to annul corporate rights.

The chief justice also appeared to be on shaky legal ground when he turned to the contract clause. It "can require no argument," he declared, to prove that a charter of a corporation (including presumably those issued by state legislatures) is a contract. But he was unable to cite conclusive precedents—because there were none. In addition, he had to admit that the framers had not exactly intended to include corporation charters under "contracts" in Article I, Section 10. But Marshall believed it was enough that such an interpretation fit the spirit of the Constitution and was not prohibited by it. Having hypothesized the rule, he then concluded that the case at hand was not so exceptional as to escape it.

The consequences of the chief justice's improvisations were far-reaching. First, privately endowed educational corporations were now protected by law against state interference, thus guaranteeing the legal and financial future of private education in America. Marshall clearly understood this result because as a young lawyer he argued a similar issue in *Bracken* v. *College of William and Mary* (1790) using the same common-law arguments about eleemosynary corporations. But the doctrine of the *Dartmouth College* case also extended to the new business corporation—and in 1819 there were about one thousand such corporations for every fifty private educational ones. State legislative charters creating corporations were now contracts within the meaning of Article I, Section 10, of the Constitution; once granted they could no longer be altered, even for the public good.

It was Story's concurrence perhaps more than Marshall's majority opinion that drove home this economic message. It was also Story who introduced a modest note of judicial restraint by assuring states that they could regulate the corporations they chartered providing the right to do so was explicitly stated in the charter. This "reservation clause doctrine" softened the pro-corporate impact of the decision somewhat, but hardly eliminated it given the vulnerability of legislatures to special-interest lobbying. Assured of the stability of charter grants and strategically placed to exact choice ones, the private corporation was ready for business.

Dartmouth College v. *Woodward* was the first of three great pro-business, anti-state decisions of the 1819 term. The other two were *Sturges* v. *Crowninshield* and *McCulloch* v. *Maryland*. The latter, as we have already seen, served national commerce by legalizing the Second Bank of the United States, which stabilized national currency and encouraged Congress to enact a national system of internal improvements (by promising in advance that it had the constitutional authority to do so), and by curtailing state taxing powers. The *Sturges* case dealt with the constitutionality of a New York bankruptcy law. Most authorities agreed that clear and equitable laws regulating bankruptcy were imperative in the new age of commerce when business failures were a regular thing. The question was whether these laws should be passed by Congress or by the states. Article I, Section 8, of the Constitution gave Congress the power to enact uniform bankruptcy laws for the nation, and Congress passed a bankruptcy law in 1800—"the high-water mark of debtor relief in the eighteenth century," as Bruce Mann called it in his *Republic of Debtors* (2002). The Jeffersonians repealed it, however, because of its commercial bias. Thereafter, until the ill-fated national Bankruptcy Act of 1841, bankruptcy remained the exclusive domain of the states, which made the Court's decision in *Sturges* especially critical.

The New York bankruptcy legislation raised two questions: Did the constitutional grant vesting Congress with the power to pass national bankruptcy laws automatically prohibit state bankruptcy legislation? And, assuming it did not, what limitations if any did the contract clause of the Constitution impose on such legislation? Marshall's opinion for the Court held that the states had the power to pass bankruptcy laws in the absence of congressional legislation on the subject. He went on to say, however, that such laws were governed by Article I, Section 10, which prohibited states from impairing the obligation of contract. Marshall read this prohibition to mean that state bankruptcy laws could alter only the remedy but not the substance of the contract. Because the New York law applied to contracts made before its passage he struck it down as a violation of the contract clause.

Unfortunately the decision was not as clear as Marshall intended. Those who attended to his stern words on the sanctity of contracts assumed that the decision was a practical prohibition of all state bankruptcy laws. Others, including some of the justices, emphasized Marshall's doctrine of concurrent power and assumed that the opinion gave states wide discretion to pass bankruptcy laws so long as they applied to contracts made after the passage of the act. The business community and the politicians waited anxiously for clarification. When the Court finally ruled (in *Ogden* v. *Saunders* [1827]) that prospective bankruptcy laws were constitutional, the chief justice entered a passionate dissent.

The ambiguity of the *Sturges* decision suggests what Don Roper's article on the "Unanimity of the Marshall Court" demonstrates: that the Marshall Court was not monolithic. Even so, when one fits the political, economic, and legal pieces together, the Court's plan for economic greatness was remarkably coherent. Starting from the assumption that morality and capitalism are synonymous, the Court made the corporation the vehicle of economic expansion by identifying it with the enterprising individual. And because the Court viewed the corporate charter as a private contract immune to legislative interference, the corporations were able to attract sufficient capital to develop new productive techniques and operate on a national scale. The Court then secured that national field of operations for the business corporation by striking down state obstructions by using doctrines of constitutional nationalism (as in *McCulloch* and *Gibbons* v. *Ogden*).

All the advantages of mercantilism, and none of its disabilities, were extended to the entrepreneurs who came forth. Implied powers meant that Congress could pass promotional legislation; actual practice guaranteed that no national regulation would accompany this paternalism. Though the states were prevented from interfering with property, they were free, through the granting of corporate charters and other legislation, to subsidize enterprise (a story recounted in the classic studies of Louis Hartz on Pennsylvania and Oscar and Mary Handlin on Massachusetts).

At both the state and national level, then, the legal foundation was laid for the promotional, non-regulatory state of post–Civil War America. As the chief justice saw it, the entrepreneurial spirit of Americans operating in the emerging national market would obliterate sectionalism and would forge lasting bonds of national union. The new conservative class of businessmen and lawyers who rose to guide the forces of capitalism would replace the vanishing gentleman-ruler of the old republic and counterbalance the newly emergent class of professional politicians. American enterprise, generated by self-interest, liberated by free trade, facilitated by uniform commercial law (the kind Story taught at the newly founded Harvard Law School) would bring national prosperity. Men like Story and Webster allowed themselves to think that the capitalist spirit might even transcend nationalism to establish the basis of a *pax Atlantica.*

Retreat under Fire

In the brief period following the War of 1812, American sentiment appeared to be in tune with the Court's nationalism. The financial panic of 1819 and the subsequent depression, plus the Missouri debates over slavery, changed all that. The slaveholding states, newly conscious of their vulnerability to northern political dominance, came to fear that market capitalism would undermine their way of life. Increasingly they came to believe that the pro-national, pro-commercial jurisprudence of the Marshall Court was the source of the problem. Spurred to action by *McCulloch* the states' rights theorists, first in Virginia and then in other southern states, launched an all-out assault on the Court—and on the chief justice personally. In the last years of Marshall's tenure as in the first years, the fate of the Supreme Court was on the line.

The allegations against it were sweeping. Judicial review, once widely accepted, was now viewed by southern critics as flat-out usurpation. This power, they argued, was not granted by the Constitution and, because of the prejudices of the justices, it would always "be on the side of power and of the government which feeds them." By unauthorized judicial amendment, the Court undermined the constitutional system of limited government and dual federalism. (Jefferson described the process as "sapping and mining" and "twistification.") If, as John Taylor proclaimed (echoing the Virginia and Kentucky Resolutions of 1798), the state legislatures were "the people themselves," then the Court struck at democracy itself. Rather than viewing the Court as an impartial tribunal for preserving the constitutional settlement of 1787 (which was Marshall's view), critics depicted it as an agent of northern capitalists, which threatened to turn democratic government, rooted in state-based agrarianism, into an oligarchy ruled by a national, moneyed aristocracy.

However unfairly, the states' rights politicians of Virginia blamed John Marshall. By cunning and insinuation, they complained, he bewitched and befuddled his weak-willed associates—including Republican appointees. He subverted the democratic procedures of the Court by eliminating separate opinions and then by writing the Court's opinions himself. In short, he made the Court his own bully-pulpit from which he read Hamiltonian political and economic principles into constitutional law. Convinced by *McCulloch* that the Court was out to subvert their way of life, the Old Republicans of Virginia (typified by John Randolph) and nascent southern sectionalists joined forces and set out to convert the rest of the nation.

This new conservative phalanx, led by John Taylor of Caroline County and Judge Spencer Roane of the Virginia Court of Appeals, and urged on behind the scenes by Jefferson, countered the Marshall Court's opinions with ever more radical states' rights correctives. In 1822, for example, Jefferson pleaded with Justice William Johnson to break Marshall's hold on the Court and prevent the practice of "cooking up opinions in conclave" by reinstituting the practice of separate opinions. Johnson obliged with a barrage of dissenting opinions. States in the South and West were prepared to resist unpopular decisions by force, while more permanent remedies against "judicial tyranny" were considered.

There were numerous suggestions. Some thought the Senate should be made the supreme appellate court, others that the justices should have six-year terms like senators. And Congress actually considered requiring a majority of at least five of seven justices in constitutional decisions, or giving the Senate appellate jurisdiction in questions involving state sovereignty. Most threatening was the effort to repeal or modify Section 25 of the Judiciary Act, since it could be done by a simple majority in Congress. The election of Andrew Jackson in 1828 on a states' rights platform that promised to eradicate "neo-Federalism" seemed to seal the Court's fate. Sensing the danger, John Marshall cast his vote for J. Q. Adams in 1828—his first vote in a presidential election since becoming chief justice in 1801.

The Court did have enthusiastic supporters who rallied to its defense, especially in the middle and northern states. The "wise and the good and the elevated in society," as Story called the friends of the Court, had their own diagnosis of the nation's ills: Thomas Jefferson, whose "loose and visionary" ideas were demagogic tools to gain popular power and gratify an insatiable ambition. He hated the Court because, in checking the "wild impulse of the moment," it curtailed his own power. And it was Jefferson who inspired and guided the assault on the judiciary. The destruction of the Court, its defenders firmly believed, was only the first step in a process that would subvert the Constitution itself. Across the nation, conservatives toasted John Marshall as a national hero and looked to the Court, in the words of Timothy Pickering, as "the high Controlling *Authority*; the *Moral Scepter,* of the Nation."

The Court rode out the storm because the Jacksonians, including the president, were more interested in capturing the Court than in destroying it—and because the Court under the astute generalship of Marshall worked strategically to save itself. But it was not the "old Court" that survived. That court had been remarkably stable. From 1811 to 1823, there had not been a new member, and together the justices had accumulated 123 years of experience. There was disagreement among the justices to be sure—even between close friends like Marshall and Story—but mutual respect, communal living, and shared principles held dissent to a minimum. Working in harmony as never before or since, the justices exploited the opportunities for lawmaking afforded by post-1815 nationalism.

The inevitable change began in 1823 with a raft of new appointments. Henry Brockholst Livingston died in that year and was replaced by Smith Thompson. Robert Trimble replaced Thomas Todd in 1826, only to be replaced himself three years later by President

Jackson's appointee, John McLean. Henry Baldwin's appointment in 1830 to fill the chair of Marshall's friend Bushrod Washington was another blow to the old solidarity. The selection of Richard Peters as Supreme Court reporter in 1828—against considerable opposition within the Court—added to the disunity. Gone were the old camaraderie and accord, and gone too, in some measure, was Marshall's unique position of authority. As Donald Morgan's biography of Justice William Johnson shows, it was Johnson's determination to salvage a few Jeffersonian principles that brought the division among the justices into the open. During the ten years following 1823, Johnson wrote twenty-seven separate opinions, eighteen of which were dissents, and the new justices followed his example.

The chief justice was still a force to reckon with, however (witness his masterful opinions in the Cherokee Indian cases in 1831, and 1832), but age, the death of his beloved wife in 1831 and the onset of illness took a toll. On top of everything else the justices abandoned the tradition of communal living that had been a major factor both in the Court's unity and in Marshall's influence. There was much truth in his heartfelt complaint to his old friend Story, that there was a "revolutionary spirit" on the Court.

Beleaguered from the outside and radically changed within, it seemed certain that the Court would have to modify its high nationalism to fit the new age. The question—and it was one on which the institutional future of the Court hung—was whether the modification would be a rout, or an orderly retreat to solid nationalist ground. A sign of the change came, with symbolism to match the doctrine, in the case of the *Steamboat Thomas Jefferson* (1825). To the surprise of the profession, Justice Story's opinion refused to extend federal admiralty jurisdiction over the great system of inland lakes and rivers. Story based his opinion on the English doctrine that admiralty jurisdiction was confined to waters where the tide ebbed and flowed, but almost certainly the attack on the Court played a role. Coming from the champion of federal admiralty jurisdiction at a time when the steamboat made uniform admiralty law on the inland waters imperative, Story's jurisdictional retreat prompted *The North American Review* (January 1826) to remark, with some justification, that "high political sentiments and political emergencies" had brought the age of great judicial lawmaking temporarily to a close.

"Political emergencies"—that is, the rising state opposition to the nationalism of the Marshall Court—also influenced the Court's interpretation of the commerce clause. Here the retreat was decorous, if not entirely logical. To be sure, *Brown* v. *Maryland* (1827) revealed some of the old nationalist boldness and showed the Court's reluctance to abandon its high nationalism. But even here Marshall added an uncharacteristic note of judicial restraint by suggesting that "it might be premature to state any rule as being universal in its application" until the case demanded it. In *Willson* v. *Black Bird Creek Marsh Co.* two years later, the Court implemented the new spirit of restraint by refusing to void a Delaware law authorizing a bridge over a navigable stream that interfered with interstate commerce—though it clearly might have done so on the basis of precedent. As in the *Brown* case, Marshall's opinion made no attempt to draw a precise line between state and national commerce powers, but it did leave intact for later use its authority to do so. And still intact also were the nationalist principles of *Gibbons* v. *Ogden*.

Curtailing nationalism in contract clause cases was less subtle and more revealing of the Court's inner tensions during this period of transition. In the *Sturges* opinion of 1819, when the Court struck down the New York bankruptcy law that applied to contracts made before the act, it touched only tangentially on the constitutionality of such a law when it applied only to subsequent contracts (that is, to those made after the passage of the law). This issue came before the Court in *Ogden* v. *Saunders* (1827), and it soon became apparent that the Court was bitterly divided—and had been divided even in 1819. Justice Johnson's majority opinion was appropriately Jeffersonian in rhetoric. He held that, in the absence of federal bankruptcy legislation, a state act that applied to subsequent contracts was valid, even if it altered the substance of the agreement. Dismayed at this new tolerance for state regulation of property rights (although it was both a plausible and practical interpretation of the contract clause), Marshall made explicit what he only inferred in his *Sturges* opinion: that under no circumstances could a state law obliterate the substance of a contract. For the first time in twenty-six years, he dissented from his colleagues on a major constitutional issue. The company of Story and Duvall was little consolation.

"Ogden's case marks an epoch in our constitutional and judicial history," said the *United States Magazine and Democratic Review* later. "Painfully convinced that their constructive bow had been shot with vigor beyond the law, the Supreme Court, *de guerre lasse,* made a halt; and soon afterwards began retreat and atonement." *Providence Bank* v. *Billings* (1830) and several other cases of this period confirm the *United States Magazine*'s diagnosis. The question in the *Billings* case was whether a Rhode Island banking corporation was, by the implication of its charter, immune from a state tax on banking capital. Ignoring contrary precedents, which were pressed vigorously by counsel, Marshall affirmed the "vital importance" of the taxing power to the state and refused to diminish it. When Chief Justice Taney fell back on *Providence Bank* v. *Billings* seven years later to quash the doctrine of implied property rights, conservatives declared that that ruling was no "legitimate principle of constitutional interpretation." But the language of the decision is very clear.

The Court continued to moderate its use of the contract clause against state power in *Hawkins* v. *Barney's Lessee* (1831). Taking its cue from Kentucky states' rights opposition rather than its own decision in *Green* v. *Biddle*, the Court upheld the validity of the state's occupying claimant laws. Marshall's final constitutional opinion two years later was another concession to state power. The question in *Barron* v. *Baltimore* (1833) was whether the Fifth Amendment, and by extension the first eight amendments, restricted the states as well as the nation. Marshall refused to countenance the idea. The Bill of Rights, he said, was intended to prevent the "general government" from encroaching on the essential liberties of the people and, unless explicitly stated, it could not be used to limit state power.

Perhaps Marshall sensed the irony of presenting an essay on limited government in his last constitutional opinion. If so, it reinforced his mounting conviction that the Court he knew was under siege once again. More and more the Court was doing just what Jefferson and John Taylor said it should do—make decisions, not law. And increasingly it was harder to do even that. Hampered by ideological divisions, vacancies, and sickness, the justices fell behind in their docket. With the single exception of the Cherokee Indian Cases, the great constitutional questions of the day were continued from term to term, leaving them to be settled by the states' rights court of Roger Taney.

The confrontation between Georgia and the Cherokees, who occupied the northwest corner of the state, encapsulated the dilemma faced by all indigenous American tribes: whether they could coexist peacefully with the militarily dominant white Americans who believed it was their God-given destiny to rule and own the continent. Against the forces of Manifest Destiny, the Cherokees had only the word of the federal government in the treaties of 1790 and 1802, which guaranteed them continued sovereignty over the territory they did not voluntarily cede. Discouraged by the slow pace of cession, frightened by the economic, literary, and legal progress made by the Cherokees, and spurred on by the discovery of gold on Cherokee land, the Georgia legislature asserted control over Cherokee land in 1828. When the Democratic Congress at the urging of President Jackson passed an act in 1830 for the removal of the Cherokees west of the Mississippi, the Indians retained William Wirt as their chief counsel and turned to the Supreme Court as their last best hope.

That hope was seemingly dashed by the Court's decision in *Cherokee Nation* v. *Georgia* (1831), when it ruled that the Cherokees were neither a foreign state nor a state of the Union, and therefore could not sue under original jurisdiction (which they had attempted to do). In a remarkable obiter dictum, however, the chief justice went on to declare that the Cherokees were a "distinct political society" capable of self government—a "domestic dependent nation" in his famous words—and that a case brought properly before the Court would be favorably considered.

Such a case arose fortuitously in 1832, when two New England missionaries, Samuel Worcester and Elizur Butler, were arrested and imprisoned for preaching in Cherokee territory without a state license. Worcester appealed the state court decision upholding his conviction to the Supreme Court under Section 25. Marshall's opinion for the Court in *Worcester* v. *Georgia* (1832) held first that the Cherokees, as a self-governing political community, could negotiate treaties with the federal government; and second, that the treaties they had negotiated guaranteed their rights against Georgia. Federal treaties trumped state law; Georgia's act of 1828 was unconstitutional.

Marshall's "domestic dependent nation" concept, formulated in *Cherokee Nation* and implemented in *Worcester*, has since become the foundation of modern Indian law—and perhaps (as Gerald N. Magliocca has argued in the *Duke Law Journal*, 2003), an early example of equal protection jurisprudence as well. Unfortunately it did not help the beleaguered Cherokees. When Georgia refused to obey the Court and Jackson refused to back it, their only hope was the American voter. After Jackson's reelection in 1832, there was little choice for the Cherokees but to head West on the Trail of Tears. Several thousand died on the way and when they arrived, they discovered the lands promised by Congress were occupied by other tribes. "The Court has done its duty," as Story put it; unfortunately the American people did not do theirs.

Worcester's principled challenge to states' rights was evidence of the chief justice's continued influence and his determination to stand firm. Yet, accommodation rather than confrontation characterized the late Marshall Court. The substance and method of this accommodation have led historians to tone down the image of a monolithic Court dominated by a chief justice who handed down impeccably certain law. Unfortunately, there are no extant sources dealing with the internal divisions on the Court during this period, but the doctrinal compromises in cases involving state power tell the story. So, too, do complaints from the legal profession and business community that the doctrinal modifications of the late Marshall period left the meaning of the law uncertain. The extent to which the Taney Court was able to maneuver within that uncertainty (as Gerald Garvey perceptively observed in "The Constitutional Revolution of 1837 and the Myth of Marshall's Monolith" [1965]) proves their point.

The pattern of state defiance to Court decisions further signaled the end of the "golden age": for example, the quiet nonenforcement of *New Jersey* v. *Wilson*, the vigorous opposition to *Martin* v. *Hunter* in Virginia, and *Green* v. *Biddle* in Kentucky, Ohio's threatened violence in *Osborn* v. *Bank of the United States* and Georgia's open repudiation of *Worcester* v. *Georgia*. This is not to mention the legislative circumvention (through the reservation clause) of *Dartmouth*

College v. *Woodward*; or the shift in political power that dissipated both the doctrinal and economic impact of *McCulloch* v. *Maryland.* Clearly (as Michael Klarman reminds us) some of the Marshall Court's great decisions, when measured by their impact on actual events, were not as controlling as the words of the Court would lead us to believe.

Marshall himself sensed this fact and died fearing that the Court was permanently disabled and its doctrines vitiated. He was mostly wrong. Constitutional nationalism was not in the ascendancy, to be sure, but the nationalist principles proclaimed in *Gibbons, Fletcher,* and *Dartmouth College* were still available for future courts—thanks to Marshall's decorous retreat. The Second Bank of the United States was gone but not the doctrine of implied powers, even though it was temporarily shelved by the Jacksonians. And most important of all, the Court's power of decision had not been impaired. Whether the Court could or would preserve the principles and tradition of constitutional jurisprudence fashioned under Marshall—given the obvious politicization of the appointment process—was another question. The answer, and ironically history's appraisal of Chief Justice Marshall, rested squarely with the Jacksonian Court of Roger B. Taney. It was precisely this fact that worried the conservatives.

Associate Justice Samuel Chase (1741–1811)
Maryland
Appointed by George Washington
Served 1796–1811
Library of Congress, LC-USZ62-065448

Associate Justice Bushrod Washington
(1762–1829)
Virginia
Appointed by John Adams
Served 1798–1829
Library of Congress, LC-USZ62-56703

Left: Chief Justice John Marshall (1755–1835)
Virginia
Appointed by John Adams
Served 1801–1835
Portrait by John B. Martin
Collection of the
Supreme Court of the United States

Associate Justice William Johnson (1771–1834)
South Carolina
Appointed by Thomas Jefferson
Served 1804–1834
Library of Congress, LC-USZ62-915

Associate Justice Joseph Story (1779–1845)
Massachusetts
Appointed by James Madison
Served 1811–1845
Library of Congress, LC-USZ62-10382

Associate Justice Smith Thompson
(1768 [?]–1843)
New York
Appointed by James Monroe
Served 1823–1843
Library of Congress, LC-USZ62-10382

Chief Justice Roger Taney (1777–1864)
Maryland
Appointed by Andrew Jackson
Served 1836–1864
Portrait by James S. King
Collection of the
Supreme Court of the United States

Left: Associate Justice Levi Woodbury (1789–1851)
New Hampshire
Appointed by James K. Polk
Served 1845–1851
Library of Congress

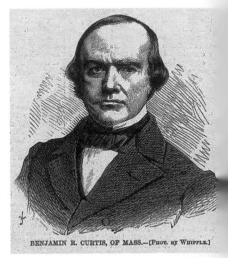

BENJAMIN R. CURTIS, OF MASS.—[Phot. by Whipple.]

Right: Associate Justice Benjamin Curtis (1809–1874)
Massachusetts
Appointed by Millard Fillmore
Served 1851–1857
Portrait from Harper's Weekly, *April 18, 1868*

The Old Senate Chamber, where the Court sat from 1860–1935. Collection of the Supreme Court of the United States

CHAPTER FOUR

The Taney Court: Democracy Captures the Citadel

The President will nominate a Democratic chief justice, and thus, we hope, give some opportunity for the good old State-Rights doctrines of Virginia of '98–'99 to be heard and weighed on the Supreme Court.
Richmond Enquirer (July 28, 1835)

The old constitutional doctrines are fast fading away, and a change has come over the public mind, from which I augur little good.
Justice Joseph Story (1837)

Unlike its illustrious predecessor, the Taney Court (1836–1864) was not an immediate favorite of historians due primarily to the *Dred Scott* decision of 1857. Before that decision the Court's popularity rivaled that of the Marshall Court, and Chief Justice Taney was widely considered to be a worthy successor to John Marshall. *Dred Scott* obliterated the memory of twenty-one years of effective judicial government and burdened the Court with the moral obloquy of slavery, along with a heavy share of war guilt. The Civil War itself—which secured

89

both freedom for the slaves and national consolidation—made the Taney Court appear un-American and historically irrelevant. The great multivolume histories of the early postwar period—like those of Rhodes, Schouler, and Von Holst—hardly mention the Taney Court, except for the shame of *Dred Scott* and the folly of judicial pretensions.

Historiographical bias progressively diminished, however, as the passions of war subsided and the Taney Court justices were replaced with Republican appointees (who ironically narrowed the reach of the Civil War amendments to accommodate the realities of northern racism). *Dred Scott* was not forgotten, but in 1891, Hampton Carson (whose two-volume *Supreme Court of the United States* was one of the first general histories of the Court) concluded that the Taney Court had adjusted, not destroyed, Marshall's constitutional system. He went on to say that—slavery excepted—its accomplishments were "quite as essential to the full realization of our welfare as a nation" as those of "any preceding epoch in the history of the Court." In the meantime, the Court discovered Taney precedents worth citing, including some nonslavery aspects of the *Dred Scott* decision itself. Edward Corwin's scholarly essay on that decision in the *American Historical Review* in 1911, though by no means uncritical, signaled the beginning of a more dispassionate consideration of the Taney era—and of Taney himself.

The implications of Carson's generous assessment of the Taney years were spelled out more fully in volume two of Charles Warren's *The Supreme Court in United States History* (1922) and also in Charles Grove Haines and Foster H. Sherwood, *The Role of the Supreme Court in American Government and Politics 1835–1864* (1957), the first general account devoted entirely to the Taney Court. Monographs by Felix Frankfurter (on the commerce clause) and Benjamin F. Wright (on the contract clause) also contributed to a more balanced view of the Taney period. Judicial biographies—Francis Weisenburger on John McLean; John P. Frank on Justice Peter Daniel; Alexander A. Lawrence on James Moore Wayne; Robert Saunders on John Archibald Campbell; and James McClellan and R. Kent Newmyer, respectively on Joseph Story—also presented a more nuanced appreciation of the Taney Court, as did Carl Brent Swisher's biography of Taney (1936) and most importantly his authoritative volume, *The Taney Period,* in

The O. W. Holmes Devise History of the Supreme Court of the United States (1974).

Newer scholarship on the Taney Court recognized that its chief accomplishment was to adjust the constitutional legacy of its predecessors to the political and economic realities of the Age of Jackson. Unlike the Marshall Court, the Taney Court inherited a substantial body of decisional law. Because its prestige and authority depended on it, whenever possible the Taney justices modified the old law without appearing to abandon it—this while dealing with the disruption caused by new appointments and increased personal discord on the bench. The challenge was different from the one the Marshall Court had faced, but no less difficult. The accomplishment, most historians are inclined to concede, was impressive—with the obvious exception of *Dred Scott* v. *Sandford.*

The historical changes that brought the Jacksonians to power in 1828 and established a new frame of reference for the Taney justices amounted to a major transformation in American society. Freed from the restraints of British mercantilism by the Revolution, the Lockean tradition coalesced with romantic Protestantism and abundant economic opportunity to create a climate of militant individualism. The democratization of the political process reflected and simultaneously supported the new intellectual and economic egalitarianism: universal white male suffrage was achieved by the mid-1820s; direct election of electors by the 1830s; caucus nomination gave way to the national convention; and elective offices multiplied. As the national two-party system took permanent shape in the 1830s, the twin principles of deference and noblesse oblige, which had conditioned politics since the colonial period, disappeared. Government by as well as for the people seemed close to realization—a fact the Taney Court accommodated to a remarkable degree.

This new democratic America was fully committed to the dream of inevitable economic progress but badly divided on what that progress meant and how to achieve it. Driven by new technology, market capitalism continued to expand, but it was no longer universally welcomed as it had been in the brief period of national euphoria following the War of 1812. Nor was it universally assumed that national mercantilism was the road to utopia. The Panic of 1819 and the

Missouri Debates of 1819–21 brought to light sectional differences that, as Henry Clay painfully discovered, could not be served equitably by a single national plan. The admission of twelve new western states during the Taney period further complicated the problem. In the new age of rampant sectionalism, it seemed clear that less economic nationalism, not more, was the order of the day.

Whigs and Jacksonians alike were obliged to adjust to the new egalitarian spirit and to face the fact that unity on national economic policy, if it had ever existed, had vanished. Only the Jacksonians got the message. The Jacksonian party organization—based on an intricate network of local, state, and national units, popular electioneering, and presidential patronage and prestige—was ideally structured to exploit the potential of mass participatory democracy. Jacksonian economic policy was a combination of egalitarian assumptions and the recognition that, in the face of growing sectional diversity, national economic planning would be fatal to political popularity and power.

In short, the Jacksonian commitment to liberal economics was a negative one. Not only was national economic planning abandoned but planners like Daniel Webster, Henry Clay, and Nicholas Biddle (president of the Bank of the United States) were effectively branded as enemies of the people. It was both democratic and practical to let the states take the initiative if governmental action were required. This emphasis on state power, moreover, appealed to the state-based reform movement in the North, allowed the southern states to do what they wanted with slavery, and, at the same time, permitted the Jacksonians to identify with the states' rights democracy of the Jeffersonians. With Andrew Jackson as living proof that states' rights was not incompatible with national Union, the United States pushed on with the capitalist revolution, promising that its benefits would be equally dispersed and that the honesty and other simple virtues of the golden agrarian age would be preserved.

King Andrew's Court

To the immense discomfiture of conservatives, President Jackson brought the Supreme Court into harmony with Jacksonian Democracy by virtue of six appointments. Before Marshall's death in 1835, the president had already put three Democrats on the bench—John McLean (1829), Henry Baldwin (1830), and James Wayne (1835). Roger Taney's appointment as chief justice in 1836, along with the appointments of Philip Barbour the same year and John Catron in 1837, gave the Democrats an easy majority. Martin Van Buren, Jackson's handpicked successor, appointed two more stalwart Democrats, John McKinley and Peter Daniel, leaving only Joseph Story and Smith Thompson as holdovers from the Marshall Court. As a result of the judicial reorganization act of 1837, the Court now numbered nine justices (where it has remained, except for a brief interlude during the Civil War).

The Jacksonian justices clearly represented a new generation in antebellum history. The differences were significant—and distasteful to many. The Whigs lamented the seven Democrats on the Court. The northern states distrusted the six judges from the South and West and felt increasingly underrepresented, a fact that they blamed on the "slave power conspiracy." The new justices lacked the common experience in the Revolution and the Confederation periods that had rallied the Marshall justices to the nationalist cause. And, like the rest of the age, they were contentious ("a gaggle of squabbling prima donnas," as David P. Currie aptly observed) and unabashedly political. Whereas Marshall strove to keep the Court out of politics, many of the new justices were frank about their political affiliation and open in their friendship with politicians.

Not all of them were up to the job of judging, either: Fourteen justices served from 1836 to 1864. Of the longer serving, only Story, Taney, and Curtis were really gifted and the latter had served only six years, from 1851 to 1857, when he resigned in protest. Duvall's deafness, Baldwin's sporadic madness and consistent paranoia, and Daniel's noncompromising agrarian radicalism (which manifested itself in chronic dissent) also detracted from the Court's efficiency. McClean's perennial presidential aspirations further hurt the Court's image, although he did carry his share of the Court's work (which was not true of many of his colleagues). Opposition to Court Reporter Richard Peters (one of whose inadequacies was a handwriting that not even he could read) and the struggle over his removal in 1843 turned latent dissension on the Court into outright factionalism. But even before that, institutional unity had all but vanished.

More than anything else, it was seeing Roger Taney in John Marshall's chair that chilled the spirits of the old Court's friends. Marshall had become synonymous with the Court and after him, none could please. Story, who came closest, wanted the chief justiceship badly (and clearly deserved it), but resigned himself to being passed over by his omnipotent political enemies. But the conservative mind veritably boggled at the prospect of Taney, that "supple, cringing tool of power." Taney was the champion of states' rights and the coauthor of Jackson's veto message that condemned the Second Bank of the United States; he was also the secretary of the treasury who executed the sentence. Stooped, sallow, and a Catholic too, Taney did not fit the Marshall mold.

The prophets of gloom were correct in predicting change but were badly mistaken in assuming that a changed Court was no Court at all. Less paranoid contemporaries saw much ground for hope, and history soon confirmed their optimism. Not the least of the new Court's assets, as it turned out, was its chief justice. Roger Taney suited the complex and contradictory middle period of American history as well as any man could. He was a southerner who loved his country, a champion of states' rights who was dedicated to the Union, a slaveholder who manumitted his slaves, and an aristocrat with a democratic political philosophy. In Maryland he had practiced law and politics simultaneously and succeeded in both. After abandoning Federalism as a losing cause, he rose to the top of the state's Jacksonian machine. As United States attorney general (1831–33) and secretary of the treasury (1833), he revealed an anti-monopolistic, state mercantilist, democratic bias that made him one of President Jackson's closest advisers. He brought this bias to the chief justiceship, along with an impressive legal mind, a lucid writing style, and a kind and gentle manner that worked to keep his discordant colleagues on task.

Corporations and the Court: The New Look

The chief justice made his debut wearing long trousers instead of the small clothes (or knee breeches) of the Marshall period, a sartorial omen that a new age had begun—a sure portent, one journal remarked grimly, of a "modern sans-culotte-ism." The three great constitutional cases of the 1837 term confirmed conservative fears. Each had been argued before the Marshall Court, but because of divisions and absences, none had been decided. In each of its decisions, the new Court modified a doctrine of the "old law"; together, these decisions presented a rough outline of the democratic posture of the Court in the new age.

Of these three cases, the *Charles River Bridge* v. *Warren Bridge* (1837) was the most dramatic and revealing. The facts raised crucial and delicate issues. In 1785, the Massachusetts legislature chartered the Charles River Bridge Company to build a bridge across the Charles River connecting Boston and Cambridge. In return for building and maintaining the bridge, the charter granted the company the right to collect tolls for forty years, a privilege later extended to seventy years. The charter did not explicitly grant the company the exclusive right to tolls, however, although the proprietors no doubt assumed that it did. In 1828, while the toll rights of this company were still in force, the legislature chartered the Warren Bridge Company, giving it authority to build an adjacent, toll-free bridge. The question was whether the imprecise wording of the old charter implicitly conferred a monopoly on the Charles River Bridge Company which the new bridge encroached upon, thus violating the contract clause of the Constitution and the *Dartmouth College* ruling.

As Stanley Kutler's insightful account of the case shows, this technical legal question reflected the major political, economic, and constitutional issues of the age, issues that sharply divided the Whigs from the Jacksonians. Warren Dutton, speaking for the Charles River Bridge Company and for the Whigs, reminded the Court that the free bridge which had been built next to the old toll bridge had, in effect, by nullifying the toll rights of the old bridge company, extinguished half a million dollars in property outright and jeopardized another ten million. He wanted the Court to declare the Warren Bridge charter unconstitutional so that the proprietors of the old bridge company might receive compensation for their losses. If the Court failed to do so, he predicted public faith in the government's promises would evaporate, along with the venture capital so critical to corporate development.

Lawyers for the new bridge company cited precedents to support their argument but relied primarily on the fact that the community needed a toll-free bridge connecting Boston and Cambridge to accommodate the rapid growth in population. In serving the public, the legislature should not be hamstrung by the acts of its predecessors—especially when there was no explicit legal obligation to do so. As for private property and economic progress, supporters of the new bridge insisted that the old bridge had already paid for itself several times over. Furthermore, asked counsel for the new bridge company, how could new modes of transportation, such as the railroad, be developed if every dilapidated turnpike and canal company could entrench itself behind an implied monopoly?

The chief justice spoke for the majority in an opinion that disconcerted his critics by its persuasiveness ("smooth and plausible," admitted Webster, who was counsel for the Charles River Bridge Company, "but cunning and jesuitical"). Taney mobilized Anglo-American law and Jacksonian politics and economics against the doctrine of implied contracts. It was a rule of common law, he declared, known in every case "without exception" and supported by fifty years of American "usage and practice," that "any ambiguity in the terms of the contract, must operate against the adventurers, and in favor of the public." "While the rights of private property are sacredly guarded," Taney continued in good Jacksonian style, "we must not forget that the community also have rights, and that the happiness and well-being of every citizen depends on their faithful preservation." In addition, both equality of opportunity and economic progress militate against implied monopoly, the legal pivot on which the case turned. If every turnpike and canal company could take refuge behind implied monopoly, said Taney, following the lead of counsel, then "modern science" would be throttled and transportation set back to the last century. Neither economic progress nor the state's power to serve the public good could be interdicted on the shaky grounds of legal inference and construction. The charter of the new bridge was constitutional.

Justice Story liked public welfare and economic progress as much as the chief justice but, believing them inseparable from the absolute security of private property, he dissented bitterly from the "speculative niceties and novelties" of his new brethren. His scholarly refutation of Taney convinced only his old colleague on the Court, Justice

Thompson. Across the land, however, conservatives read his learned dissent as good law—and they were right. But mistakenly, they concluded that a revolution had occurred in American law.

The Court had, in fact, neither opposed the corporation per se, nor departed from the *Dartmouth College* ruling that a corporate charter was a contract protected by the contract clause. Had the rights claimed by the Charles River Bridge Company been explicitly granted, there is little doubt that the Court would have upheld them. The real significance of the *Bridge* decision was the Court's refusal to extend the rule of the *Dartmouth College* case by implication. Instead, following Jacksonian priorities, the majority recognized that the new corporate device, by combining economic privilege and political power, posed a danger to the public welfare. Especially was this true when select economic interests were given monopolistic powers by special legislative charters. By allowing the state legislature to override its own charter, the Court showed a new tendency to defer to the will of the people and the authority of state government.

What it did not recognize, as Kutler points out, was the fact that the new bridge movement was driven by real estate interests who stood to profit from the location of the second bridge. Seen from this angle, the *Bridge* case was as much a battle between static and dynamic capitalist groups as it was a populist uprising against monopoly. By siding with dynamic capital, the Court laid the cost of economic development on the stockholders of the old bridge company. Had the old bridge company been compensated for its loss—which was really what the plaintiffs hoped for—the cost of economic development would have fallen on the taxpayers of Massachusetts where, in fairness, it rightfully belonged.

The *Bridge* decision was unmistakably Jacksonian in tone and substance—the sign that a significant shift in constitutional law was underway. The decision did not mean that the Jacksonians were hostile to corporations (they were not), or that the Court intended to take charge of corporate law (it did not). In fact, nearly all law regulating corporate behavior during this period emanated from state governments. State legislative charters specifying limitations on corporate operations were the primary means of regulation. And the interpretation of such grants took place largely in the state courts. (As it turned out, the problem of effective control was less a legal one of judicial construction than a political one of getting meaningful regulations through state legislatures that were pressured by powerful lobbies and burdened by incompetence.) In other, more direct, ways state judiciaries entered the regulatory field. Writs of mandamus and quo warranto—the former designed to compel the performance of duties stipulated in the charter, and the latter to obtain a forfeiture of the charter in case of nonperformance—were devices available in the state courts for use against corporations. As early as 1807, state courts acted to protect the public from corporate abuses by holding corporations liable for torts, that is, for private or civil wrongs committed independent of contract.

Nevertheless, the Supreme Court did touch various phases of this regulatory process at vital points. And under Taney its actions were guided by the spirit of economic realism and judicial self-restraint regarding state law apparent in the *Bridge* decision. The interpretation of corporate charters was a case in point. Charters, especially those extending unusual privileges—such as the monopoly granted to a railroad corporation in *Richmond F. & P.R.R.* v. *Louisa R.R.* (1851)— were construed narrowly and viewed with an eye to the public welfare. In *Ohio Life Insurance & Trust* v. *Debolt* (1854), the Court conceded the constitutionality of a state charter granting tax exemption to a bank, but refused to extend such a privilege by implication. Taney made clear that its refusal was based on a recognition of some unpleasant realities in business life. Bills of incorporation, he noted, were almost always drawn up by the parties "personally interested" in getting concessions rather than by impartial representatives of the public. Moreover, such bills "are often passed by the Legislature in the last days of its session when, from the nature of our political institutions, the business is unavoidably transacted in a hurried manner, and it is impossible that every member can deliberately examine every provision in every bill upon which he is called on to act."

In addition to this strict construction of corporate charters, the Court also endorsed the use of mandamus, quo warranto, and tort law by state courts against unauthorized corporate power. And in *West River Bridge Co.* v. *Dix* (1848), in a rare majority opinion written by Justice Daniel, the Court sanctioned the doctrine of eminent domain, permitting the state of Vermont to take corporate property (a bridge with a hundred-year charter) for public use with just compensation (which turned out to be a mere $4000). The case was remarkable not the least for the fact that the takeover upheld by the Supreme Court was originally ordered by the Vermont County Court. The *Dix* ruling, boasted the democratic *Boston Post*, heralded a "new era" of popular rights over corporate monopoly. Daniel Webster, on the other hand, feared that the Taney Court's concession to state sovereignty would unleash "levelling ultraisms" like "Antirentism or Agrarianism or Abolitionism."

In denouncing the Court's radicalism, Webster seems to have overlooked its decidedly pro-corporation, pro-property decision in *Bank of Augusta* v. *Earle* (1839). That decision, an instrumental one in encouraging the interstate operation of the corporation, concerned bills of exchange (the primary source of commercial credit in antebellum United States) purchased in Alabama by agents of three out-of-state banking corporations. When the bills came due, the men who had issued them cynically refused payment on the grounds that foreign banking corporations were not permitted to operate in Alabama. Justice McKinley heard the case on circuit, and, as Justice Story recalled, "frightened half the lawyers and all the corporations of the country out of their properties," by upholding the defaulters. Had the Supreme Court affirmed McKinley's opinion, it would have dealt a mortal blow to the interstate operation of corporations.

The Jacksonians were still rejoicing and the Whigs were still lamenting when the Court reversed McKinley's sweeping interdict. Taney tactfully applied the doctrine of comity (the "full faith and credit" clause in Article IV, Section 1), holding that if a corporation founded in one state was authorized by charter to do business in another, it could do so unless specifically prohibited by the law of the other state. Silence would be interpreted to mean that the state had no objection to foreign corporations doing business within its boundaries. Taney found nothing to undo this presumption in the Alabama case.

Compared to the radical democracy of McKinley's circuit opinion, the Taney decision seemed—and was so labelled by democratic purists—a sellout to the corporation. In fact, it was an expedient concession to the realities of American economic life that was generally consistent with the Court's Jacksonian posture. The decision armed the state with great potential power to prohibit the operation of foreign corporations, and it also denied Webster's contention that the corporation was a citizen with all the constitutional rights and privileges thereof (although there was material at hand for such an interpretation). Taken with Justice Thompson's circuit decision in the *Warren Manufacturing Co.* v. *Aetna Insurance Co.* (1837)—upholding a law making a Connecticut corporation doing business in Maryland subject to suit in the latter's courts and making judgments in such cases subject to review in federal courts—it was clear that the Court had no intention of leaving the state at the mercy of interstate corporations. If the states failed to control such corporations, it was because they saw the economic advantages offered by the growing national market of which the corporation was a vital part.

Briscoe v. *Commonwealth Bank of Kentucky*, the second of the three leading cases of the 1837 term, concerned state banking. Of all the corporate issues of the period, banking was the most comprehensive and the most likely to bring the Court under political and economic attack. Because the Bank of the United States was in competition with state banks, bank policy became the battleground in the contest between state and national mercantilism. Moreover, as credit and currency manipulation were alien to the mentality of the small farmer, banking became a focal point in the debate over honest labor and the good life that divided the agrarian- and commercial-minded. Not surprisingly, both Jacksonian policy and Jacksonian rhetoric were shaped in the war against the parasitic "monied aristocracy" associated with "Mr. Biddle's Bank." As champions of state banking, the Jacksonians not only broadened economic opportunity, but also unleashed the forces of laissez-faire capitalism.

The *Commonwealth Bank of Kentucky* fit neatly into the Jacksonian economic plan. Though nominally a private corporation, the bank's stock was owned solely by the state, its president and board of directors were chosen by the legislature, and its notes circulated as money. The crucial issue was whether these notes were bills of credit prohibited by Article I, Section 10, of the Constitution. John Marshall's answer was well-known to the Court. In the parallel case of *Craig* v.

Missouri (1830), he had in a narrow 4-3 decision ruled against state issuance of paper money. And when the Kentucky case was argued in 1834, he was prepared to bring it within the scope of the *Craig* ruling.

In 1837, however, circumstances were different. President Jackson had made good his promise: Nicholas Biddle's Bank was dead. And by default, state banks now constituted the main source of national currency and credit. Justice McLean, in the majority opinion, accommodated both this blunt economic fact and Jacksonian principles by holding that the notes of the Commonwealth Bank of Kentucky were not bills of credit interdicted by the Constitution, even though the state owned the bank and the notes circulated by state law as legal tender. McLean went through the motions of distinguishing the Kentucky from the *Craig* case. But it was obvious that technical law had given way to economic and political expediency. As McLean admitted, an opinion against the Kentucky bank would be "a fatal blow against the state banks, which have a capital of near $400,000,000, and which supply almost the entire circulating medium of the country."

Justice Story stood on the *Craig* decision and in a bitter, solitary dissent condemned the new spirit of expediency that had set the Court "adrift from its former moorings." Delivered with "profound reverence and affection" for John Marshall, Story's dissent marked the distance the new Court had strayed from the path of the "old law."

The Taney Court and the Commerce Clause

Thanks in large part to the Marshall Court, the commerce clause became the key constitutional instrument for allocating power between the states and the nation. And given the American tendency to view fundamental economic and political problems in terms of the balance of power in the federal system, it was inevitable that it should become the center of constitutional debate. Some adjustments were clearly in order (a subject discussed concisely in Frankfurter's book on the commerce clause). The Marshall Court had painted with broad strokes. The new age needed a lighter touch and more subtle shading. Both North and South desired an expansive national commerce, but neither took kindly to commerce-clause decisions that encroached on their special concerns: slavery in the South and state-based reform legislation (including antislavery laws) in the North. A delicate interpretation of the commerce power was needed, one that would please both North and South and would, at the same time, encourage national commerce. *New York* v. *Miln* (1837) brought the Court face to face with the problem. New York had passed a law in 1824 requiring masters of all vessels arriving at the port of New York from foreign countries or from other states to report the names, ages, and occupations of all passengers, and to take bond that none should become wards of the city. This law was designed to keep the city from being overwhelmed with indigents it was not prepared to care for. It seemed clear, and the state so argued, that such legislation fell within its authority to protect the health and welfare of its citizens. But just as clearly, the law regulated interstate commerce. The question was whether this law was an unconstitutional encroachment on congressional commerce power as set forth in Article I, Section 8, as interpreted by the Marshall Court.

The Court might have closed the door on state power by opening the one to exclusivism deliberately left ajar by Marshall's *Gibbons* opinion. Story, for one, believed that the grant of commerce power to Congress automatically excluded state authority from the field, and he argued that Marshall agreed. Justice Barbour's opinion for the majority followed Jacksonian priorities, however, rather than those espoused by Marshall and Story. The New York regulation, he said, was a valid exercise of police power, which he defined vaguely as state authority to legislate for the safety, happiness, and general welfare of the people within its jurisdiction.

Barbour cited Marshall's tangential references to police power in the *Gibbons* and *Brown* opinions as his authorities, but his contention that police power was "unqualified and exclusive" went far beyond anything that precedent or practice could justify. In assuming that police regulations could be entirely separated from interstate commerce, he flatly contradicted the *Gibbons* opinion, which gave federal law priority in case of conflict, and ignored both the Tenth Amendment to the Constitution and Article VI by establishing, simply by definition and assertion, an area of state power that was prior to, outside the scope of, and superior to the power delegated to Congress. Story saw the oversimplifications, was appalled at their radical import, and dissented forcefully on the basis of *Gibbons* v. *Ogden*.

The scholarly Story wanted to settle the law; the majority wanted to settle the case and they did so in a result-oriented decision that permitted New York to address a pressing practical problem. As a result, however, the justices remained bitterly divided over the basic questions of whether congressional power over interstate commerce was exclusive or concurrent with the states, and whether and to what extent it extended to slaves. The amorphous concept of police power (not even its advocates could agree on a definition) was at best an expedient means of avoiding open division on the Court; but, as rendered by Justice Barbour, it was not even that. When Barbour delivered his opinion on the last day of the term, several of his colleagues were shocked to discover that the opinion's assertions about the scope of police power went beyond the position accepted in conference, and did not have the concurrence of a majority.

Confusion and uncertainty about the meaning of the commerce clause continued in the License Cases (1847) and the Passenger Cases (1849). Both raised the question of whether state welfare and reform legislation affecting interstate commerce was an unconstitutional encroachment on congressional authority. At issue in the License Cases were the temperance laws of Massachusetts, Rhode Island, and New Hampshire. In the first two states, the contested laws required state licenses for retailers of imported liquor in less than bulk quantity; in the latter the statute required a license, whether the liquor was sold wholesale or retail, without distinction as to quantity.

As in *Miln* the Court decided the case but not the law. Nine justices agreed in multiple separate opinions that the laws were valid but were unable to agree on their reasons for thinking so. Taney's opinion upheld the Massachusetts and Rhode Island laws by Marshall's "just and safe" *Brown* ruling, which permitted states to tax imports once the "original package" had been broken. The New Hampshire law was a different matter, since it licensed bulk as well as retail sales. In upholding this law, Taney explicitly repudiated exclusivism and supported the power of states to legislate concurrently with Congress in the field of interstate commerce, although he made it clear that in case of a conflict between state and national laws, the latter were "superior and controlling." He went out of his way to play down the police power concept, which he thought extraneous and "nothing more or less than the powers of government inherent in every sovereignty to the extent of its dominions."

With a convenient suspension of logic, Justice McLean undertook to refute Marshall's original package rule: he insisted on the exclusive power of Congress, but then avoided the impractical consequences by supporting an extreme version of police power. Peter Daniel rejected the hairsplitting of his colleagues, the "glosses of essay-writers, lecturers, and commentators," and substituted instead the proposition that states controlled all the property within their jurisdictions, regardless of derivation. He went on, as Barbour had ten years earlier, to reverse the whole concept of reserved powers by declaring: "Every power delegated to the Federal government must be expounded in coincidence with a perfect right in the States to all that they have not delegated. . . ." Justice Woodbury paid respects to Daniel's extreme position as well as the concurrent power concept, but he subscribed to the Jacksonian proviso that doubtful cases be resolved in favor of the states. John Catron relied on concurrent power, Robert Grier on police—though he was not bold enough to say what it meant. Justice Nelson sided with Catron and Taney. Altogether the Court agreed on nothing and left its decision without a reasoned justification.

Doctrinal chaos also prevailed in The Passenger Cases two years later. At issue were the laws of Massachusetts and New York, which taxed immigrants coming into the ports of the state. Massachusetts, once the seat of constitutional nationalism, was now sharply divided between those advocating national commerce through national power, and those who wanted sufficient state power to keep out undesirable aliens and to tax for the public welfare. The rising forces of antislavery were among the champions of state power, because they saw this power as a weapon against the fugitive slave law. (Daniel Webster was embarrassed by the schism and berated his state for its "ultraism, mock-morals, false philanthropy and illiberal laws infringing trade and commercial intercourse.") To add to the confusion, the southern states violently objected to the North's use of police power and states' rights against slavery, but they were obliged to support the doctrines themselves to defend their own laws prohibiting the immigration of free negroes.

The Court's decision, reflecting these contradictory desires, made no constitutional sense. After three arguments, the justices came up with eight separate and discursive opinions running to nearly two hundred pages. A precarious majority of five struck down the laws as conflicting with federal law but continued to disagree on their reasons. Despite Justice Wayne's attempt to reduce the majority position to order, the Court reporter had to conclude that there was no opinion of the Court.

Not only were the judges unable to agree, but they foolishly vented their previous disagreement in *New York* v. *Miln*. Wayne took particular care to diminish the authority of that decision by noting that Barbour's last-minute discourse on the commerce clause (printed in the *Reports* with the apparent sanction of the chief justice) went beyond the decision of the conference and was supported by only two justices. Taney, seconded by Daniel, answered Wayne's charges, reminding him that if the authority of the opinions could be undone by one justice's "individual memory," the "public confidence" in the Court was done for. That confidence had already been shaken to the extent that neither lawyers nor legislators knew where the Court had been nor where it was going.

Not until *Cooley* v. *Board of Wardens* (1852) did the Court inject some constitutional order into its interpretation of the commerce power. The facts brought the disputed issues into sharp focus. In 1803, Pennsylvania passed a pilotage law for the Port of Philadelphia that required ships entering or leaving the port to take on pilots or pay half the pilotage fee into a fund for the relief of distressed pilots. Since pilotage was obviously connected with navigation and thus with commerce, the Pennsylvania law raised a clear question of state power to regulate foreign and interstate commerce. Congress had twice legislated on pilotage, but in neither instance was there any conflict with the Pennsylvania law. The precisely defined question was whether the constitutional grant of commerce power to Congress automatically prohibited state regulation of interstate commerce or whether states could regulate as long as such regulation did not actually conflict with congressional legislation. Such was the fundamental issue on which the Court had been divided since 1837, if not 1824.

Justice Benjamin R. Curtis, who replaced Woodbury in 1851, helped break the deadlock. He had no strikingly original ideas on the problem and in fact drew liberally on his predecessor's opinion in the License Cases as well as on Webster's *Gibbons* argument. But he did have a sharp mind and a lucid pen, and, since he was not identified with either side, he was able to provide the neutral ground for a compromise.

His clear and refreshingly short opinion started from the undeniable proposition that the commerce power granted to Congress did not expressly exclude the states from exercising authority over matters of interstate commerce. Exclusive congressional jurisdiction in an area, he went on, could only come when the subject matter itself made this jurisdiction imperative. But the subject of commerce was vast and various and did not require exclusivism. Some matters, he said, needed a "single uniform rule, operating equally on the commerce of the United States in every port." Some just as certainly required diversity. Curtis then expounded a rule to cover the complex nature of commerce: Power follows necessity. If the matter in question requires uniformity, then the power belongs to Congress; if diversity, it belongs to the states. Since the regulation of pilots in the port of Philadelphia fell into the latter category, the Pennsylvania law was constitutional.

McLean and Wayne, whom Curtis called the "most high-toned Federalists on the bench," dissented. Taking up Story's role as the preacher of gloom, McLean prophesied that this retreat from nationalism would return the republic to the chaos of the confederation period. Justice Daniel concurred in the majority verdict but not in its reasoning, upholding the Pennsylvania law by reference to his doctrine of "original and inherent" state power.

"Selective exclusiveness," as the Court's approach came to be called, was not a certain and final answer to the problem of allocating the commerce power between state and nation as subsequent attempts to apply the rule revealed. Curtis gave no clues beyond the case as to which aspects of commerce required uniformity, which diversity. Nor did he supply any specific criteria for determining these essential categories. In fact, the significant feature of the decision was not the formulation of a definitive doctrine but the Court's tacit agreement to stop looking for one, as well as its decision to operate case-by-case on the basis of practicality, common sense, and economic realism. This new spirit was evident not only in the repudiation of exclusivism and the undogmatic solution of "selective exclusiveness," but also in the Court's reasoning. The opinion was ten pages long, was deliberately limited to the case at hand, made no reference to precedent (not even to *Gibbons* and *Brown*), and was guided by the principle that the rule of law should conform to the facts of life. By insisting on rigid doctrine and objecting to the majority's pragmatic definition of power, McLean and Daniel merely highlighted the majority's new pragmatism.

In retreating from constitutional formalism, the Court willed to do what it had previously done unwillingly: it decided cases without a definitive pronouncement of doctrine. The important difference now was that the Court devised a rule of thumb to guide the process of decision-making, thus giving clarity and some predictability to its efforts. Thanks to its nondoctrine-like doctrine and the elegance of Curtis's prose, *Cooley* remained a beacon in commerce-clause litigation well into the next century.

The *Cooley* decision represents the Taney Court at its best—and best illustrates how it differed with the Marshall Court. Gone was the "grand style" and gone too was the search for comprehensive doctrine. Without surrendering its authority to decide, the Court restrained itself—when judicial restraint was the order of the day. Gone too from the days of Marshall was the working assumption that the states were axiomatically untrustworthy. If the democratic majority was no longer tyrannous, the Court no longer needed to present itself, as it had tended to do in the days of Marshall, as the platonic guardian appointed to save the people from their legislative impulses. Chief justice Taney had sounded this new theme in his *Bridge* opinion and his colleagues— Daniel in the License Cases, Wayne in the Passenger Cases, and Woodbury in *United States* v. *New Bedford Bridge* (1847) to mention a few—followed suit. As Taney put it in 1837, the Court, "acting on its own views of what justice required," should not raise up an implied contract, "by a sort of judicial coercion," when the legislature had chosen not to do so.

In the Dorr Rebellion case of *Luther* v. *Borden* (1849), the Court was even more precise about what it should not do. "Political questions," Taney said, belong to the political branches and are beyond the competence of the judicial process. And the rival governments' conflicting claims to legality in Rhode Island (as well as the issue of domestic violence) fell within that nonjudicial category. While the Court "should always be ready to meet any question confided to it by the Constitution, it is equally its duty not to pass beyond its appropriate sphere of action."

And even in spheres less clearly "political," the chief justice advised caution. When the majority attempted to judge the competing claims of railroads and steamboats in *Pennsylvania* v. *Wheeling and Belmont Bridge Co.* (1851), for example, Taney and Daniel sharply dissented. Without legislative guidelines from Congress, argued the chief justice, the Court should not substitute its discretion for that of the state. Because of the "narrow scope of judicial proceedings," there are many duties that the Court "is utterly incapable of discharging." Six years later in *Dred Scott* v. *Sandford*, the chief justice and his associates proved the validity of that simple truth—by ignoring it.

Continuity Versus Change: The Haunting Presence of John Marshall

When the conservatives took stock at the end of the 1837 term, they found "the whole fair system of the Constitution beginning to dissolve like the baseless fabric of a vision." Yet ten years later Justice Wayne, a Jacksonian, felt compelled to praise the Marshall period as an age of "giants" and to rejoice that "the structure raised by them for the defense of the Constitution, has not this day been weakened by their successors." Henry Clay agreed that the "structure" was still intact and revised his previous condemnation of Taney to read: "No man in the United States could have been selected, more abundantly able to wear the ermine which chief justice Marshall honored."

What obviously had not occurred was the constitutional upheaval prophesied by Story, Kent, and Webster. No less than its predecessor, the Court was committed to private property (especially the dynamic kind), economic progress, and market capitalism. Dramatic changes in the latter forced the Taney Court to modify the decisional law from the Marshall period—or even in rare cases to abandon it entirely. For the most part, however, the new Court worked within the framework of law created by the old Court. Even when adjustments were in order, the Taney justices found themselves grappling respectfully with the constitutional reasoning of the old Chief and his colleagues. This kind of grappling, it might be argued, is what constitutional government is all about.

The Taney Court's solicitude for large speculators in land was one conspicuous area of continuity. Here the spirit of *Fletcher* v. *Peck* lived on. Considering American land greed and the southern and western complexion of the new Court, it is not surprising that agrarian capitalism continued to have high priority. The Taney Court did resist some of the most exorbitant demands of large speculators and occasionally a dissenting justice (Daniel, for example, in *Arguello* v. *United States* [1855]) spoke for the little man. But the majority of the Court permitted land speculators to acquire hundreds of thousands of acres of public domain, often against the arguments of government counsel. The governing assumption, soon to be the mantra of the bumptious capitalism of the antebellum period, was that what helped the big investors would trickle down to the ordinary citizen.

The Taney Court's solicitude for capitalism, as the *Charles River Bridge* decision prophesized, was not limited to the agrarian kind. The opposition to charter rights by implication in that decision stemmed not from hostility toward but rather solicitude for commercial expansion and corporate enterprise. The disagreement on the Court was over means not ends: Story argued that absolute contractual sanctity was essential for capital investment, while Taney and the majority insisted that monopoly would deter it. A number of "sound lawyers" (like Daniel Webster) and businessmen of established wealth (like Harrison Gray Otis) never learned to live with Taney's opinion; nor did the stockholders in the old bridge company who lost everything.

But the new wave of entrepreneurs and their professional allies, along with some of the old guard, such as the counsel for the new bridge company Simon Greenleaf, or Charles Sumner, or Court Reporter Richard Peters—all friends of Story— saw Taney's opinion as an encouragement to corporate development. The phenomenal growth of the corporate enterprise in the thirty years following the *Bridge* decision proved them correct.

The *Bridge* decision also continued to guide the Taney Court in subsequent contract-clause cases. These cases, according to David Currie, constituted a major part of the Taney Court's docket (by his count, thirty of the Court's one hundred-plus constitutional decisions). Those involving the state debtor relief laws growing out of the depression of 1837 were especially revealing of the Court's conservative disposition. In *Bronson* v. *Kinzie* (1843), Taney did, to be sure, uphold the state's right to regulate contractual remedies (the means of enforcing the contract) and the right to impose regulations on subsequent contracts. But in four other cases, such laws, though presumably passed to protect the "common man," were struck down as violations of the contract clause. In *Rowan et al.* v. *Runnels* (1847), the Court made clear that state courts had no more right to void contracts than did state legislatures.

Legislative grants of tax exemption to banking corporations (public contracts according to *Fletcher* v. *Peck*) were also consistently upheld by the Court—even though one might have inferred from the *Bridge* decision that the Court would have given high priority to the state's taxing power. Consider, for example, the unanimous opinion in *Gordon* v. *Appeal Tax Court* (1845), which cited Marshall's conservative opinion in *New Jersey* v. *Wilson* for authority to uphold a state law granting tax exemptions to state banks. *Piqua Branch of the State Bank of Ohio* v. *Knoop* (1853) went even further in this direction. That case raised the question of whether a state legislature could surrender its sovereignty to the extent of granting perpetual corporate tax exemptions. Against bitter state opposition and the dissent of Taney and three other justices, the Court upheld the grant as coming under the protection of the contract clause. When the Ohio constitutional convention countered with an amendment repealing such tax exemptions, the Court also struck it down (in *Dodge* v. *Woolsey* [1855]). The chief justice, who did not view state banks with the same suspicion as he did other corporations, went with the majority. But the southern agrarians—Catron, Daniel, and Campbell—dissented, charging the corporation with turning the republic into a Turkish empire. Many Democrats across the country, who had cut their political teeth on Jackson's war against the "monster Bank," no doubt sided with the dissenters.

In these cases the Court helped corporate capitalism by letting the states help corporations. In *Bank of Augusta* v. *Earle* (1839), as previously noted, it provided some essential help of its own. The issue was whether states could prohibit the operation within their borders of corporations chartered in other states. Ignoring both the commerce clause and the comity clause in Article IV, Taney ruled that states could do so. By ruling further that legislative inaction implied consent, however, the Court recognized the centrality of the business corporation to the emerging market economy. As the *New York Courier* put it, "Taney's opinion was as far from Loco-Foco doctrine as Alexander Hamilton himself could have desired."

One favor called for another. Corporations chartered in one state but doing business in another feared discrimination in the courts of the second state and insisted on jurisdictional access to the more impartial, hopefully pro-business, federal courts. Marshall's opinion in *Bank of the United States* v. *Deveaux* (1809), which had brought corporations under federal diversity of citizenship jurisdiction, seemed at first to cover the situation. But subsequent rulings—that cases under diversity jurisdiction would be barred if any stockholder of the corporation were a citizen of the same state as that of the opposing party—took back most of what had been given—especially with the increasingly broad base of stock ownership. In *Louisville Railroad* v. *Letson* (1844), the Court eliminated this "great anomaly in our jurisprudence," as Story called it, holding that for jurisdictional purposes, the corporation would be presumed to be a citizen of the state in which it had been chartered. The subsequent explosion of corporate litigation in the federal courts suggests that corporate interests realized some of the anticipated advantages. One such was the gradual development of a uniform body of commercial law governing interstate business.

In the famous case of *Swift* v. *Tyson* (1842), the Court confronted the problem of uniform commercial law head on. The issue, coming to the Court under its diversity jurisdiction, concerned the negotiability of bills of exchange (commercial notes drawn by one party and accepted by another, specifying an amount of money to be paid at a certain date). Such bills circulated among merchants, sometimes changing hands dozens of times, before they were presented for payment. Such transactions, according to Story (who was writing a treatise on the subject) constituted two-thirds of all mercantile credit in the country. The question in *Swift*, on which the viability of the entire system rested, was whether each bill carried with it the equities that existed between the original parties. If payment could be defeated by circumstances that remote endorsers of the bill had no way of apprehending, no prudent businessman would accept the bill in payment for goods and services.

Story's opinion for a unanimous Court was revolutionary both in its jurisdictional reach and its ruling on the merits. In diversity cases the Court was obliged by Section 34 of the Judiciary Act of 1789 to rule according to the laws of the state in which the suit was brought. On the point at issue in *Swift*, however, there was no controlling statute and New York courts had established no conclusive ruling. Justice Story took this opportunity to rule that "laws" in Section 34 did not include state court decisions and that, in the absence of a controlling statute, federal courts were free to apply general principles of commercial law. After arming the Court with the power to make national commercial law, Story struck a blow for negotiability, holding that remote endorsers could not escape payment by calling on defenses available to original parties to the transaction.

Story's effort to create uniform commercial law—one of the most audacious acts of judicial creativity in the Court's history—worked for several decades but ultimately failed because state courts refused to withdraw from the field of commercial law and also because federal judges, less learned than Story, could not agree on what the "general law" of commerce was. *Swift* was unceremoniously declared "unconstitutional" in *Erie R.R.* v. *Tompkins* (1938).

How a court that prided itself on states' rights and judicial restraint could have rendered a decision like *Swift* is hard to explain—except for the fact that a majority of the justices were fully committed to the ongoing commercial revolution. Such, too, was the implication of Taney's opinion in *The Genesee Chief* v. *Fitzhugh* (1851), which overturned *Steamboat Thomas Jefferson* (1825). In that decision, Story ruled that the admiralty and maritime jurisdiction of the federal courts followed the ebb and flow of the tide, and accordingly did not extend to rivers and other inland bodies of water. In effect, the decision turned over to state courts and legislatures the job of governing the steamboat commerce on the great inland system of navigable lakes and rivers. The result was legal chaos. In an explicitly pragmatic response to commercial necessity, Taney reversed the earlier decision as founded in mistaken law and bad policy, and declared jurisdiction over the entire system of inland waterways. In this case at least, national commerce trumped the Court's preference for states' rights and its respect for stare decisis as well.

The Case for Judicial Statesmanship

The Taney Court discourages easy evaluation. Its preference for expediency over doctrine, the resulting uneven mixture of change and continuity, its unheroic style, and the perpetual squabbling among the justices all obscure the direction of the Court's jurisprudence and provide few great moments to celebrate. This much seems clear: before entering the vortex of the slavery controversy, the Court shaped constitutional law to serve the political and economic imperatives of the new age. This it did without dismantling the basic constitutional doctrines established by its predecessor. By building on the Marshall Court (rather than repudiating it), the Taney Court advanced its own institutional status.

The Court's claim to statesmanship, in short, is that it chose what to preserve and what to change with discrimination and historical discernment. Among the historical constants that the Taney Court recognized were the basic cultural premises of American capitalism. Commercial law—contracts, agency, bills and notes, insurance, tort—continued to rest on the nineteenth-century assumption that citizens were rational enough to know what they were doing and moral enough to accept responsibility for what they did. Though divided and contentious, the justices agreed that economic enterprise and social progress went hand in hand, and they acted on the corollary assumption that the law served the latter by encouraging the former. In this spirit the Court under Taney put constitutional law on the side of the rising business corporation. Despite the states' rights ideology of many of the justices, they also managed to agree on a viable constitutional basis for interstate commerce. Finally, modified though it was, the contract clause remained in full force as the basic constitutional shield for private property.

Not only did the Court carry on the capitalist-oriented law of the Marshall Court, but it did so while introducing changes compatible with Jacksonian political priorities. As national mercantilism declined and the business corporation rose, for example, the Court modified constitutional federalism to accommodate the new responsibilities that fell to the states in banking, internal improvements, and in economic promotion generally. Facing the realities of corporate power that the Marshall Court had ignored, the Taney Court recognized the state not only as a promotional agency, but also as a regulatory one. Gone was the Marshall Court's working assumption that state power was inherently hostile to the public interest and fatal to the Union. Since it was free from antidemocratic, anti-state prejudices, the Court under Taney could grasp the central fact of early nineteenth-century government: the states, as Jacksonian Justice Levi Woodbury put it, were the "great fountains of legislation" and the vital source of experimentation in both policy and administration.

Above all, the Court understood and acted on the theory—the same theory on which Jacksonian political and economic policy was predicated—that the states, not the nation, were best able to handle the diverse and conflicting economic demands of a sectionally divided nation. Viewing the states in a new historical light, the Court devised a fresh approach to state power. As Justice Woodbury put it in *Planter's Bank* v. *Sharp, et al.* (1848), the states, when acting "in matters of general interest," "must be presumed to act from public considerations, being in a high public trust." And "in the true spirit of the age . . . the disposition in the Judiciary should be strong to uphold them."

As applied after 1837, this rule altered the balance between state and national power. The alteration, however, was achieved not by repudiating the nationalist doctrines of the Marshall Court but by selective application and modification. In contract-clause litigation *Fletcher* v. *Peck* pretty much ruled supreme. Even the *Dartmouth*

College holding was unchallenged, although significantly the Taney Court refused to extend it by implication. In commerce-clause litigation, *Gibbons* also remained good law, although the Taney Court extrapolated from it by exploring the concurrent commerce power and state police power. The exclusivist interpretation of *Gibbons*, championed by Webster and Story, was rejected outright. And in *Cooley*, the Court introduced the new doctrine of selective exclusiveness without mentioning *Gibbons* at all. Because old law and new interpretations continued to exist side-by-side, and because changes were often introduced in sharply divided opinions, confusion abounded. What the Court's view of federalism lost in coherence, however, it gained in practicality. In a strange way the chaos on the Court and in its jurisprudence fit the dynamically chaotic history of the late antebellum period.

Surprisingly the changes introduced by the Taney Court did not seriously disrupt the course of its institutional development. There were some subtle changes, to be sure, as the Court moved away from its eighteenth-century moorings. The common-law idiom still infused constitutional decisions, but with less frequency as the Court began to work within its own precedential tradition. Reference to natural law also receded into the background. Even when the Taney justices modified the old law, however, they generally did so respectfully and without hubris. The days of Marshall were gone, but the spirit of the old chief justice lived on. As Story ruefully put it, "Hardly a day now passes in the court he so dignified and adorned, without reference to some decision of his time as establishing a principle which, from that day to this, has been accepted as undoubted law. . . ." By building on the tradition of the Marshall Court, the Taney Court enhanced its own stature.

No less than its predecessor, the Taney Court also wanted to preserve national union. States' rights manifestoes sometimes issued from the radical agrarians on the Court (almost always in cases involving slavery), but the majority tended to avoid extreme language and doctrinaire solutions. Conspicuously absent were "the good old State-Rights doctrines of Virginia of '98 and '99" the *Richmond Enquirer* had hoped to see. What the politically minded justices did recognize was that the Union rested on a pragmatic federalism that allowed the states a new measure of authority to address the problems of the new age. Such concessions to the states were as necessary in the period after 1830 as they had been in 1787 or would be in 1877.

This nondoctrinaire approach to the Constitution was probably due more to the collective disagreement of the justices than to their collective wisdom. In any case, internal disagreement was a detracting feature of the Taney Court. Justices Story and McLean, who spoke for the constitutional nationalism of 1819 were on one end of the spectrum. On the other end were the southern agrarians—Daniel of Virginia, Catron of Tennessee, and Campbell of Alabama—whose consistent dissents showed their disagreement with the policy of moderation. What they wanted—although they differed among themselves as to degree—were fewer concessions to corporate capitalism and more to states' rights. In a formal sense this group left hardly a ripple on the mainstream of American jurisprudence.

Through the prism of southern agrarianism, however, they saw things their more moderate colleagues frequently missed. They perceived (what history was later to verify) that the business corporation was a revolutionary development in political and economic power that might hurt as well as help the public interest. In disagreeing with the majority, they openly acknowledged that the Court was making policy, and for this reason, they became vociferous spokesmen for judicial self-restraint (at least until *Dred Scott*). If nothing else, their extreme views made compromise necessary, when compromise was the order of the day. Thanks to the leadership of Chief Justice Taney, it was also the hallmark of his Court.

When Daniel Webster bemoaned the absence of a great "leading mind" on the Court, he was longing for the days when Marshall mobilized the Court. Taney's contribution, however, was not to mobilize the Court but to keep it from being immobilized—to keep it on task and on track as an institution. He lacked the charisma of Marshall, but as Carl Swisher's fine biography demonstrates, he possessed that "intrinsic authority" that Frankfurter called the "test of leadership." Wisely, he did not use that authority to consolidate the Court or to impose his own ideas on it. Instead, he recognized the inevitability of division and made a democratic virtue of necessity. By tact, innate gentleness, and infinite patience, he succeeded in moderating the personal conflict that accompanied disagreement—with the serious exception of *Dred Scott*. In the resulting atmosphere of tolerance, he was able to bring together a majority that willy-nilly translated difference of opinion into constitutional moderation. Considering the obstacles, it was a considerable feat of leadership.

While adjusting itself and its law to the new age, the Court not only preserved its authority but also expanded its jurisdiction in corporation law, admiralty and maritime matters, and general commercial law. But its approach to power, its internal procedures, its methods, and its style differed from the that of the Marshall Court. Separate opinions, division, and dissent became regular occurrences. And, although not necessarily virtues in themselves, they reflected a new internal democracy that was congenial to a democratic age. The Court respected stare decisis, but it also felt free to correct past errors. And, appropriately, as it relaxed its imperial posture, the Court softened its magisterial rhetoric. Notions of natural law and constitutional finality gave way to a more realistic view of law as a process and of the Court as an instrument of adjustment rather than an oracle of certitude.

To adjust, however, the Court still had to win popular and professional approval for its decisions. To the great surprise of its detractors, the Taney Court went up in popular reputation as it came down from the Olympian heights. Because it dealt moderately and respectfully with the work of the Marshall Court, it inherited the earlier Court's high reputation. By undertaking less and heeding the democratic imperative of the age, the Court won the respect of the political branches and the confidence of the people. Consequently, by 1850, the national prestige of the Court was as great as it had been in the golden age of Marshall. Ironically, this popularity tempted a majority of the justices to believe the Court could save the Union by putting the Constitution on the side of human slavery.

CHAPTER FIVE

The Court's Time of Troubles: Slavery, Sectionalism, and War

But if the Supreme Court is ever composed of imprudent or bad men, the Union may be plunged into anarchy or Civil war.

Alexis de Tocqueville (1835)

Had the Taney Court rested on its laurels in 1856, it would surely have gone down as one of the most popular and effective Courts in our history. Taney's tactful leadership, his simple eloquence, and his demonstrated legal ability would have assured his reputation as a worthy successor to the great John Marshall. But a slave named Dred Scott caused the Court and its chief justice to lose this commendation. In a single decision, the Court abandoned its moderation, threw away its popularity, and jeopardized its very institutional existence. Instead of a great judicial statesman, Roger Taney became a "mere man," as one northern paper called him, or, in a less generous appraisal, a minion of southern slavocracy and a traitor to the Marshall tradition.

It is a paradox that slavery should have become so important a factor in appraising the Court's statesmanship—as well as the main focus of its historiography—for, by ordinary standards it was an issue peripheral to the Court's work. Of all the cases decided by the Marshall and Taney Courts, hardly more than a hundred dealt with slavery, and most of those did so indirectly. Only a handful of these cases are remembered; not one, including *Dred Scott* v. *Sandford* (unless one counts the unintended lesson on judicial humility), contributed any lasting principle to American law. However, more than any other issue, slavery raised fundamental constitutional and institutional questions that put the Court to the supreme test.

Slavery was rooted in state law and firmly embedded in the federal Constitution as part of a compromise between "the great northern and southern interests," as James Madison noted. The question which has plagued historians (as it also plagued the Taney Court) was whether those provisions merely recognized the existence of state-based slavery without endorsing it, or whether, either individually or collectively, they made slavery a constitutionally mandated and thus a national, institution. Scholarly efforts to answer the question by determining the intent of the framers have failed, although, as Don Fehrenbacher observed, it is significant that they omitted the word "slavery" from the text of the Constitution. Equally suggestive is the fact that the Constitution treats slavery piecemeal and always in conjunction with other subjects.

The pieces themselves are unclear, however, even with the benefit of Madison's *Notes*, which first became available in 1840. For example Article I, Section 2, paragraph 3, apportions direct taxes and representation by "adding to the whole number of free persons . . . including those bound to service for a term of years, and excluding Indians not taxed, three fifths of all other persons." The contrast between "free persons," and "all other persons" seems clearly to acknowledge slavery but concedes no more than is necessary for the purpose of determining representation and taxation. Article I, Section 9, which prohibits Congress from interfering with the "migration or importation of such persons as any of the States now existing shall think proper to admit," is likewise subject to various readings. By giving Congress the right to prohibit the foreign slave trade (which it did in 1808) and by limiting the right of importation to existing states, the clause appears to put slavery on the way to extinction. On the other hand, the same clause gives constitutional protection (for twenty years) to the buying and selling of human beings and the infamous "middle passage."

Article IV contains three more clauses devoted to slavery—two directly, and one by implication. All three are ambiguous on the larger question of whether the Constitution endorsed the institution. Section 1, paragraph 3, declares that persons held to "service or labor" in one state who escape to another state, shall not be freed by "any law or regulation" in the latter, "but shall be delivered up on claim of the party to whom such service or labor may be due." Did that clause endorse and nationalize slavery or did it simply recognize the state-based nature of the institution? Was it self-enforcing or did it need implementing legislation? The answers were not clear until the Court spoke in *Prigg* v. *Pennsylvania* (1842). Two other slave-related provisions in Section IV were also left to be clarified—or obfuscated—by judicial decision. One was the comity clause in Section 1, which declared that "full faith and credit be given in each State to the public acts, records, and judicial proceedings of every other State." The other provision, on which the fate of the Union ultimately came to hinge, was Section 3, paragraph 2, which authorized Congress to "make all needful rules and regulations" respecting the territories.

About the only thing that seems clear from these provisions is that those who framed and ratified the Constitution could read into them pretty much what they wanted. Dissatisfied extremists on either end of the political spectrum went along with the spirit of compromise in the interests of national union. Whether slavery was local or national, whether the Constitution looked to slavery or freedom, were questions left to future generations—and ultimately to the Supreme Court.

Unhappily for the Court, developments in the antebellum period all worked against the slavery compromise of 1787. Not only did that arrangement become progressively less satisfactory to extreme elements in the slave and free states, but slavery came to subsume and to symbolize the whole range of political, economic, and moral differences between the sections. The process began as the exploitative spirit in both the North and the South fulfilled the economic logic of climatic and geographic differences. Encouraged by the cotton gin, new types of cotton seed, and rising prices, the South made cotton and slave labor the economic basis of its society. Soil exhaustion in the seaboard South, augmented by the expansionist impulse, carried cotton culture into the deep South. In the North, industrial capitalism replaced agriculture and commercial capitalism as the dynamic economic force.

On these contrary economic foundations, each section erected a distinctive culture—one tending to corporateness and conservatism, the other to radical individualism and liberalism. The Panic of 1819 and the Missouri Debates helped turn these differences into sectional self-consciousness, and the militant abolitionism of the 1830s changed this self-consciousness into a sectional narcissism that defined the Union, and the good life, in strictly sectional terms. And at precisely the time that the North and South were growing socially, economically, and psychologically apart, they were thrown into unavoidable contact by the transportation and communications revolution of the 1840s and by competition for control of the West.

In this super-heated atmosphere, the constitutional provisions that lay buried in the spirit of compromise and conciliation were now resurrected by radical theorists in both sections. In the North, as William Wiecek has brilliantly demonstrated, abolitionists either condemned the Constitution as a "compact with the devil," or discovered that it was a charter of freedom. Southern theorists, first in Virginia and then in South Carolina, looked on the slave provisions of the Constitution increasingly as a national guarantee that northern states were bound to respect as the price of Union. Beginning in the last days of the Marshall Court, and with growing insistence during Taney's tenure, these radical theories infused arguments of counsel in slave-related cases (see George Berrien's brutally racist argument, for example, in *The Antelope* in 1825, or John Quincy Adams's fiery speech for freedom in the *Amistad* case in 1841).

Like the politicians, the justices were pressured to fashion decisions that decided cases without offending the radicals in each section—or the majority of the American people in the North and South on whose goodwill the Court depended for its authority. The problem was that by the 1850s—thanks to the propagandizing of radical abolitionists and proslavery firebrands—little of the undecided middle

122 THE SUPREME COURT

remained. Half the nation wanted the Constitution to support freedom; the other half wanted it to support slavery. In this situation there
was no margin for constitutional error, little respect for constitutional
objectivity, and in fact, probably no viable constitutional solution available to the Court.

The Court and Slavery

Most slavery cases before the Marshall and early Taney courts afforded little opportunity for either policymaking or judicial miscalcu-
lation. Most of them came from the states and turned on questions of
state law, which meant that the Court was obliged to treat the slave as
property. Reduced to chattel, the slaves were callously disposed of in
wills, deeds, mortgages, bills, and notes according to the formal rules
of common law. Cases concerning the foreign slave trade (generally
coming under the Court's admiralty and maritime and prize jurisdiction) permitted somewhat more creative leeway (and accordingly revealed more of the internal divisions among the justices.) In one such
case, the gross evils of the slave trade tempted Justice Story on circuit
to abandon legal technicality for the morality of natural justice. *United
States* v. *Le Jeune Eugenie* (1822) won the praise of rising antislave
forces because of its condemnation of the slave trade, and by implication, slavery itself as "repugnant to the great principles of Christian
duty, the dictates of natural religion, the obligations of good faith and
morality, and the eternal maxims of social justice."

Three years later in *The Antelope*, the majority resisted Story's
moral solution. Marshall reminded his colleague and friend that his
noble sentiments had nothing to do with international law governing
the foreign slave trade. As a consequence of the Court's narrow ruling, most of the newly enslaved Africans in the case were returned to
their Spanish and Portuguese owners—their identity to be chosen by
lot. The American slave trade—though it was prohibited by congressional act in 1808 and deemed piracy in 1819—continued until the
Civil War, with a large share of the profits going to the North.

The Court first confronted domestic slavery in cases coming under the commerce clause. The loaded question was whether persons
(meaning slaves and free blacks) were commodities and thus subject
to congressional regulation by Article I, Section 8. If so, then state

control over slavery would be weakened at several vital points. One such point was southern state police laws that prohibited the entrance of free blacks into the state in the interest of social order. Some justices insisted on grappling with the issue. On circuit in 1823, Justice Johnson "hung himself on a democratic snag," as Marshall put it, by striking down one such South Carolina law as an encroachment on the power of Congress to regulate commerce—a ruling that the state proceeded to condemn and ignore. The decision was not appealed, and the Marshall Court was never forced to rule on the slavery–commerce clause question.

The Taney justices were not so fortunate. In all of their commerce-clause decisions slavery played a role, either indirectly or directly. Indeed, the doctrinal confusion previously discussed in *Miln* (1837), the License Cases (1847), and the Passenger Cases (1849) was clearly attributable to slavery, although that issue was not before the Court. In *Groves* v. *Slaughter* (1841), the issue was whether the section of the Mississippi Constitution that prohibited the importation or sale of slaves unlawfully encroached on Congress' power to regulate interstate commerce. The issue was explosive, since any curtailment of state control over slavery was sure to be met with southern resistance. Justice Thompson's opinion for the majority dodged the danger by holding that the Mississippi constitutional prohibition had not been implemented by necessary legislative action. Taney, McLean, and Baldwin entered separate concurring opinions that, predicting the chaos to come in the License and Passenger cases, went in radically different doctrinal directions.

The Fugitive Slave Question

As long as the Court could deal with slavery and not the slave, as long as it could talk of bills and notes, wills, deeds and statutory interpretation, and not of humanity, it could avoid arousing moral fervor and dividing popular opinion. All such avoidance came to an end in 1841 because enslaved Africans persisted in escaping the law that made them somebody's property.

The fugitives in *United States* v. *Schooner Amistad* (1841) were not American slaves but Africans on their way to enslavement. On June 30, 1839, en route from Havana to another port in Cuba, they rose up, killed the ship's captain, and forced two Spanish slavers to steer the ship back to Africa. Instead, the Spaniards directed the *Amistad* to United States waters where the vessel was seized by the United States brig *Washington*. The officers and crew, claiming salvage rights, brought the Africans before the federal district court in Connecticut.

By the time the case reached the Supreme Court it had gone far beyond the question of salvage and treaty rights under which the Spanish owners claimed the Africans as property. As former president John Quincy Adams, counsel for the imprisoned men, wrote, the issue was that of "humble Africans" asserting their right to be free men against the machinations of two powerful governments. Adams had not practiced for decades, but he was, as Justice Baldwin observed, "charged to the muzzle" with moral indignation. Forgetting his seventy-four years (and often the legal issues before the Court) he spent three days in powerful and bitterly sarcastic argument in an effort to get the moral issue across to the Court and the nation.

Justice Story's deliberately restrained opinion, which used principles of municipal and international law to free the Africans, did not avert a sectional response. Northerners, who were not put off by the Court's moderation, rallied to its defense of freedom; the South looked on and drew dark conclusions from the North's enthusiastic reaction. As a concession to the South, the administrations of Tyler, Polk, Pierce, and Buchanan all pressed for reparations to the Spanish owners, presumably at taxpayers' expense. Congress refused.

The *Amistad* case dramatized the evils of the slave trade and the courage and humanity of the enslaved Africans (a story told with admirable clarity in Howard Jones's *Mutiny on the Amistad* [1987]). One year later, with the passions generated by that decision still running high, the Court faced another fugitive slave case—this time of a domestic nature. The Court chose not to dodge the constitutional issue. The events leading to *Prigg* v. *Pennsylvania* (1842) began when a professional slave-catcher named Edward Prigg was dispatched to Pennsylvania by a Maryland slave owner to recover Margaret Morgan, who had escaped from slavery and lived as a free person in the free state of Pennsylvania for five years. Prigg returned her and her children (one of whom had been born in Pennsylvania) to slavery in

Maryland. Prigg was subsequently indicted in the Pennsylvania courts (apparently in an agreed-upon case involving the two states) for violating that state's personal liberty law of 1826, which established procedural safeguards in rendition cases. The question was whether Pennsylvania's law violated the fugitive slave clause of the Constitution and the 1793 Act of Congress passed to implement it. Maryland and the South viewed the Pennsylvania law as a palpable deprivation of their constitutionally guaranteed property rights. Pennsylvania did not contest the fugitive slave law, but demanded the right to protect free blacks living in the state from the incursions of slave-catchers.

Justice Story, recognizing the combustible nature of the case (both on and off the Court), would have preferred not to write for the majority—especially since he was personally opposed to slavery. He took the job out of a sense of duty—and because he thought he could settle the fugitive slave issue in a way that was true to the Constitution and acceptable both to the slave and free states, and also to his badly divided colleagues. Some of his improvisations were highly questionable, however, particularly his holding that the Pennsylvania law was a violation of the clear, constitutional, statutory obligation to return fugitives. This holding may have been part of the price Story paid to enlist a majority of his colleagues, but it was questionable law because the Pennsylvania statute did not in fact prevent the return of fugitives but only provided procedural guarantees that those returned were really slaves.

So far the South was pleased, but the cheering stopped—and Taney, Daniel, and Thompson dissented—when Story went on to say that power over fugitives belonged exclusively to the national government. Story appears to have carried a bare majority with him on this point, which is somewhat surprising given the fact that there is nothing in the Constitution to support it. However, the exclusivist ruling permitted Story to argue that the free states were not obliged—indeed were not constitutionally able —to assist in the return of slaves. On this point, he lost the support of the majority.

If Story hoped that *Prigg* would calm the troubled waters, he was wrong. Extremists in both sections abused the Court—proslavery firebrands for not going the whole distance with slavery; and northern abolitionists for going too far. (William Lloyd Garrison proposed the

immediate withdrawal of free states from the Union, and the Massachusetts Anti-Slavery Society reckoned that an "overthrow of the
Constitution and the government" might be necessary.) Moderate
southerners settled for the immediate victory and the judicial assurance of their constitutional rights. Northern criticism subsided temporarily with the belief that the burden of state compliance with the
1793 statute had been lifted; six northern states passed laws prohibiting such compliance.

In this sense, perhaps, Story's conviction that he had struck a
blow for "liberty" was true. But the fact remained, as Don Fehrenbacher
observes, that the decision was fundamentally racist, since it failed to
address the "kidnapping problem"—"a refusal that would have been
inconceivable if the victims had been white." Ominously, *Prigg* confirmed what the statute of 1793 had implied: that the national government was the "guardian" of the rights of slaveholders—even in states
where slavery did not exist. This point was driven home by Story's
dicta that the obligation to return fugitive slaves was mandated by the
Constitution itself and did not require legislative implementation.

In averting the immediate crisis (by giving something to both the
free and slave states), *Prigg* prepared the way for a greater one. By
discouraging state cooperation in returning fugitives, the decision
undercut the Fugitive Slave Act of 1793, making necessary the more
brutal Fugitive Slave Act of 1850. The South now looked to the federal government for a national resolution to the crisis, and the Court
pledged itself in advance to support such a solution. Ironically, the
justices and perhaps even the American people began to think of the
Court as uniquely constituted to quell the agitation over slavery. Un-
knowingly, it had taken a giant step down the path leading to *Dred
Scott*.

The issues in *Prigg* remind us, as they must have reminded the
justices, that slavery in the federal system was at fundamental odds
with the theory that it existed only as a municipal (state) institution.
So too did a series of cases involving slaves in transit to and through
free states (a complicated subject treated authoritatively in Paul
Finkelman's *Imperfect Union: Slavery, Federalism, and Comity*, 1981).
Sometimes the issue was whether slaves who escaped into free states
became free; or, sometimes it was whether slaves who accompanied

their masters into or through free states became free. In every instance, however, the question was whether freedom trumped slavery or whether property (in slaves) trumped freedom.

Americans, who loved both freedom and property, had been conscious of the comity issue ever since Lord Mansfield's famous ruling in *Somerset* v. *Stewart* (1772), that a slave brought to England was freed because only positive law could support such an "odious" institution. The problem with *Somerset* in America, however, was Article IV, Section 3, and the Fugitive Slave Act of 1793, especially as interpreted in *Prigg*. The justices personally opposed to slavery did not relish enforcing that harsh decision, as Robert Cover's *Justice Accused* (1975) shows. But there were many cases where they had little option—except to resign. As Justice Levi Woodbury explained in *Jones* v. *Van Zandt* (1849), the Constitution had struck a bargain with slavery that Congress and the Court subsequently recognized, leaving the Court no recourse but to "go where that constitution and the laws lead, and not to break both, by travelling without or beyond them."

The Court followed Woodbury's principle of restraint two years later in *Strader* v. *Graham* (1851). The question was whether slaves who had visited the free state of Ohio as travelling musicians and returned to the slave state of Kentucky, and then later escaped to Canada, had became free by virtue of the laws of Ohio and the prohibitions against slavery in the Ordinance of 1787. Writing for a unanimous Court, the chief justice refused jurisdiction on the ground that the Kentucky slave law as interpreted by the Kentucky Supreme Court was controlling once the slaves returned to the state and that consequently, no federal question was involved. By not ruling the Court had, in fact, ruled for slavery; it had also kept itself out of the slavery spotlight. Had the Court followed the *Strader* precedent six years later in *Dred Scott*, as it initially decided to do, the history of the republic might have been quite different.

Slavery in the Territories

The fugitive slave issue aroused bitter sectional feelings, but it was the question of slavery in the territories that fully joined the issue between the North and the South. The South considered the right to extend slavery into the territories basic to its future existence. Given the soil depletion in the slave-holding states in the seaboard South, the acquisition of new land for slave-based agriculture in the West was an economic imperative. The admission of new slave states would also bolster southern representation in Congress, especially in the Senate, which was immune from the population advantages held by the free states in the House. Finally, southern honor demanded the right as a reward for its services to the Union and as an indication of the good intentions of the North.

Unfortunately, the North was not in an obliging mood. This is not to suggest that free staters were immune from racism or that they had been converted to abolitionism; neither proposition was true. But the abolitionists, though a distinct minority, framed the slavery issue in moral and religious terms that northerners found hard to resist. And those who were not drawn out on the moral issue were increasingly persuaded that slavery and free labor could not coexist. So it was that the North joined the South in believing that its future—and that of the Union—was at stake in the territories. The bloody civil war raging in Kansas territory showed that members of each side were willing to kill and die to defend their claims.

Such was the situation when the Court took up *Dred Scott* v. *Sandford*. At issue was the meaning of Article IV, Section 3, which gave Congress the authority to make "needful rules and regulations" for the territories. Unfortunately for the Court, there was no way of knowing whether "needful rules and regulations" included the authority to regulate, and possibly prohibit, slavery in the territories. Political logic and common sense said that it did, since only Congress possessed the machinery for patching together a compromise solution satisfactory to both the free and slave states. In fact, Congress had immediately assumed this power and used it to keep sectional peace. In his scholarly dissent in *Dred Scott*, Justice Curtis counted fourteen instances of congressional legislation on the question between 1789 and 1848: six of these acts, all before 1822, had recognized and continued slavery; eight, following the precedent of the Northwest Ordinance, had prohibited it. The most important prohibition, and the one addressed in *Dred Scott*, was the Compromise of 1820, wherein Congress excluded slavery from the entire Louisiana Purchase territory north of 36° 30', excepting Missouri.

If long practice determines constitutional doctrine, as the Court had consistently asserted, then Congress had plenary power over slavery in the territories. Thus far it had used that power to strike a balance between slave and free states. And so far as the Court said anything on the subject, (which was mainly in *American Insurance Co.* v. *Canter* [1828]), it supported congressional authority to rule on slavery in the territories. Presidents from Washington to John Quincy Adams did the same.

Following the Missouri Compromise, however, circumstances began to erode both the spirit of congressional compromise and the theory of congressional power on which it rested. The abortive Denmark Vesey slave rebellion in 1822, as well as the very real Nat Turner insurrection in 1831, increased southern paranoia and stimulated ever more aggressive efforts to secure the slave system—which meant expanding it into the new territories. The territorial issue heated up during the debate over the admission of Texas in the late 1830s and came to a boil in 1848 with the acquisition of territory following the Mexican War. Fought to validate the annexation of Texas and to lay claim to more Mexican territory, the war was seen in the free states as conclusive evidence of a "planter conspiracy" to control the West and gain dominance in Congress. The South, on the other hand, viewed David Wilmot's 1846 resolution banning slavery permanently from any territory acquired from Mexico as evidence of the North's intentions to use its growing numerical strength in Congress to deny southern rights in the new territories.

With paranoia rampant in both the North and the South, Congress was hard put to satisfy sectional demands regarding the land ceded by Mexico following the war—and accordingly, was increasingly less interested in claiming the power to do so. While the politicians in Congress held back, extremists from both sections rushed forward with constitutional theories tailored to their own interests. Reminded of its declining power by the passage of the Wilmot Proviso in the House, the South began to question how much control Congress should have over the territories. More to the point, it came to believe (in the spirit of *Prigg*) that the federal government—looked upon in southern theory as the agent of the sovereign states—was constitutionally obliged to protect slavery in the territories. For their part, antislavery northerners were willing to accept congressional power in the territories, but only as long as it worked for them. When it did not, they turned to their own view of the Constitution and failing that, to a still "higher law." With the decline of congressional effectiveness, and with both the North and South demanding a definitive solution—within the Constitution if possible, outside it if necessary—the stage was set for the Court's entrance.

Before it set out to save the nation, however, there remained one possible political solution to the problem, which promised to satisfy northern and southern moderates, to take Congress off the hook, and to keep the Court from getting involved. Founded on the "great fundamental principle of self-government," as Illinois Senator Stephen Douglas noted, popular sovereignty left the people of the territories "free to form and regulate their domestic institutions in their own way, subject only to the Constitution of the United States." What did the Constitution require? When would the settlers act? By what political mechanism? With what finality? The beauty of popular sovereignty was that no one really knew, so politicians could read their own self-serving interpretation into the confusion—or so Douglas hoped. The one sure thing was that Congress would be relieved of the obligation to act, without having surrendered the theoretical power to do so.

Popular sovereignty was not original with Douglas. Congress had applied the idea, coupled with the right to appeal disputed matters to the Supreme Court, in dealing with the territories of New Mexico and Utah in 1850. But the real test came four years later as a consequence of the Kansas and Nebraska Act. Both territories lay within the upper reaches of the Louisiana Purchase and, by the terms of the Missouri Compromise, would have been organized as free territories, except for the intrusion of presidential politics. As an aspirant for the Democratic nomination for the presidency, Senator Douglas favored a compromise solution to the territorial problem, which would hold the northern and southern wings of his party together.

Popular sovereignty appeared to serve that end. By applying the principle of self-determination to Kansas and Nebraska rather than the Compromise of 1820, Douglas could win southern support in the Senate for his bill to organize the new territories, and at the same time provide a rallying ground for the northern and southern wings of the

Democratic party. Accordingly, the Kansas-Nebraska Act of May 1854, which Douglas pushed through the Senate, declared "inoperative and void" the 36° 30' provision of the Missouri Compromise. Introduced in its place was the "principle of non-intervention by Congress with slavery in the States and Territories." Instead of having Congress guarantee free territories, the people of the new territories were now given the dubious privilege of choosing for themselves.

Pro- and antislave settlers in Kansas immediately implemented the vague formula by killing one another and dividing the territory into two armed camps, one slave and one free. The turmoil in Kansas split the Democrats in Congress along sectional lines, with Senator Douglas and the moderates desperately laboring to make enough sense out of popular sovereignty to reunite the party. At the same time, a new sectional party called the Republicans, which opposed slavery in the territories, forged unity from the flames of Kansas and waited to pick up the reins of power that the divided Democrats seemed certain to drop.

Enter Dred Scott

At the height of the Kansas crisis, with extremism rampant and the national party structure tottering, President Buchanan casually dropped a bombshell in his inaugural address of March 4, 1857. Admitting, in what was surely the understatement of the decade, that the "happy conception" of popular sovereignty had raised some questions, he went on confidently to promise that they were of "little practical importance." In any event, the whole dispute was "a judicial question" which was about to be "speedily and finally settled." Thanks to the confidential information given him by Justices Grier and Catron, the president knew whereof he spoke. The case of *Dred Scott* v. *Sandford*, which had been on the Court's docket since 1854, was decided two days after his inaugural promise.

Sam Scott, known as Dred, was the property of Dr. John Emerson, a surgeon in the United States Army and a resident of Missouri. Emerson took Dred with him on a tour of duty, first to Fort Armstrong in the free state of Illinois in 1834, and then in 1836 to Fort Snelling in the upper Louisiana Purchase territory, which was free under the

Missouri Compromise. In 1838 Emerson removed Scott, who now had a wife and baby daughter, back to the slave state of Missouri. Emerson died in 1843, willing the Scott family to his widow.

After an unsuccessful effort to purchase freedom for himself and his family, Dred sued in the lower state court of Missouri, arguing that residence in a free state and free territory had made him free. The Scotts (his wife's case was a companion suit) won their freedom in the lower court only to lose it before the Missouri Supreme Court. Caught up in Missouri's bitter slavery politics, the state supreme court went against the strong current of its own previous decisions, ruling that the slavery prohibition in the Missouri Compromise and the laws of Illinois had no extraterritorial effect in Missouri. Citing Taney's opinion in *Strader* v. *Graham* (much of which was obiter dictum), the Missouri Supreme Court concluded that when Scott returned to Missouri, the slave law of that state determined his status.

Had Scott's lawyer Roswell Field taken the case on a writ of error from the state court to the Supreme Court, the usual mode of appeal in such cases, it would surely have turned out differently, because the Court would have been confined to reviewing the legal correctness of the lower court's decision. Since the Missouri court relied on *Strader*, the Supreme Court almost certainly would have affirmed its holding. Dred's case would then have been thrown out because he was a slave and not a citizen, and thus could not bring a diversity suit in the federal courts. It was to avoid this outcome that Field entered the case, again under diversity jurisdiction, suing John Sanford of New York for assault and false imprisonment. (Sanford, misspelled Sandford in the Supreme Court Reports, was Mrs. Emerson's brother and had come into possession of Dred and his family, either as agent for his sister or possibly as the actual new owner.) Otherwise, the evidence and arguments in support of Scott's freedom were identical to those used in the state court.

Sanford pleaded to the jurisdiction of the circuit court, contending that since Scott was a a slave and a "negro of African descent," he could not be a citizen of the United States capable of suing in the federal courts. Scott demurred to this plea, i.e., admitted that he was an African American, but argued that this did not bar him from citizenship and the right to sue. Sanford pleaded over, i.e., he accepted

Scott's plea regarding his citizenship and right to sue and then pleaded not guilty on the merits. The circuit court (following Sanford's plea) ruled that Scott was a citizen capable of suing in the federal courts. On the merits, however, the court agreed with the state supreme court that the Missouri Compromise and the laws of Illinois were not controlling once Scott returned to Missouri. So instructed, the jury brought in the verdict that he was a slave by state law. This decision was appealed to the Supreme Court, docketed in December 1854, argued (this time by Montgomery Blair) first in February 1856, reargued after conference in December 1856, and finally decided on March 6, 1857.

Because the case came from the federal circuit court rather than the state supreme court, all the questions raised in the previous litigation were properly before the Court. First was the question of Dred's citizenship (since the Court's jurisdiction depended on it). This in turn raised the comity question, i.e., whether Missouri was obliged to recognize Dred's freedom on the basis of his residence in the free state of Illinois. Finally, and most importantly, was the question of whether Dred became free by virtue of having resided in a free territory (made free by the Missouri Compromise). The territorial question was not covered by *Strader* and it raised the most explosive question of all: whether Congress had the authority to prohibit slavery in the territories at all.

All of the key issues were now before the Court; whether, and how, the justices would consider them was a matter of judicial discretion. Given the bloody civil war in Kansas and the resulting chaos in the American party system as the presidential election approached, restraint appeared to be the order of the day. In fact, after the first argument in February 1856, a majority of the Court prudently decided to deny jurisdiction on the ground that Dred was a slave by Missouri law and therefore could not sue under federal diversity. Justice Nelson drafted a decision to this effect. Sometime between February and December, however, this strategy of avoidance was abandoned in favor of an all-out doctrinal assault on the problem. The result was nine separate opinions (two in dissent) covering 234 pages, announced two days after the presidential election of the Democrat James Buchanan.

Discovering what the majority had actually decided has occupied historians for decades, but contemporaries assumed that Taney spoke for the Court (and most scholars now agree that he did). His opinion placed the Court in the eye of the storm. After establishing the Court's right to consider all aspects of the case, the chief justice turned to the initial and controlling question: whether Dred Scott was a citizen with the constitutional right to sue in the federal courts. The circuit court below had ruled in favor of Scott's right to sue, but it had not elaborated on the meaning of citizenship. Taney did just the opposite: he denied Scott's right to sue and expounded on the meaning of citizenship, for the first time in the Court's history.

There were, he said by way of explanation, two separate categories of citizenship, one state and the other national. State citizenship was municipal only and could not confer the right to sue in federal courts. National citizenship was controlled by the Constitution itself. That document, asserted Taney, recognized a "perpetual and impassible barrier" between whites and blacks. The latter were "subjugated by the former," indeed, were a "subordinate and inferior class of being" with no rights except ones which "those who held the power and the government might choose to give them." Though African Americans might be free, or even be state citizens, they could never be citizens of the United States within the meaning of the Constitution. Dred Scott was an African American (and possibly still a slave) and thus could not sue in the nation's courts.

It is hard to imagine an opinion better calculated to offend the antislavery forces in the North—unless it was Taney's further ruling on the territorial question. Dred's argument for freedom was based on his residence in the free state of Illinois and his residence in the upper Louisiana Territory (later Minnesota), made free soil by the Missouri Compromise. Because the former issue was presumably settled by *Strader*, the territorial issue was now front and center—and was pressed on the Court by the proslave arguments of Sanford's lawyers.

Taney gave them all they could have hoped for. The Constitution, he observed, did not give Congress plenary power over the territories. The "needful rules and regulations" clause of Article IV, Section 3, and Marshall's opinion in the *American Insurance Company* case (1828), usually cited in support of such congressional power, were inadequate authorities. The former applied only to territories already possessed by the government in 1787; the latter applied only to the Florida territory. Indeed, far from granting plenary power, the Constitution imposed severe limitations on congressional authority over the territories.

And here the chief justice introduced the southern states' rights theory that had taken shape in response to the Wilmot Proviso. The federal government might acquire territory and govern it, he conceded. But when it did, it acted as the trustee of the people of the several states and for their common benefit. And whatever Congress did in the territories, it must respect the rights of persons and property of the citizens of the states, not excluding those southern states that recognized slaves as property. This obligation, continued Taney, was not left to inference—the Fifth Amendment prohibited the government from depriving persons of life, liberty, and property without due process of law. As it had been traditionally understood, this clause did not confer the absolute rights of life, liberty, or property, but meant only that those rights could not be abridged except according to established processes of law. Taney shifted the meaning from procedure to substance. Congress, he declared categorically, could not deprive persons of property; since slaves were property, Congress could not prohibit slavery in the territories. Accordingly, the 36° 30' provision of the Missouri Compromise (effectively repealed by the Kansas-Nebraska Act in 1854), had been unconstitutional from its inception. Therefore, Scott's residence in Louisiana Purchase territory did not and could not make him free.

Justice McLean and Justice Curtis both dissented in separate opinions. Curtis's dissent, as persuasive as it was passionate, admonished the majority for its lack of restraint and refuted Taney's opinion on both historical and constitutional grounds. First, national citizenship followed state citizenship and, he noted, as early as 1787 five states had conferred citizenship on African Americans. Second, Congress had consistently exercised authority over slavery in the territories with the Court's support, and prescription was recognized by the Court as evidence of constitutionality. Finally, a correct appreciation of the rules governing conflict of law between states, as well as a correct understanding of Missouri law, would show that Scott retained his freedom on his return to Missouri. The anti-slave North, which had previously condemned Curtis for upholding the fugitive slave law, now embraced him. Even before the delivery of the Court's opinion, they printed and circulated his opinion as the true law of the Constitution.

Rarely has the Court undertaken so much—and settled so little. Taney's doctrine of dual citizenship was ignored in the northern lower federal courts as soon as it was expounded; in 1868, the Fourteenth Amendment laid it to rest for good. The Court's settlement of the territorial question was neither final nor controlling: Section 8 of the Missouri Compromise, which the Court voided, had already been re-pealed by Congress. Free-soilers in Kansas settled their problem without reference to *Dred Scott* by voting down the proslavery constitution of 1858 and entering the Union as a free state in 1861. The Republican Party platform of 1860, based on the prohibition of slavery in the territories, casually overlooked the decision. So did Congress in June, 1862, when it outlawed slavery in all existing territories without compensation.

Even the Court's determination of Scott's fate was reversed three months later when Calvin Chaffee, the abolitionist husband of widow Emerson, manumitted the Scott family. To be sure, the conservative post–Civil War Court cited Taney's opinion in support of the emerging substantive interpretation of the Fifth and Fourteenth Amendments. But that interpretation did not depend on precedent. It is even doubtful that the *Dred Scott* decision advanced the doctrine of judicial review of congressional acts. To be sure, it was the second time the Court had nullified an act of Congress and the first time an act not dealing with the judicial branch was involved. But the decision did more to jeopardize judicial power than any decision the Court has ever made.

The immediate (and unintended) results of the decision were far-reaching and deleterious. The Court's hard-won prestige dissolved immediately. Personal division among the judges—so bitter that Justice Curtis resigned—became a matter of public gossip. (It was rumored, and was in fact true, that Taney had added several pages of argument to his opinion after it had been read in Court and before it was printed.) On top of all this, the opinions were so numerous and diffuse that not even the profession was certain what had been decided.

The nation was in no mind to pick legal bones, however, and it accepted Taney's proslavery opinion as the Court's final word. The South, of course, felt vindicated and came to the defense of the Court. But northern newspapers, congressmen, and state legislators endorsed popular opinion in their section by heaping abuse on the decision and the Court that had made it. The justices had become "mere men." The Court's majority—"five slaveholders and two doughfaces," Greeley's *Tribune* called them—were depicted as agents in a plot to aggrandize the South. On the Senate floor, William Seward charged conspiracy between Buchanan and the proslavery justices, and Lincoln expanded the cabal to include "Stephen [Douglas], Franklin [Pierce], Roger [Taney], and James [Buchanan]."

Lincoln (who had great respect for the authority of the Court and who once argued for a judicial solution to the territorial problem) now suggested that a Court capable of handing down such a decision might hand down another forcing slavery on the free states. An opinion so contrived, asserted the *Tribune*, was entitled to "just so much moral weight as would be the judgment of those congregated in any Washington barroom." With its reputation at this new low, with cries for basic reform coming from all directions, the Court confronted the constitutional crisis of the Civil War.

Dred Scott damaged the machinery of political compromise even more than it hurt the Court. Because the decision made the position of the Republican party (whose raison d'être was opposition to slavery in the territories) constitutionally untenable, it was forced to denounce the Court. This strengthened abolitionist sentiment within party ranks, which in turn further alienated the South. This state of affairs left the Democratic party as the only national party and thus the sole institution capable of working out a compromise. Whether it would do so depended on the willingness of the two wings of the party to accept Douglas's doctrine of popular sovereignty. But as Lincoln put it to Douglas at Freeport, Illinois, if the Constitution and the Supreme Court prohibited both Congress and the territorial legislatures from excluding slavery, by what authority could the settlers themselves do so? Perhaps they could, Senator Douglas responded, by refusing to pass the police legislation necessary to enforce slavery. This refined logic failed to allay the misgivings of northern Democrats, however. And, even if they had accepted popular sovereignty, how could the southern Democrats be expected to forgo the certain advantage of *Dred Scott* for the contingency of a popular decision? When they refused to do so at the national convention in Charlestown in 1860, the Democratic party split along North-South lines. Hope for political compromise was now all but gone.

Dred Scott did not of course cause the Civil War. But it did make it almost impossible to contain the forces that did. By bolstering slavery with constitutional law, the decision forced the North to go beyond the Constitution, which in turn led the South to reject it as a worthless promise. And without the Constitution, there was nothing left but the grim logic of marching men.

Pitfalls of Judicial Discretion

When the Court decided *Dred Scott*, it put itself on trial. And historians soon rushed in with a collection of opinions so various and divergent as to confound analysis. Not until Fehrenbacher's *Dred Scott Case* appeared in 1978 did students of the Court feel confident in assessing the decision. Whether they judged the decision tolerantly as an "error in judgment" or harshly as "judicial egoism" or a "monstrous piece of judicial effrontery," their general verdict was that the Court undertook what was judicially impossible. Viewed as a case study of the nature and limitations of judicial power—which is a common theme of most scholarship—*Dred Scott* has much to offer. There remain many puzzling questions. Why, for example, at the peak of its popularity, after skillfully navigating the troubled sea of federalism for twenty years, did the Court head into the treacherous political realm of slavery in the territories? Why, once there, did the justices decide as they did? Were they "mere men," "bad" men, or merely "imprudent"?

History's harsh verdict rests on the fact that the Court need not have made itself a key player in the political crisis of the 1850s. This is not to say, as historians once argued, that Taney and the majority exceeded their legal authority by ruling on the merits after finding that Dred had no standing to sue. The Court was justified, perhaps even compelled, to explain its decision to the American people. The explanation, however, did not have to be a full and final statement on every point in dispute. To say that it did is to prefer the formality of law over the art of judicial statesmanship. Since the days of Marshall, the Court has been able to employ calculated vagueness in times of crisis.

That something less than a comprehensive and lucid treatment of the case was possible is obvious from the Court's early conference decision to ignore both law and logic by affirming the circuit court decision below, thus escaping the question of slavery in the territories. Justice Nelson wrote such an opinion for the majority, relying heavily on *Strader* v. *Graham*. He delivered it finally as his own opinion, but with the majority "we" still intact. *Strader* did not address the territorial question—but that was the whole point. Obfuscation has its uses in law as well as in politics. In any case, the real tragedy was not that the "opinion of the Court" was hopelessly confused, but that it seemed clear.

What drew the Court from the path of expediency into the arena of politics? A proslavery conspiracy composed of the president, Democratic congressmen, and the "black robes," said the North. The opinions followed sectional lines. The five southern justices, joined by the "two doughfaces" from New York and Pennsylvania, where pro-southern sentiments were strong, were ranged against those from Ohio and Massachusetts, centers of abolitionism. The lawyer opposing Dred was Reverdy Johnson, a close friend of the chief justice, who, it was said, pressured Taney to decide as he did. (Northern advocates of conspiracy conveniently ignored the fact that Justice Curtis' brother was counsel for Dred.)

Adding to the conspiracy hypothesis was the fact that President Buchanan, whose pro-slavery sympathies were evident in his Kansas policy, wrote letters to Justices Catron and Grier urging a judicial solution. Assurance came in Catron's return letter. The hundreds who saw the president and the chief justice chatting confidentially before the inaugural announcement drew the easy conclusion that Buchanan's subsequent promise of a judicial solution meant that the decision was rigged. The Court's enforcement of the fugitive slave law, the repeal of the Missouri Compromise in 1854, and the Court's pronouncement of it as void in 1857 prepared the North to believe the worst.

This belief, however, was wrong. The Court was imprudent perhaps but not conspiratorial. An intricate combination of general and specific factors accounts for its imprudence. One fact, though not the chief one, was Justices McLean's and Curtis's determination to explore the whole question, despite the early majority decision in conference to escape the problem via the *Strader* precedent. Both were moved by conviction, but McLean had a personal motive as well. To get the Republican presidential nomination in 1856—which he desperately wanted—he needed to publicize his antislavery views. McLean's ambition was no secret (and in fact he broadcast his views on the territorial question in northern newspapers), and may have contributed to the decision to postpone the second argument until after the November election. But common sense says that the justices would have done so anyway.

In any case, McLean and Curtis cannot be blamed for the Court's final determination to abandon its moderate course. What counted most was a deep-seated desire among the majority justices to stamp out, as fatal to the Union, the radical anti-Court, anti-Constitutional notions of the abolitionists. Moreover, as Fehrenbacher shows, certain justices had deep sympathy for, if not slavery itself, then the southern way of life that depended on its continuance. And this was especially true of the chief justice who, on the slavery question appears to have become the "leading mind" that Webster had once found wanting on the Court.

All the majority needed was assurance that the slavery issue was amenable to a judicial solution. Unfortunately, there was much to encourage this prideful conclusion. After all, the Court was at the apogee of its prestige among moderates in both sections. Statesmen—including at one time or another, Lincoln, Clay, Douglas, Webster, and presidents Pierce and Buchanan—and leaders of the bar were increasingly intrigued with a judicial cure for the nation's illness. This inclination was, in turn, fortified by a tendency of the age to fall back in emergencies on the Constitution, which, while it was being threatened, became even more venerable and more subject to doctrinal rigidity.

Most important (and Wallace Mendelson makes the point in "Dred Scott's Case—Reconsidered" [1953]), because Congress was desperate to shrug off the responsibility, it gave the Court the legislative go-ahead to save the nation. In 1848, the Clayton compromise bill tied to the scheme of congressional noninterference the additional principle that the question of slavery in the territories should rest on the Constitution as expounded by the territorial courts, with the right of appeal to the Supreme Court. This bill passed the Senate but failed in the House; the principle of a judicial solution, however, was incorporated in 1850 into the bills organizing the territories of Utah and New Mexico, and in the Kansas-Nebraska Act of 1854. Desirous of smashing radicalism, made confident by past success, encouraged by presidential and congressional importuning, the Court took up the Constitution and set off to rescue the fortunes of the Union.

Though the Court was damned for acting, it would just as surely have been damned for doing nothing. Perhaps, then, the real problem was the way the Court acted. It is tantalizing to speculate on the results of an opinion upholding congressional authority over slavery in the territories. Such a decision would have been consistent with both practice and with the Court's oft-stated rule that it was guided by well-established usage. Popular sovereignty as a compromise solution would then have become constitutionally feasible. To be sure, the northern Democrats in 1860 would have had to accept the 1854 repeal of the Missouri Compromise, but, with the prospect of a free Kansas, they might have done so. And without *Dred Scott* to fall back on, it is possible that the South would have settled for popular sovereignty as the best available alternative. The Democratic party, the potential vehicle for compromise, might then have held together. Congress would have been given back the responsibility it had passed on so unchivalrously. The Court could have escaped the devastating moral burden that *Dred Scott* placed on it. It might be insisted, of course, as Taney himself did insist, that his statement on slavery and the rights of free African Americans fit the framers' intent. The argument, though not entirely true, was neither entirely preposterous. On the other hand, if there was any controlling principle of constitutional law established during the age of Marshall and Taney, it was that the Constitution of 1787 could change to meet the various crises of the American people. Slavery in 1857 was a new crisis.

So much for the "ifs." Once in the breach, the Court's course of action was predictable. As John R. Schmidhauser shows in "Judicial Behavior and the Sectional Crisis" (1961), the background influence of party and section were never absent from decision-making on the

Taney Court. (Schmidhauser's scalogram analysis of decisions on the sectionally sensitive issues of commerce, corporations, and slavery makes the point conclusively and conveniently rates the justices from 1837–60 according to their varying susceptibility to party preferences and regional views of social and economic issues.) Such influences were frequently not controlling, rarely gross; but in a subtle way they influenced the outlook and thus the opinions of the judges.

Considering that seven of the nine justices—all of those who sided with Taney—were Democrats, it is not remarkable that *Dred Scott* fit neatly into the Jacksonian scheme. By denying Congress the authority to prohibit slavery in the territories, the Court limited the authority of the national government. The Jacksonians curtailed congressional authority over commerce, banking, and internal improvements when it threatened state or sectional interests. Why not curtail it over slavery? The Court protected the property interests of corporate capitalism; should not its guardianship embrace the property interests of southern agrarian capitalism as well? In answering these questions— questions that could affect the fate of southern civilization so markedly—time-ingrained values and sentiments could not be suppressed. The "five Southerners and two doughfaces" did not conspire; they succumbed.

The War Years: The Court Survives

Fought to preserve the Constitution, the war in fact laid siege to it (a story told with remarkable concision in Daniel Farber's *Lincoln's Constitution* (2003). The magnitude and unprecedented nature of that crisis called forth a flood of decisions that went beyond the regular channels of constitutional law and swept over the classic constitutional barriers against governmental abuse of power. An effective two-party system faded into Republican dominance, though it remained theoretically alive. Separation of powers gave way, in fact if not in theory, as wartime decisionmaking shifted to the president. Many if not most of Lincoln's decisions—his order blockading southern ports; his decision to raise volunteers; his suspension of the writ of habeas corpus; and his Emancipation Proclamation, to mention the most obvious—raised fundamental constitutional questions. The delicate balance between state and federal powers that the Court had labored to maintain was also permanently disrupted as the federal government consolidated the duties—military, financial, and administrative—that the states could not perform. The necessities of war took priority over individual freedom and private property. Order and the rule of law grappled feebly with chaos and expediency.

The Civil War reminds us, as it must have the justices themselves, that the Court shares the lawmaking process with the other branches and with the people, and that its power depends on historical circumstances. The Court functions most effectively in periods demanding and permitting moderate adjustments in the constitutional system. As Arthur Bestor wrote, during the Civil War "the question of how the Constitution ought to operate as a piece of working machinery was superseded by the question of whether it might and should be dismantled." Even if the Court had been popular, vital, and united—and thanks to *Dred Scott*, the Taney Court was none of these—it would have been hard pressed to maintain constitutional integrity against what a morally aroused populace and a determined Congress and president decided was military necessity.

With the Republican victory in 1860, the Court confronted a party whose platform of opposition to slavery in the territories directly challenged the *Dred Scott* decision. With the secession of the southern states, the Court presided over a northern nation that condemned it. Powerful anti-Court forces in and out of Congress cried for retribution. Some demanded the repeal of Section 25 of the Judiciary Act of 1789, some wanted to pack the Court to make it representative, and others wanted to abolish it and start from scratch. In addition, the Court was internally weak. The frequent illnesses of Catron, Grier, Wayne, and Taney greatly reduced efficiency and vitality. Institutional continuity was disrupted by deaths, resignations, and the creation of a new judicial circuit, which meant that six new justices were appointed between 1857 and 1864. In short, it was not just a question of whether the Court could save the Constitution but whether it could save itself.

The Court survived at the price of personal and doctrinal "Republicanization." Fortunately, Lincoln and his party were more interested in dominating the Court than in destroying it. By 1862, the president had appointed three justices of acceptable political persuasion, and two more by 1865, including abolitionist Chief Justice Samuel Chase. And by then, Congress had reorganized judicial circuits giving preponderance to the North. But even before these changes, the Court demonstrated a willingness to accept Lincoln's war powers.

The exception was the old chief justice himself. In *Ex parte Merryman* (1861) he single-handedly set out to put the president in his place. The issue was Lincoln's suspension of the writ of habeas corpus in the border state of Maryland, an action taken to curb pro-southern mob violence, which had the potential to hinder the transit of northern soldiers through the state, or worse, lead to secession. Taney, who once supported Andrew Jackson's threatened use of force against South Carolina secessionists, now ruled that the power to suspend the writ (listed in Article I not Article II) belonged exclusively to Congress (even though Congress was not in session at the time of the suspension). Because the opinion was not an official decision of the circuit court but an opinion written at chambers by Taney acting as chief justice, it was unusually personal. To emphasize that point, Taney sent a copy to Lincoln, who quietly ignored the insult.

The *Merryman* case never reached the Supreme Court, but in *Ex parte Vallandigham* (1864), the Court had a chance to rule on the constitutionality of military rule in an area where the civil courts were active. It begged off on jurisdictional grounds. The chief justice, undaunted to the end, was prepared to strike down the Legal Tender Act (a wartime measure which made government notes legal tender for all public and private debts), national conscription, and the emancipation of the slaves, if these questions came before the Court—but they never did.

Only once, in the Prize Cases of 1863, did the Court directly confront constitutional issues raised by the War. Here it showed its dexterity in making certain that necessity found a law. The questions raised were of a fundamental nature. The first was whether the president had the power to proclaim a blockade in the absence of a congressional declaration of war. The Court sanctioned executive action, arguing that a state of war already existed even though it had not been recognized by Congress; in effect, the president had merely responded to the grim reality.

Having acknowledged the existence of a state of war, the Court was then faced with the thorny problem of defining its legal nature, i.e., whether it was a conflict between nations or an insurrection or rebellion by private persons against a legal government. Recognition of the full belligerent status of the Confederacy would acknowledge the legality of secession, invite foreign countries to recognize the southern nation, and tie the hands of the administration in dealing with southern persons and property. To define the clash as an insurrection would avoid these dangers and actually strengthen the powers of the executive in meeting the emergency. But the southern blockade was an act of war inferring belligerency, and there were advantages, regarding prisoners and other matters, in granting a qualified belligerent status to the South. By assuming that the conflict was a war and at the same time an insurrection, the Court let the administration have it both ways. The job of determining when it was which was left to the political departments, and the Court willingly accepted their decisions as binding.

Filled with Republican justices, headed by an abolitionist, and responsive to the requirements of the war effort, the Court recovered popularity and prestige. Cooperating with the executive and Congress on Reconstruction came naturally, and by the 1870s, the Court was ready to launch out on a remarkable spree of judicial activism, which (as Christopher Wolfe has so ably shown) carried the doctrine of judicial review far beyond what John Marshall had envisaged in *Marbury v. Madison.*

Clearly the Court survived, but it did little during the war to keep alive the axiom of constitutional government—that law, and not men, should rule. That the rule of law was maintained at all, J. H. Randall concluded in his *Constitutional Problems Under Lincoln* (1964), was due more to Lincoln's respect for the Constitution (even while he was straining it) and to the "American people's sense of constitutional government," than to the efforts of the Court. Yet it must be added that the people's "fundamental sense of respect" for constitutionalism owed much to the dedicated and educative statesmanship that the Marshall and Taney Courts displayed for over sixty years.

CHAPTER SIX

The Legacy of the Supreme Court under Marshall and Taney

Is there any better plan, whatever imperfections our present one may have, for securing a reasonably continuous, nonpartisan and philosophical exposition of the Constitution than by regarding it as the supreme law of the land to be applied in actual cases and controversies through the exercise of judicial power?

Charles Evans Hughes (1928)

History is a stern judge. By its standard, past accomplishments are rated according to their relevance with regard to the changing present. Such has been the case with the Marshall and Taney Courts. Each had a distinct constitutional character and style of its own; each has faced the test of historical relevancy on its own unique merits.

The Marshall Court has fared well. Resonating to the spirit of the Revolution and the intent of the framers, it worked for a united, politically independent and economically self-sufficient nation—one dedicated to market capitalism and "invested with large portions of that sovereignty which belongs to independent states," as Marshall wrote in *Cohens* v. *Virginia*. What the modern age refers to as civil liberties was left to the states, along with much else. That is to say,

Marshall's nationalism was not consolidationist, just as his concept of national capitalism was a far cry from that of modern America. But Marshall and his Court undertook to strengthen the national government when the dominant political forces of the age were opposed to it. In the short run he lost, as radical states' rights gained the upper hand, but his vision of the nation was vindicated by American history—starting with the northern victory in the Civil War.

Power and with it responsibility have moved inexorably from the local and state levels to the nation; the United States itself has risen to the pinnacle of world power. Sectional versions of the good life, so dominant in the age of Marshall and Taney, have given way to a standardized American dream. Since the Civil War, nationalism and capitalism have been inseparable. Because it was instrumental in the development of both, the Marshall Court has retained its relevance and its favored place in American historiography. Critics of big business and big government, of course, have found less to extol. But even the reformers have been hard pressed to make an effective case against the Marshall Court, because—at least since Woodrow Wilson—they too have relied on the power of the federal government to implement their programs when it was expedient to do so.

By 1901, if not sooner, Chief Justice Marshall had become, by common agreement, *the* representative figure of American law. Because Marshall and his Court were identical in the popular mind, the Marshall Court itself took on heroic proportions. It was uniquely situated to do so. It was the first Court to speak in a single voice, and its constitutional decisions were precedent-setting. Its constitutional nationalism, moreover, rightly perceived in the large sweep of American history, is as of a single piece with that of the framers. Because Marshall succeeded in identifying the Court with the written Constitution, he made it and himself part of a creation myth that historians have found irresistible.

History and historians have not treated the Taney Court (or chief justice Taney) so well (a story recounted insightfully in Timothy S. Huebner's *The Taney Court: Justices, Rulings, and Legacy* [2003]). There were few truly memorial constitutional moments and few truly outstanding justices—except Story (a holdover from the Marshall Court), Taney himself, and Benjamin Curtis. For all of his legal ability the chief justice was unable to mobilize the Court and accordingly, it was often bitterly divided and doctrinally confused. The Taney justices were also much more overtly political than ever before or since.

Finally, there was the problem of slavery. It may be true that the members of the Taney Court did not differ greatly from Marshall and his colleagues on this subject. They did not conspire with southern slaveholders. And what the Taney Court did to African Americans was no worse than what subsequent generations of Americans were to do. Yet the stark fact remains that the majority in *Dred Scott* did choose, from several alternatives, to make slavery the law of the land. However slowly and painfully, American society has been moving toward meaningful freedom for African Americans; understanding the Taney Court's dilemma cannot put it on the winning side of this epic struggle.

If the Taney Court was reactionary regarding slavery, it was also —as Robert J. Harris reminds us in "Chief Justice Taney: Prophet of Reform and Reaction" (1957)—forward-looking and reform-minded in other respects. It did not challenge capitalism and nationalism head-on. However, taking its cue from the states' rights philosophy of the Jacksonians, it sensed the threat to democracy from corporate interests that were in league with government. It appreciated the often innovative nature of state governments and more than the Marshall Court, permitted them to regulate the new economic forces in the interest of the public and for the benefit of the common American. In doing so, the Taney Court acknowledged the importance of legislative government and the corresponding need to impose realistic limits on judicial policymaking (as in *Luther v. Borden*).

It is not likely that some future revival of Jacksonian states' rights sentiment will carry the Taney Court to historiographical glory. Two factors, however, have produced modest, if cyclic, periods of appreciation. One is the diminishing issue of slavery (already a fact by the 1870s). The second is the recognition—common wisdom among recent conservatives on and off the Court—that federalism rather than separation of powers is the most reliable constitutional corrective for overweening power at the national level. While Taney's own reputation has been unable to escape the shadow of *Dred Scott*, it has been partially redeemed by scholars and jurists who have acknowledged the timeliness of the constitutional philosophy he espoused and the quality of his legal craftsmanship.

The Marshall and Taney Courts, though distinct in many ways, also occupied much common ground. They contributed jointly to the continuous development of the Supreme Court as an institution. Though their emphases may have been different, both courts agreed that the duty of government was to maximize the creative energy of the people, both collectively and individually. In this regard, the two courts were influenced by the symbiotic relationship between law and social change (described generally in Willard Hurst's *Law and Social Process in United States History* [1960]). During these formative years, basic propositions of national culture took shape and were given legal form. Property was identified with liberty and vice versa. Material progress became the measure of individual merit and national greatness. And the corollary principle—that government should serve both individual and national progress by aiding capitalism—was established as well.

The Supreme Court did not create these social axioms, but neither did it merely reflect them. The courtroom was a forum where individual parties came into direct contact with state authority, where economic conflicts could be resolved peacefully, where conflict could be transmuted into economic rules designed to facilitate market transactions. And when the highest court in the land decided cases, it put the collective authority of the people behind one set of interests and gave priority to the social values on which they rested. In the process of resolving the controversies of Americans over a period of sixty-four years, the Supreme Court formulated the legal principles and the intellectual justification for the free enterprise system. In doing so, it facilitated the transition from the unified corporate society of the eighteenth century to the atomistic one of the twentieth—the transition, in Sir Henry Maine's classic phrase, "from status to contract." Far from being overwhelmed by this cultural transformation, the Court presided over it.

In laying the legal foundation for free enterprise, the Court under Marshall and Taney proved itself to be a representative institution in the broadest sense. One hastens to add that it did not represent all Americans. Capitalism Horatio Alger–style meant little to the pieceworker of Philadelphia who labored fourteen hours a day for as many cents, or to the women and children in northern factories, or to millions of African Americans both slave and free. Then as now, the law was often inaccessible to these anonymous poor, and they aspired outside and often against it. The price they paid presents a vital corrective to the myth of the "happy republic."

The legal principles of capitalism, however, made sense to the dominant power groups and to the large middle class of Americans who also shared in American affluence. For these classes, for those who aspired to move ahead without losing what they already had, a constitutional system that permitted change and yet kept it in trustworthy hands was appropriate. De Tocqueville missed the point when he pitted judicial government against majoritarian democracy. The Court may have restrained the majority by forcing it to justify its means and ends in terms of law, but far from opposing majority will, the Court most often served it. Because it did, the American democrat was willing to talk the language of law and order and be educated to the virtues of conservative change. The Court, to no small degree, thus made constitutional conservatism the other face of majoritarian liberalism.

Whether the legal principles fashioned to serve free enterprise in the heroic age continue to be entirely relevant today is another question. The basic assumptions that property and liberty are identical and that freedom means free enterprise have lost much of their meaning in an age when property is often a quarterly dividend rather than the extension of one's creative self; and they have no meaning at all to the millions with no real stake in society. It cannot be said that the rule of law, which the early Court did so much to institutionalize, has become irrelevant. But that great principle is not self-sufficient and it has not ensured social justice. Frequently, it has been invoked to prevent necessary reform rather than to check reckless change. In other words, law is not synonymous with morality. If it did nothing else, *Dred Scott* showed that the two are distinct and sometimes at odds. It was not due process of law, but rather a bloody civil war that freed the slaves. The Court's contributions to law and order should be justly praised, but it must not be forgotten that the vitality of the political process, and indeed the constitutional process, in America has relied and continues to rely on extralegal, sometimes illegal, radicalism. The Constitution is a living document not just because nine judges in black robes made it so, but because those not originally included—African Americans, indigenous Americans, women, and labor and other groups—fought their way into its protective orbit. It took the lives of 650,000 young men between 1860 and 1865 to reverse *Dred Scott*.

To say that the Court is answerable to the large forces of history, that some of its cherished doctrines have been repudiated over time, does not mean that the legacy of the antebellum Court is irrelevant. Its truly great achievement is that in formulating legal principles for its time, it refused to stamp them with categorical finality. The Court accepted without question the cultural assumptions of the age. But it also saw that change was the essence of the American experience and it accommodated the Constitution to this central fact. Because it did, the Court survived its mistakes and shortcomings. In surviving, it left a vital institutional legacy: established judicial procedures, proven techniques of judicial statecraft, nascent judicial self-consciousness, and a tradition of pragmatic responsiveness to the facts of American life. When the modern Court has reacted to social crises in the twentieth century, as it did after 1937 when it stopped trying to regulate the economy and took on the task of protecting individual liberty from government power, it built on the foundation laid by the early Court. So too does the present, conservative-leaning Court when it strives to roll back the excessive liberalism of the New Deal court. Whether liberal or conservative, the modern Court continues to work within an institutional tradition fashioned by the Supreme Court under Marshall and Taney.

In short, constitutional law under Marshall and Taney was a victory of constitutional process over constitutional doctrine. The process, it needs to be emphasized, was not always tidy. Nor was it always successful—witness the Taney Court's doomed effort to permanently implant the institution of slavery into American constitutional law. The victory, imperfect though it may be, was embodied in a vital, organic Constitution capable of ordering, yet responsive to, historical change. The Supreme Court was not, of course, the only instrument of change, but it was uniquely equipped if not to originate change, then to preside over and formalize the changes introduced by the executive and legislative branches and by the American people. Without the Supreme Court operating as an equal branch of government—the joint accomplishment of the Court under Marshall and Taney—the Constitution would have been either mired in the past or transformed by countless amendments into a mere legal code. The system was adumbrated by the framers of the Constitution, implemented and amplified by the Marshall Court, and tested and refined in its own chaotic fashion by the Taney Court. In reply to Charles Evans Hughes, it is a constitutional system that the American people have accepted as the best they can get.

BIBLIOGRAPHICAL ESSAY

Understanding of the Constitution in its historical context is the indispensable foundation for the study of the Supreme Court under Marshall and Taney. The logical starting point, beyond the document itself, is Max Farrand, ed., *The Records of the Federal Convention of 1787*, rev. ed., 3 vols. (1966) and James H. Hutson, ed., *Supplement to Max Farrand's Records of the Federal Convention of 1787* (1987). Also see Hutson, "The Creation of the Constitution: The Integrity of the Documentary Record," in *Interpreting the Constitution*, ed., Jack N. Rakove, (1990). A broad collection of historical documents that influenced the writing of the Constitution can be found conveniently arranged by subject matter ("Principles of Structure," "Principles of Federalism," for example) in Neil H. Cogan, ed., *Contexts of the Constitution* (1999). Philip B. Kurland and Ralph Lerner, eds., *The Founder's Constitution*, 5 vols. (1987), is a marvelous collection of sources keyed to the "major themes" in the document and to specific clauses within it. The definitive edition of the ratification debates in the several state conventions is the multivolume *Documentary History of the Ratification of the Constitution* (1971–) published by the State Historical Society of Wisconsin, under the current editorship of

John P. Kaminski and Gaspare J. Saladino. Although constitutional law is only one of many categories of law treated, special attention should be given to Morris L. Cohen, *Bibliography of Early American Law*, 6 vols. (1998), also available on CD-ROM. This massive work of scholarship identifies, locates, and indexes almost every printed document related to the development of American law from the early seventeenth century to 1860.

Among the voluminous works of secondary scholarship on the origins of the Constitution, the following are worthy of note: Forrest McDonald's trilogy, especially *E Pluribus Unum: The Formation of the American Republic, 1776–1790* (1965) and *Novus Ordo Seclorum: The Intellectual Origins of the Constitution* (1985); John Phillip Reid, *Constitutional History of the American Revolution*, 3 vols. (1986–1993); Gordon S. Wood, *The Creation of the American Republic, 1776–1787* (1969); Jennifer Nedelsky, *Private Property and the Limits of American Constitutionalism: The Madisonian Framework and Its Legacy* (1990); and Jack N. Rakove, *Original Meanings: Politics and Ideas in the Making of the Constitution* (1996). Two recent books revisit old ideas with new research: Robert A. McGuire, *To Form a More Perfect Union: A New Economic Interpretation of the United States Constitution* (2003) takes up where Charles Beard left off; and Max M. Edling, *A Revolution in Favor of Government: Origins of the U.S. Constitution and the Making of the American State* (2003) argues that the framers were concerned mainly with creating a state armed with sufficient power to survive in a hostile world; Saul Cornell, *The Other Founders: Anti-Federalism and the Dissenting Tradition in America, 1788–1828* (1999) explores the impact of the antifederalists in creating the Constitution they opposed.

Also consider Edward Corwin's *The "Higher Law" Background of American Constitutional Law* (1959); J. T. Main, *The Anti-Federalists: Critics of the Constitution, 1781–1788* (1962); Staughton Lynd, *Class Conflict, Slavery, and the United States Constitution* (1967); and Stanley Elkins and Eric McKitrick, "The Founding Fathers: Young Men of the Republic," *Political Science Quarterly* 76 (1961). Richard Kay emphasizes the truly radical nature of the founding in "The Illegality of Constitution," *Constitutional Commentary* 4 (1987). Further references, especially to the abundant periodical literature, can be found in Kermit L. Hall, comp., *A Comprehensive Bibliography of American Constitutional and Legal History, 1896–1979*, 5 vols. (1982).

Foremost among the contemporary commentaries on the Constitution that shaped judicial interpretation during the Marshall and Taney period is *The Federalist* by Alexander Hamilton, James Madison, and John Jay (available in various editions). A classic essay on the context of Madison's ideas is Douglass Adair, "'That Politics May Be Reduced to a Science,': David Hume, James Madison, and the Tenth Federalist," *Huntington Library Quarterly* 20 (1957). There are numerous anthologies of antifederalist writings, but the definitive collection is Herbert J. Storing, ed., *The Complete Anti-Federalist*, 7 vols. (1982). Students of judicial review might want to compare Hamilton's *Federalist* 78 and the Letters of Brutus (for the antifederalist view).

The Supreme Court and the Judicial Process

The study of the Supreme Court logically begins with Article III of the Constitution (which creates and defines the federal judiciary) and Article VI (which makes the Constitution the supreme law of the land). For context consult the debates at the Philadelphia Convention and those in the various state ratifying conventions. The Judiciary Act of 1789, vol. 1, *U.S. Statutes at Large* 73, fleshes out the entire system of federal courts and can profitably be read in conjunction with Maeva Marcus, ed., *Origins of the Federal Judiciary* (1992) and volume four of Maeva Marcus, ed., *The Documentary History of the Supreme Court of the United States: Organizing the Federal Judiciary* (1992). Also see Wilfred J. Ritz, *Rewriting the History of the Judiciary Act of 1789*, eds., Wythe Holt and L. H. La Rue (1990).

The changing organization, jurisdiction, and practice of the Court is analyzed in Felix Frankfurter and J. M. Landis, *The Business of the Supreme Court* (1928), and in Homer Cummings and Carl McFarland, *Federal Justice* (1937). These accounts are supplemented by Curtis P. Nettels's analysis of how politics and sectionalism shaped the structure of the federal courts in "The Mississippi Valley and the Federal Judiciary, 1807–37," *Mississippi Valley Historical Review* 12 (1925).

A useful compendium of information on the Court is *The Oxford Companion to the Supreme Court of the United States*, ed. by Kermit L. Hall (1992).

The foundation blocks of all scholarship on the Court are, of course, its official decisions. Although it is good strategy to consult a general account of the Court first, the serious student will want to go directly to the *Supreme Court Reports*. The first ninety volumes (through 1874) are cited according to the name of the "official" reporter: thus 4 *Peters* 514 (1830) refers to volume 4 of Peters's *Reports* at page 514 for 1830. Various unofficial editions of the *United States Reports* (the Lawyers' Edition is the standard one) are "star paged" (e.g.,*514) to indicate pages in the original reports. Excerpts of the Court's leading opinions are available in a number of recent collections. One of the few emphasizing cases of historical interest is Stanley Kutler's *Supreme Court and the Constitution* (1969). James B. Thayer's *Cases on Constitutional Law*, 2 vols. (1895), remains the most comprehensive collection of cases for the nineteenth century. Justices on the Marshall and Taney Court also served as circuit court judges (where they sat twice yearly with the federal district judges in their respective circuits). The most complete and accessible collection of circuit court decisions before 1880 is the thirty-volume series called *Federal Cases*.

A wide variety of materials useful in reconstructing the legal world in which the antebellum Court operated is now available. The first American law periodical (Hall's *American Law Journal*) appeared in 1808 and, by the end of the Marshall period, several more (the *American Jurist and Law Magazine* being the most broad-based and inquiring) had appeared with a notable advance in coverage and sophistication. Complete runs of these revealing journals are now available in the *American Periodical Series,1800–1850* (University Microfilms, Ann Arbor, Mich.). Newspapers are also important sources of information relative to the Court's work (as for example in Charles Warren's *The Supreme Court in United States History*, 2 vols. (1926).

For a discussion of commentaries on the Constitution, a vital part of the constitutional discourse of the age, consult Elizabeth K. Bauer, *Commentaries on the Constitution, 1790–1860* (1952). Justice Joseph Story's *Commentaries on the Constitution of the United States,* 3 vols.

(1833), although it was opposed by southern constitutional theorists, was the single most influential work on the Constitution in the nineteenth century. Chancellor James Kent's *Commentaries on American Law,* 4 vols. (1826–30), covering all of American law, is one of the great works of nineteenth-century legal scholarship (especially see Oliver Wendell Holmes, Jr.'s definitive 12th ed.). Perry Miller excerpts the writings of Kent, Story, and many other contemporaries in *The Legal Mind in America* (1962). Charles Haar's superb collection of essays, letters, and speeches in *The Golden Age of American Law* (1965) also provides ready access to the central legal ideas of the formative period and dispels the notion that American legal thought began with Holmes. Worthy of mention for its unique combination of historical documents and scholarly essays relating to them is Kermit L. Hall, ed., *Major Problems in American Constitutional History: I: The Colonial Era Through Reconstruction* (1992).

There are several general histories of the Supreme Court. The most comprehensive and authoritative are the relevant volumes in *The O. W. Holmes Devise History of the Supreme Court of the United States,* starting with Julius Goebel, Jr.'s *Antecedents and Beginnings to 1800* (1971). The pre-Marshall Court is also the subject of William R. Casto, *The Supreme Court in the Early Republic: The Chief Justiceships of John Jay and Oliver Ellsworth* (1995). The Marshall Court gets three volumes in the *Holmes Devise History*: George L. Haskins and Herbert A. Johnson, *Foundations of Power, 1801 to 1815* (1981); and in volumes 3–4 of G. Edward White, *The Marshall Court and Cultural Change, 1815–1835* (1988). Carl B. Swisher, *The Taney Period, 1836–64* (1974) is the definitive account of the Taney Court by Taney's distinguished biographer. In addition to extended treatment of the Court's decisions, these volumes discuss the justices who sat on the Court, the lawyers who argued before it, and its mode of operation.

Among the other general works on the Court are Harold M. Hyman and William M. Wiecek, *Equal Justice Under Law: Constitutional Development, 1835–1875* (1982) and Charles Warren's classic work, *The Supreme Court in United States History,* 2 vols. (1926). Gustavus Myers' socialist *History of the Supreme Court* (1912) and Louis Boudin's *Government by Judiciary,* 2 vols. (1932) are unique in their critical take on the Court. Boudin sets out to demonstrate that, from the start, judicial power has encroached on the "legitimate rights of legislature, executive and people"; though massive in its scholarship, it is marred by excessive special pleading. Not until the publication of Charles Grove Haines's *The Role of the Supreme Court in American Government and Politics 1789–1835* (1944) and the companion volume by Haines and Foster H. Sherwood (1957), covering the period from 1835 to 1864, was there a comprehensive answer to Warren's pro-Court, nationalist interpretation. William W. Crosskey, in *Politics and the Constitution in the History of the United States,* 2 vols. (1953), attempted to swing the interpretive pendulum back by arguing that the Constitution established a unitary government. His massive research is full of keen insights, but his provocative thesis has left most scholars unconvinced. For an incisive critique of leading cases, see David P. Currie, *The Constitution in the Supreme Court: The First Hundred Years, 1789–1888* (1985). Among the more streamlined histories of the Court are: Robert G. McCloskey, *The American Supreme Court,* 2d ed., rev., Sanford Levinson (1994); and William M. Wiecek, *Liberty Under Law: The Supreme Court in American Life* (1998).

Among the several constitutional histories that discuss Congress and the executive as well as the Court, four are notable: the most recent (and most provocative) is Bruce A. Ackerman, *We The People: Foundations* (1991) and *We the People: Transformations* (1998), which argue that the American electorate, working outside the formal amendment process, plays a central role in constitutional change. Andrew C. McLaughlin, *A Constitutional History of the United States* (1935) led the way and, although in need of revision, it still merits attention. Carl B. Swisher's *American Constitutional Development,* 2nd ed. (1954) is distinguished by its incisive scholarship. Alfred H. Kelly, Winfred A. Harbison, and Herman Belz, *The American Constitution,* now in its seventh edition, is outstanding for its comprehensiveness and its extensive bibliography.

No discussion of general scholarship on the Court would be complete without special mention of Edward S. Corwin. With a mastery of institutional history and legal and political philosophy he combined hard-nosed judicial realism and a dedication to historical truth. Corwin's great synthetic work was never written, but in some twenty monographs and countless articles and reviews he supplied the ideas that enriched the whole field of constitutional literature. The best of his essays, collected by Alpheus T. Mason and Gerald Garvey in *American Constitutional History: Essays by Edward S. Corwin* (1964) reads like an interpretive history of the Court.

The Close View: Monographs and Articles on the Marshall And Taney Courts

Some of the most thought-provoking scholarship treats special themes or phases of the Court's work. The classic theoretical analysis of judicial review is Alexander M. Bickel, *The Least Dangerous Branch: The Supreme Court at the Bar of Politics* (1962). An essential work that puts in historical perspective judicial review during the Marshall and Taney period is Christopher Wolfe, *The Rise of Modern Judicial Review: From Constitutional Interpretation to Judge-Made Law* (1986). Also interesting in this regard is William E. Nelson, "Changing Conceptions of Judicial Review: The Evolution of Constitutional Theory in the States, 1790–1860," *University of Pennsylvania Law Review* 120 (1972). On contending theories of constitutional interpretation see Jack N. Rakove, ed., *Interpreting the Constitution: The Debate Over Original Intent* (1990), especially (for the Marshall and Taney periods) the "The Original Understanding of Original Intent," by H. Jefferson Powell.

Felix Frankfurter's *The Commerce Clause under Marshall, Taney, and Waite* (1937) provides an overview of that crucial facet of the Court's work not found in general accounts. In *The Contract Clause of the Constitution* (1938), Benjamin F. Wright does the same for that subject. John R. Schmidhauser singles out a vital function of judicial history for special treatment in *The Supreme Court as Final Arbiter in Federal-State Relations, 1789–1957* (1958). For a fuller treatment of conflict within the federal system see Forrest McDonald, *States' Rights and the Union: Imperium in Imperio, 1776–1876* (2000). Also see Edward S. Corwin, *The Commerce Power versus States' Rights* (1936).

Mitchell Wendell, *Relations between the Federal and State Courts* (1949) deals with a seriously neglected aspect of the federal-state relationship.

Several books treating the Court's often contentious relationship with Congress include: Charles Warren, *Congress, the Constitution and the Supreme Court* (1925); Donald G. Morgan, *Congress and the Constitution: A Study in Responsibility* (1966); and Raoul Berger, *Congress v. the Supreme Court* (1969). For insight into the relationship between the early Court and political parties, see Kathryn Turner, "Federalist Policy in the Judiciary Act of 1801," *William and Mary Quarterly* 22 (1965); Richard Ellis, *The Jeffersonian Crisis: Court and Politics in the Young Republic* (1971) and *The Union at Risk: Jacksonian Democracy, States' Rights, and the Nullification Crisis* (1978). Also see Peter C. Hoffer & N.E.H. Hull, *Impeachment in America, 1635–1805* (1984); and Mary K. B. Tachau, *Federal Courts in the Early Republic: Kentucky, 1789–1816* (1978)—one of the few studies of the lower federal court system in operation. Other important themes of antebellum law are treated in Benjamin F. Wright, *American Interpretations of Natural Law* (1931) and Charles G. Haines, *The Revival of Natural Law Concepts* (1930). A pioneering study in its own time, and one still worth pondering is Max Lerner, "Constitution and Court as Symbols," *Yale Law Journal* 46 (1937).

The impact of constitutional law on economic development is another subject that has received much profitable attention. Although he was not concerned primarily with the Supreme Court, Willard Hurst is the pioneer in this area. His *Law and Conditions of Freedom in the Nineteenth Century United States* (1956) is a good starting point and should be read in conjunction with Harry Scheiber, "At the Borderland of Law and Economic History: The Contributions of Willard Hurst," *American Historical Review* 75 (1970). Volume 18 (2000) of *Law and History Review* is devoted entirely to Hurst's work. One of the best accounts dealing with the interaction of law and economic development during the antebellum period is Stanley I. Kutler, *Privilege and Creative Destruction: The Charles River Bridge Case* (1971). On this decision also see R. Kent Newmyer, "Justice Joseph Story, the Charles River Bridge Case and the Crisis of Republicanism," *American Journal of Legal History* 17 (1973). Newmyer's biography of Justice Story explores the relationship between Story's jurisprudence and his vision of American capitalism.

The Court's role in bringing the Constitution to the service of private property is the subject of Corwin's classic essay, "The Basic Doctrine of American Constitutional Law," *Michigan Law Review* 12 (1914). Max Lerner's "Supreme Court and American Capitalism," *Yale Law Journal* 42 (1933) puts the Court's economic role in the cultural setting. A more detailed treatment of the same general subject is Howard J. Graham's "Procedure to Substance—Extra-Judicial Rise of Due Process, 1830–1860," *California Law Review* 40 (1952–53). Wallace Mendelson's *Capitalism, Democracy, and the Supreme Court* (1960) relates the capitalistic tendencies of American law to democratic political development and uses this economic touchstone to distinguish the Taney from the Marshall Court. The impact of economic issues on judicial opinions is treated in Harry N. Scheiber, "Instrumentalism and Property Rights: A Reconsideration of American 'Styles of Judicial Reasoning' in the 19th Century," *Wisconsin Law Review* (1975). R. Kent Newmyer's *John Marshall and the Heroic Age of the Supreme Court* (2001) deals specifically with Marshall's contribution to market capitalism. Although it treats mainly private law, Morton J. Horwitz, *The Transformation of American Law, 1780–1860* (1977) is highly recommended. Two classic studies treat the changing relationship between law and economics at the state level during the antebellum period: Oscar and Mary Handlin, *Commonwealth: A Study of the Role of Government in the American Economy: Massachusetts, 1774–1861* (1947); and Louis Hartz, *Economic Policy and Democratic Thought: Pennsylvania, 1776–1860* (1948).

No legal development in the formative period has had more impact on American history than the rise of the corporation, and on that subject E. M. Dodd's *American Business Corporations until 1860* (1954) remains the standard account. The historical background not supplied by Dodd can be obtained in John P. Davis, *Corporations: A Study of the Origin and Development of Great Business Combinations and Their Relation to the Authority of the State,* 2 vols. (1905; Capricorn Books, 1961); and Joseph S. Davis, *Essays in the Earlier History of American Corporations,* 2 vols. (1917). Very useful on selected aspects of corporate development are: Oscar and Mary Handlin,

"Origins of the American Business Corporation," *Journal of Economic History* 5 (1945), G. S. Callender, "The Early Transportation and Banking Enterprises of the States in Relation to the Growth of Corporations," *Quarterly Journal of Economics* 17 (1902), and Gerald C. Henderson, *The Position of Foreign Corporations in American Constitutional Law* (1918).

The scholarship treating specific decisions (and themes) of the Marshall and Taney Court is voluminous with *Marbury* v. *Madison* and *Dred Scott* v. *Sandford* garnering the lion's share of scholarly attention. On the former one might profitably consult: William E. Nelson, *Marbury v. Madison: The Origins and Legacy of Judicial Review* (2000); Robert L. Clinton, *Marbury v. Madison and Judicial Review* (1989); Sylvia Snowiss, *Judicial Review and the Law of the Constitution* (1990); and Jack Sosin, *Aristocracy of the Long Robe: The Origins of Judicial Review in America* (1989). Although somewhat dated, William Van Alstyne, "A Critical Guide to *Marbury* v. *Madison*," *Duke Law Journal* 15 (1969) is a useful introduction, as is James Bradley Thayer's classic essay, "The Origin and Scope of the American Doctrine of Constitutional Law," *Harvard Law Review* 7 (1893). G. Edward White has a fine essay, "John Marshall and the Genesis of the Tradition," in his *The American Judicial Tradition* (1976). A collection of interesting essays on *Marbury* can also be found in *The George Washington Law Review* 72 (2003); especially relevant are those by Philip Hamburger and Charles F. Hobson. Theodore W. Ruger explores the impact of *Marbury* and judicial review by looking closely at Kentucky during the 1820s in "'A Question Which Convulses a Nation': The Early Republic's Greatest Debate About the Judicial Review Power," *Harvard Law Review* 117 (2004).

On other leading Marshall cases (in chronological order) see: Robert K. Faulkner "John Marshall and the Burr Trial," *Journal of American History* 53 (1966); Buckner F. Melton, Jr., *Aaron Burr: Conspiracy to Treason* (2002); C. Peter McGrath, *Yazoo: Law and Politics in the New Republic: The Case of Fletcher v. Peck* (1966); Francis N. Stites, *Private Interest & Public Gain: The Dartmouth College Case, 1819* (1972); Gerald Gunther, ed., *John Marshall's Defense of McCulloch v. Maryland* (1969); On *Green* v. *Biddle* examine Paul

Gates, "Tenants of the Log Cabin," *Mississippi Valley Historical Review* 49 (1962); Maurice G. Baxter, *The Steamboat Monopoly: Gibbons v. Ogden, 1824* (1972); John T. Noonan, Jr., *The Antelope: The Ordeal of the Recaptured Africans in the Administrations of James Monroe and John Quincy Adams* (1977); Jill Norgren, *The Cherokee Cases: The Confrontation of Law and Politics* (1996); Joseph Burke, "The Cherokee Cases: A Study in Law, Politics, and Morality," *Stanford Law Review* 21 (1969). Two articles by Gerard N. Magliocca deal with the long-range impact of the Cherokee cases: "Preemptive Opinions: The Secret History of *Worcester v. Georgia* and *Dred Scott*," *University of Pittsburgh Law Review* 63 (2002) and "The Cherokee Removal and the Fourteenth Amendment," *Duke Law Journal* 53 (2003). A very interesting essay which challenges much conventional wisdom is Michael J. Klarman, "How Great Were the 'Great' Marshall Court Decisions?" *Virginia Law Review* 87 (2001).

Three interpretive articles on the Marshall period are notable because they succeed in destroying the myth of a unitary, Marshall-dominated Court. Donald Morgan traces the rise of internal division on the Court in "The Origin of Supreme Court Dissent," *William and Mary Quarterly* 10 (1953). Donald Roper's excellent article, "Judicial Unanimity and the Marshall Court—A Road to Reappraisal," *American Journal of Legal History* 9 (1965) expands Morgan's thesis by noting the composite, often compromising, nature of many key decisions of the Marshall Court. Gerald Garvey, "The Constitutional Revolution of 1837 and the Myth of Marshall's Monolith," *Western Political Quarterly* 18 (1965) makes a similar point and shows how the doctrinal flexibility of the Marshall Court left the Taney Court decisional elbow room that permitted a nonrevolutionary accommodation of old law to new history.

Generally speaking, the Taney Court, the subject of slavery excepted, has attracted less scholarly attention than that of its predecessor. The most comprehensive account is the previously mentioned volume by Carl B. Swisher in the *Holmes Devise History*. For a concise overview (and a useful bibliography) Timothy S. Huebner, *The Taney Court: Justices, Rulings, and Legacy* (2003) has much to recommend it. Also relevant are the following books and articles: Richard Longaker's "Andrew Jackson and the Judiciary," *Political Science*

Quarterly 71 (1956) corrects the misconception that President Jackson was implacably hostile to the judiciary and the law. Curtis P. Nettels' above-mentioned "Mississippi Valley and the Federal Judiciary" amplifies this revision by noting that the West wanted more federal courts, not fewer. G. Edward White touches on a key feature of the Taney Court's jurisprudence in "Taney and the Limits of Judicial Power," chap. 3 in *The American Judicial Tradition* (1976). Tony Freyer discusses the impact of *Swift* v. *Tyson* (1842) on the development of a federal commercial common law in *Harmony and Dissonance: The Swift and Erie Cases in American Federalism* (1981). A concise discussion of *Luther* v. *Borden* can be found in William M. Wiecek, *The Guarantee Clause of the Constitution* (1972). For a discussion of the Taney Court during the Civil War, see J. G. Randall, *Constitutional Problems Under Lincoln* (rev. ed., 1951); David M. Silver, *Lincoln's Supreme Court* (1956), and most recently, Daniel Farber, *Lincoln's Constitution* (2003).

Much of the literature on the Taney Court deals with slavery and the sectional controversy that culminated in the infamous *Dred Scott* decision. In this category Staughton Lynd, "The Compromise of 1787," *Political Science Quarterly* 81 (1966) starts at the beginning by going beyond the sparse documents of the constitutional period to hypothesize about the nature of the 1787 compromise on slavery. His "Abolitionist Critique of the United States Constitution," in Martin Duberman, ed., *The Antislavery Vanguard* (1965), points up the continued influence of the sectional mind on constitutional interpretation. These essays can now be found in Lynd's *Class Conflict, Slavery, and the United States Constitution* (1968).

More recent studies on the subject are Don E. Fehrenbacher, *The Slave Holding Republic: An Account of the United States Government's Relations to Slavery* (2001); and Paul Finkelman, "Slavery and the Constitution: Making a Covenant with Death," in Richard Beeman et al. eds., *Beyond Confederation: Origins of the Constitution and American National Identity* (1987). The abolitionist's treatment of the Constitution is the subject of William M. Wiecek, *The Sources of Antislavery Constitutionalism in America, 1760–1848* (1977). As a background to the Court's involvement in the constitutional debate over slavery in the territories, two articles by Arthur Bestor are superb:

"State Sovereignty and Slavery: A Reinterpretation of Proslavery Constitutional Doctrine, 1846–1860," *Journal of the Illinois State Historical Society* 54 (1961) and "The American Civil War as a Constitutional Crisis," *American Historical Review* 69 (1964).

John R. Schmidhauser, "Judicial Behavior and the Sectional Crisis of 1837–1860," *Journal of Politics* 23 (1961) uses statistical techniques to establish the vulnerability of the justices to sectional issues, including slavery. The standard compilation of slavery cases is Helen T. Catterall, *Judicial Cases Concerning American Slavery and the Negro*, 5 vols. (1937). The most comprehensive study of slavery and law is Thomas D. Morris, *Southern Slavery and the Law* (1996). John C. Hurd, *The Law of Freedom and Bondage in the United States,* 2 vols. (1858–62), is a pioneering work of scholarship which is still useful for understanding the complex legal structure that sustained slavery. On one crucial facet of that structure, Allen Johnson's "Constitutionality of the Fugitive Slave Acts," *Yale Law Journal* 31 (1920) remains the standard account. J. L. Nogee's "Prigg Case and Fugitive Slavery, 1842–1850," *Journal of Negro History* 39 (1954) throws light on that crucial case as do both William Leslie's "The Influence of Joseph Story's Theory of the Conflict of Laws on Constitutional Nationalism," *Mississippi Valley Historical Review* 35 (1948); and Joseph C. Burke's "What Did the Prigg Decision Really Decide?" *Pennsylvania Magazine of History and Biography* 93 (1969). Thomas D. Morris, *Free Men All: The Personal Liberty Laws of the North, 1780–1861* (1974) is definitive. Also see Finkelman, "Prigg v. Pennsylvania and the Northern State Courts: Anti-Slavery Uses of a Pro-Slave Decision," *Civil War History* 25 (1979). The *Amistad* case, the most widely publicized decision prior to *Dred Scott*, is treated vividly in Howard Jones, *Mutiny on the Amistad: The Saga of a Slave Revolt And Its Impact on American Abolition, Law, and Diplomacy* (1987). A broader study of the antebellum Court's response to the slave trade is David L. Lightner, "The Supreme Court and the Interstate Slave Trade: A Study in Evasion, Anarchy, and Extremism," *Journal of Supreme Court History* 29 (2004). In "Some Antecedents of the Dred Scott Case," *American Historical Review* 30 (1924), Helen T. Catterall traces the decisions that led inevitably to *Dred Scott*. Wallace Mendelson, in "Dred Scott's Case—Reconsidered," *Minnesota Law Review* 38

(1953), shows how Congress helped the Court on its way to that disaster. Also relevant is William E. Nelson, "The Impact of the Anti-Slavery Movement upon Styles of Judicial Reasoning in the Nineteenth Century," *Harvard Law Review* 87 (1974). The moral impact of slavery litigation on the judges themselves is treated brilliantly in Robert Cover, *Justice Accused: Antislavery and the Judicial Process* (1975).

On the *Dred Scott* decision itself—its antecedents and impact—Don E. Fehrenbacher, *The Dred Scott Case: Its Significance in American Law and Politics* (1978) is the leading study. For a short version of that book see his *Slavery, Law and Politics: The Dred Scott Case in Historical Perspective* (1981). Also see his *Sectional Crisis and Southern Constitutionalism* (1995). For a concise treatment of the *Dred Scott* decision, along with key documents, see Paul Finkelman, *Dred Scott v. Sandford* (1997). Finkelman's *An Imperfect Union: Slavery, Federalism, and Comity* (1981) is the best work on that important subject.

Judicial Biography

This genre (see J. W. Peltason's "Supreme Court Biography and the Study of Public Law," in Gottfried Dietze, ed., *Essays on the American Constitution* [1964]) performs a variety of historiographical functions. Above all, however, it can illuminate the relationship of human experience and character to decisionmaking and, by treating the Court from the inside, supply a realistic dimension often lacking in institutional history. For a biographical introduction to the justices one can do no better than Leon Friedman and Fred L. Israel, eds., *The Justices of the United States Supreme Court 1789–1969*, 4 vols. (1969). Volumes one and two cover the antebellum court. For a briefer compendium see Melvin I. Urofsky, ed., *The Supreme Court Justices: A Biographical Dictionary* (1987); and Clare Cushman, ed., *The Supreme Court Justices: Illustrated Biographies, 1789–1993* (1993).

None of the early justices has received as much recent attention as John Marshall, thanks in no small part to the multivolume *Papers of John Marshall*, published at The College of William and Mary under the current editorship of Charles F. Hobson. Until the recent spate of Marshall biographies the reigning authority was Albert Beveridge, *The Life of John Marshall*, 4 vols. (1916–1919). Although Beveridge is still worth consulting, his biography has recently been supplanted by several more balanced studies. Two general biographies of the "great chief justice" are Jean Edward Smith, *John Marshall: Definer of a Nation* (1996) and R. Kent Newmyer, *John Marshall and the Heroic Age of the Supreme Court* (2001). Three excellent short studies are: Robert K. Faulkner, *The Jurisprudence of John Marshall* (1968); Charles F. Hobson, *The Great Chief Justice: John Marshall and the Rule of Law* (1996); and Herbert A. Johnson, *The Chief Justiceship of John Marshall, 1801–1835* (1997). Francis N. Stites, *John Marshall: Defender of the Constitution* (1981) is a reliable concise biography, but older short studies by James Bradley Thayer (1904) and Edward Corwin (1919) are still worth consulting. Also valuable after many years is Samuel J. Konefsky, *John Marshall and Alexander Hamilton: Architects of the American Constitution* (1964). W. Melville Jones, ed., *Chief Justice John Marshall: A Reappraisal* (1956) contains a valuable collection of scholarly essays on Marshall that, as the title suggests, marks a departure from Beveridge's hagiographic approach.

Among the hundreds of articles on Marshall the following provide food for thought: Max Lerner, "John Marshall and the Campaign of History," *Columbia Law Review* 39 (1939); Justice Frankfurter, "John Marshall and the Judicial Function," *Harvard Law Review* 69 (1955); and Julian P. Boyd, "The Chasm that Separated Thomas Jefferson and John Marshall," in G. Dietze, ed., *Essays on the American Constitution* (1964). Another of the chief justice's gifted enemies is given his intellectual due in the anonymous note, "Judge Spencer Roane of Virginia—Champion of States' Rights—Foe of John Marshall," *Harvard Law Review* 66 (1953). On this subject see also: Miller F. Thornton, "John Marshall versus Spencer Roane: A Reevaluation of Martin v. Hunter's Lessee," *Virginia Magazine of History and Biography* 96 (1988); and Samuel R. Olken, "John Marshall and Spencer Roane: An Historical Analysis of their Conflict over U.S. Supreme Court Appellate Jurisdiction," *Journal of Supreme Court History* (1990). Another relevant comparison is found in Louis B. Boudin, "John Marshall and Roger B. Taney," *Georgetown Law Journal* 24 (1936). The definitive treatment of Marshall's appointment to the Court is Kathryn Turner, "The Appointment of Chief Justice John Marshall," *William and Mary Quarterly* 17 (1960).

Marshall's most distinguished colleague, Justice Joseph Story, has recently been the subject of considerable scholarship, although one might profitably begin with two works by his son: William W. Story, ed., *The Life and Letters of Joseph Story*, 2 vols. (1852); and W. W. Story, ed., *Miscellaneous Writings of Joseph Story* (1852). The three full biographies of Story are Gerald T. Dunne, *Justice Joseph Story and the Rise of the Supreme Court* (1970); James McClellan, *Joseph Story and the American Constitution: A Study in Political and Legal Thought* (1971); and R. Kent Newmyer, *Justice Joseph Story: Statesman of the Old Republic* (1985). Donald Morgan's excellent *Justice William Johnson: The First Dissenter* (1954) analyzes the constitutional career of that hard-thinking, independent Jeffersonian judge and, in so doing, throws needed critical light on the inner tensions of the Marshall Court. Justice Samuel Chase's stormy career is treated in Jane S. Elsmere, *Justice Samuel Chase* (1980); and James Haw et al., *Stormy Patriot: Life of Samuel Chase* (1980). Although not a full biography, Stephen B. Presser's *The Original Misunderstanding: The English, the Americans and the Dialectic of Federalist Jurisprudence* (1991) contains some keen insights into Chase and early national constitutional law. Donald M. Roper's *Mr. Justice Thompson and the Constitution* (1987) is the best work on that justice.

On Chief Justice Taney, Carl Swisher's outstanding biography, *Roger B. Taney* (1935) is the reigning authority, although one might also consult Charles W. Smith, Jr., *Roger B. Taney: Jacksonian Jurist* (1936); B. W. Palmer, *Marshall and Taney: Statesmen of the Law* (1966); and Lewis Walker, *Without Fear or Favor: A Biography of Chief Justice Roger B. Taney* (1965). Also see Samuel Tyler, ed., *Memoir of Roger Brooke Taney, LL.D. Chief Justice of the Supreme Court of the United States* (1872). Robert J. Harris, "Chief Justice Taney: Prophet of Reform and Reaction," *Vanderbilt Law Review* 10 (1957) treats the bifurcated nature of Taney's jurisprudence. Ferhrenbacher's *The Dred Scott Case* (1978) contains a scathing analysis of Taney's proslavery jurisprudence, especially his opinion in *Dred Scott*.

Other Taney Court justices are treated in the collective biographies of the justices mentioned above. In addition see: Henry G.

Connor, *John Archibald Campbell* (1920); John P. Frank, *Justice Daniel Dissenting: A Biography of Peter V. Daniel, 1784–1860* (1964); Francis P. Weisenburger, *The Life of John McLean: A Politician on the United States Supreme Court* (1937); and Alexander A. Lawrence's *James Moore Wayne: Southern Unionist* (1943). The best account of Justice Catron is "John Catron, Jacksonian Jurisprudence, and the Expansion of the South," by Timothy S. Huebner, in *The Southern Judicial Tradition: State Judges and Sectional Distinctiveness, 1790–1890* (1999). Richard Leach, "Benjamin Robbins Curtis: Judicial Misfit," *New England Quarterly* 25 (1952) is discerning, but B. R. Curtis, Jr., ed., *A Memoir of Benjamin Robbins Curtis*, 2 vols. (1879), remains indispensable. Another approach to judicial biography—and one essential to a full understanding of the Court—is John R. Schmidhauser, "The Justices of the Supreme Court: A Collective Portrait," *Midwest Journal of Political Science* 3 (February 1959).

GLOSSARY OF LEGAL TERMS

certiorari   a discretionary writ from a superior court calling the action of an inferior court (or a quasi-judicial body) up for review

comity   the informal and voluntary recognition by courts of one jurisdiction of the laws and judicial decisions of another

common law   the body of law developed and administered in England as distinguished from Civil or Roman law; also, the law derived from ancient usage and custom and judicial decisions as distinct from legislative or statute law; also, the law administered in courts of common law as distinguished from that in courts of equity

decisional law   law determined by reference to the reported decisions of the courts

eminent domain   power to take private property for public use

equity   a system of jurisprudence, distinct from the common law, and affording remedial justice not available in common law courts

habeas corpus   a writ directed to a person detaining another, commanding him to produce that person and show legal justification for the detention

judicial review   power of the Supreme Court to negate acts of Congress that conflict with the Constitution and to overrule

acts of state legislatures or decisions of state courts at variance
with either the Constitution or federal laws

libel   in practice, a written statement by a plaintiff of his cause of
action and of the relief he seeks to obtain in his suit

mandamus   a writ issued from a court of competent jurisdiction
commanding the performance of a particular act specified
therein

obiter dictum   an opinion expressed by a court on some question
of law which is not necessary to the decision of the case being
considered

on the merits   the inherent justice of the defendant's contention
as distinguished from technical matters such as jurisdiction or
pleading

party of record   party to a legal action whose name appears on
the record of the court

plenary   full, unqualified

private law   the law administered between citizen and citizen

public law   that branch of law concerned with the state in its
political and sovereign capacity

quo warranto   writ by which the government commences a legal
action to recover an office or franchise from a person or
corporation in possession of it

remand   to send back

salvage   in maritime law, compensation allowed to persons by
whose assistance a ship or its cargo is rescued from impending
danger or recovered in cases of shipwreck

seriatim   separately; one by one

stare decisis   doctrine of following rules or principals laid down in
previous judicial decisions, where the facts permit

sub silentio   under silence; without notice being given

tort   any wrongful act (not involving a breach of contract) for
which a civil action may be brought; a civil wrong independent
of contract

ultra vires   beyond the scope or in excess of legal power or
authority

writ of error   a writ issued from an appellate to an inferior court
commanding that the record of a case be sent up for review of
an alleged error in law of the inferior court

JUSTICES OF THE SUPREME COURT, 1801–1864

Period of Appointment

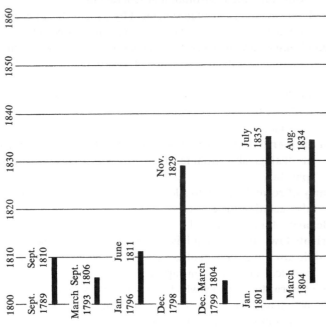

William Cushing (1732–1810), Mass., Fed.,
App. by Washington, Sept. 24, 1789

William Paterson (1745–1806), N.J., Fed.,
App. by Washington, March 4, 1793

Samuel Chase (1741–1811), Md., Fed.,
App. by Washington, Jan. 26, 1796

Bushrod Washington (1762–1829), Va., Fed.,
App. by Adams, Sept. 29, 1798

Alfred Moore (1755–1810), N.C., Fed.,
App. by Adams, Oct. 20, 1799

Chief Justice John Marshall (1755–1835),
Va., Fed., App. by Adams, Jan. 20, 1801

William Johnson (1771–1834), S.C., Rep.,
App. by Jefferson, March 22, 1804

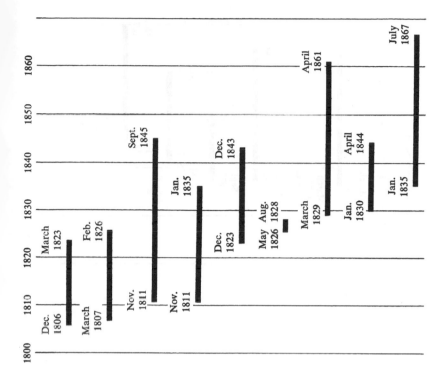

Henry Brockholst Livingston (1757–1823), N.Y., Rep., App. by Jefferson, Nov. 10, 1806

Thomas Todd (1765–1826), Ky., Rep., App. by Jefferson, Feb. 23, 1807

Joseph Story (1779–1845), Mass., Rep., App. by Madison, Nov. 15, 1811

Gabriel Duvall (1752–1844), Md., Rep., App. by Madison, Nov. 15, 1811

Smith Thompson (1768–1843), N.Y., Rep., App. by Monroe, Sept. 1, 1823

Robert Trimble (1777–1828), Ky., Rep., App. by J. Q. Adams, April 11, 1826

John McLean (1785–1861), Ohio, Dem. (later Rep.), App. by Jackson, March 6, 1829

Henry Baldwin (1780–1844), Pa., Dem., App. by Jackson, Jan. 4, 1830

James Moore Wayne (1790–1867), Ga., Dem., App. by Jackson, Jan. 7, 1835

JUSTICES OF THE SUPREME COURT, 1801–1864

Period of Appointment

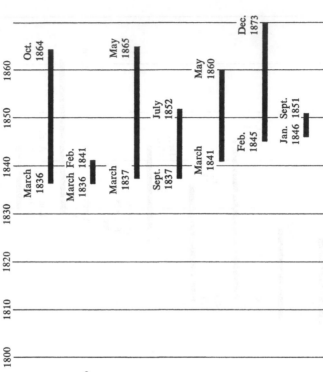

1800   1810   1820   1830   1840   1850   1860

Chief Justice Roger Brooke Taney (1777–1864),
Md., Dem., App. by Jackson, Dec. 28, 1835

Philip Pendleton Barbour (1783–1841), Va., Dem.,
App. by Jackson, Dec. 28, 1835

John Catron (1786–1865), Tenn., Dem.,
App. by Jackson, March 3, 1837

John McKinley (1780–1852), Ky., Dem.,
App. by Van Buren, April 22, 1837

Peter Daniel (1784–1860), Va., Dem.,
App. by Van Buren, Feb. 26, 1841

Samuel Nelson (1792–1873), N.Y., Dem.,
App. by Tyler, Feb. 4, 1845

Levi Woodbury (1789–1851), N.H., Dem.,
App. by Polk, Sept. 20, 1845

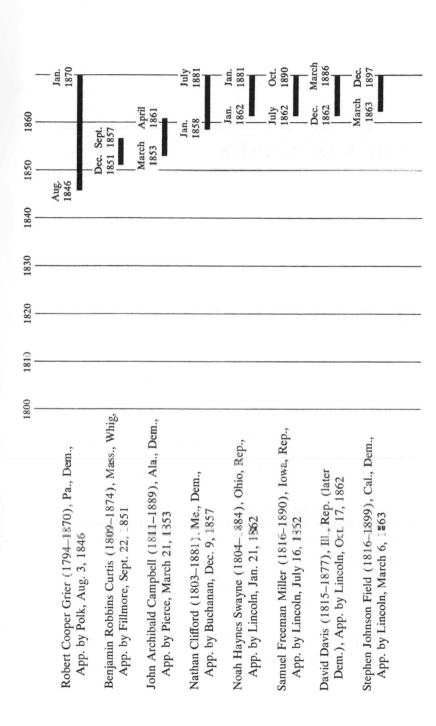

INDEX OF CASES

American Insurance Co. v. Canter, 1 Peters 511 (1828), 129, 134–35
Antelope, The, 10 Wheaton 66 (1825), 121, 122
Arguello v. United States, 18 Howard 539 (1855), 109
Ayers, Ex parte, 123 U.S. 443 (1887), 49

Bank of Augusta v. Earle, 13 Peters 519 (1839), 99–100, 111
Bank of Columbia v. Patterson's Administrator, 7 Cranch 299 (1813), 73
Bank of the United States v. Deveaux, 5 Cranch 61, (1809), 74, 111
Barron v. Baltimore, 7 Peters 243 (1833), 84
Bracken v. College of William and Mary, 5 Va. 161 (1797), 76
Briscoe v. Commonwealth Bank of Kentucky, 11 Peters 257 (1837), 100–101
Bronson v. Kinzie, 1 Howard 311 (1843), 110
Brown v. Maryland, 12 Wheaton 419 (1827), 8, 51–52, 54, 62, 83, 102, 103, 107

Calder v. Bull, 3 Dallas 368 (1798), 65
Charles River Bridge v. Warren Bridge, 11 Peters 420 (1837), 57, 95–98, 107, 109–10
Cherokee Nation v. Georgia, 30 U.S. 1 (1831), 1, 6, 82, 85
Chisholm v. Georgia, 2 Dallas 419 (1793), 25, 26
Cohens v. Virginia, 6 Wheaton 264 (1821), 8, 47, 49, 53, 146
Cooley v. Board of Wardens, 12 Howard 299 (1852), 105–7, 115
Craig v. Missouri, 4 Peters 410 (1830), 100–101

Dartmouth College v. Woodward, 4 Wheaton 518 (1819), 8, 73, 75–77, 86–87, 95, 97, 114–15
Dodge v. Woolsey, 18 Howard 311 (1855), 110

Erie R.R. v. Tompkins, 304 U.S. 64 (1938), 112

Fairfax's Devisee v. Hunter's Lessee, 7 Cranch 603 (1813), 37, 66
Fletcher v. Peck, 6 Cranch 87 (1810), 57, 62–66, 69, 87, 109, 110, 114
Fowle v. Common Council of Alexandria, 3 Peters 398 (1830), 73

Genesee Chief v. Fitzhugh, 12 Howard 443 (1851), 112
Gibbons v. Ogden, 9 Wheaton 1 (1824), 21, 49, 53–54, 60, 62, 78, 83, 87, 102,
   103, 106, 107, 115
Gordon v. Appeal Tax Court, 3 Howard 133 (1845), 110
Green v. Biddle, 8 Wheaton 1 (1823), 67–68, 84, 86
Groves v. Slaughter, 15 Peters 449 (1841), 123

Hawkins v. Barney's Lessee, 5 Peters 457 (1831), 84
Head v. Providence Insurance Co., 2 Cranch 127 (1804), 73
Huidekoper's Lessee v. Douglass, 3 Cranch 1 (1805), 68–69
Hylton v. U.S., 3 Dallas 171 (1796), 25

Jones v. Van Zandt, 5 Howard 215 (1849), 127

License Cases, 5 Howard 504 (1847), 103–04, 106, 107, 123
Louisville, Cincinnati, and Charleston Ry. Co. v. Letson, 2 Howard 497 (1844),
   111
Luther v. Borden, 7 Howard 1 (1849), 8, 108, 148

McCulloch v. Maryland, 4 Wheaton 316 (1819), 15, 31, 32, 41–49, 50, 53, 60,
   62, 77, 78, 79–80, 87
Marbury v. Madison, 1 Cranch 137 (1803), 2, 21–22, 28–39, 45
Martin v. Hunter's Lessee, 1 Wheaton 304 (1816), 36–37, 46, 48, 53, 86
Merryman, Ex parte, 17 Fed. Cas. No. 9, 487 at 144 (1861), 144

New Jersey v. Wilson, 7 Cranch 164 (1812), 66, 86, 110
New York v. Miln, 11 Peters 102 (1837), 102, 103, 105, 123

Ogden v. Saunders, 11 Wheaton 213 (1827), 78, 83–84
Ohio Life Insurance & Trust Co. v. Debolt, 16 Howard 416 (1854), 98
Osborn v. Bank of the United States, 9 Wheaton 738 (1824), 48–49, 86

Passenger Cases, 7 Howard 283 (1849), 103, 104–5, 107, 123
Pennsylvania v. Wheeling and Belmont Bridge Co., 13 Howard 518 (1851), 108
Piqua Branch of the State Bank of Ohio v. Knoop, 16 Howard 369, (1853), 110
Planter's Bank v. Sharp, 6 Howard 301 (1848), 114
Prigg v. Pennsylvania, 16 Peters 539 (1842), 120, 124–26, 127
Prize Cases, 2 Black 635 (1863), 144

Providence Bank v. Billings, 4 Peters 514 (1830), 84
Richmond F. & P. Ry. v. Louisa Ry. Co., 13 Howard 71 (1851), 98
Rowan v. Runnels, 5 Howard 134 (1847), 110

Scott, Dred v. Sandford, 19 Howard 393 (1857), 2, 3, 7, 14, 32, 89–90, 91, 108,
    116, 117, 118, 126, 127, 128, 131–42, 143, 148, 150–51
Somerset v. Stewart, Lofft 1, 98 Eng. Rep. 499 (KB 1772), 127
Steamboat Thomas Jefferson, 10 Wheaton 428 (1825), 82–83, 112–13
Strader v. Graham, 10 Howard 82 (1851), 127, 132, 133, 134, 139, 140
Stuart v. Laird, 1 Cranch 299 (1803), 31
Sturges v. Crowninshield, 4 Wheaton 122 (1819), 77–78, 83
Swift v. Tyson, 16 Peters 1 (1842), 111–12

Terrett v. Taylor, 9 Cranch 43 (1815), 67, 73, 74, 75–76

United States v. Arredondo, 6 Peters 691 (1832), 69
United States v. Burr, 25 Fed. Cas. No. 14, 693 at 55 (1807), 34–35, 39
United States v. Clarke, 8 Peters 436 (1834), 69
United States v. Fisher, 2 Cranch 358 (1805), 45
United States v. Le Jeune Eugenie, 26 Fed. Cas. No. 15, 551 at 832 (1822), 122
United States v. New Bedford Bridge, 27 Fed. Cas. No. 15, 867 at 91 (1847),
    107
United States v. Peters, 5 Cranch 115 (1809), 36
United States v. Schooner Amistad, 15 Peters 518 (1841), 121, 123–24

Vallandingham, Ex parte, 1 Wallace 243 (1864), 144
Vanhorne's Lessee v. Dorrance, 2 Dallas 304 (1795), 64

Ware v. Hylton, 3 Dallas 199 (1796), 25
Warren Manufacturing Co. v. Aetna Insurance Co., 29 Fed. Cas. No. 17, 206 at
    294 (1837), 100
Weston v. Charleston, 2 Peters 449 (1829), 45
West River Bridge Co. v. Dix, 6 Howard 507 (1848), 98–99
Willson v. Black Bird Creek Marsh Co., 2 Peters 245, (1829), 83
Wood v. Dummer, 30 Fed. Cas. No. 17, 944 at 435 (1824), 73
Worcester v. Georgia, 6 Peters 515 (1832), 1, 6, 82, 85–86

INDEX

Abolitionism, 104–5, 121–22, 128, 137, 139, 140, 142, 144, 145
Ackerman, Bruce, cited, 10
ACLU. *See* American Civil Liberties Union (ACLU)
Adams, John, 19, 25, 28, 53
Adams, John Quincy, 33, 81, 124, cited, 121
Adams-Onís Treaty (1819), 45, 69
Admiralty and maritime law, 3, 11–12, 36, 82–83, 102, 117, 122
steamboats and, 49–51, 82–83, 108, 112–13
African Americans, 8, 46, 148, 150. *See also* Scott, Dred (Sam); Slavery
Alabama, 99–100
Alien and Sedition Acts, 26, 27
American Business Corporations until 1860 (Dodd), cited, 72
American Civil Liberties Union (ACLU), 7–8
American people, 42, 46, 145, 152
individualism and, 57
representation of, 7–8, 149
Supreme Court's authority and, 2, 6, 10, 15–16, 25, 38, 54, 117
American Revolution, 13, 19, 23, 36–37, 40, 53, 66, 91, 146

Amistad (schooner), 123–24
Articles of Confederation, 13, 23, 46, 61
Attorney General (U.S.), 8, 94

Baldwin, Henry, 82, 93, 123, quoted, 124
Banking, 39, 87, 94, 114
interstate, 99–101
state and federal conflicts, 40–49, 72, 77, 100–101, 110–11, 142
Bank of the United States, 26, 72, 100
First, 42, 43, 72
Second, 8, 41–49, 77, 87, 94, 101
Bankruptcy, 77–78, 83
Bankruptcy Act (1841), 77
Barbour, Philip, 93, 102, 103, 104, 105
"Basic Doctrine of American Constitutional Law, The" (Corwin), 56, 62
Baxter, Maurice, 21, 51
Beard, Charles, cited, 3
Berrien, George, cited, 121
Bestor, Arthur, quoted, 143
Beveridge, Albert, 20, 48, cited, 33
Bickel, Alexander, cited, 3, 6
Biddle, Nicholas, 92, 100, 101
Bill of Rights, 26, 84
Blackstone, William, cited, 57
Blair, John, 24

Blair, Montgomery, 133
Boudin, Louis, cited, 56
Buchanan, James, 131, 133, 137, 139, 140
Burr, Aaron, 34–35, 39
Business corporations. *See* Commerce;
    Corporate law
Businesses. *See* Capitalism

Calhoun, John C., 47
Callender, James, 33
Campbell, John Archibald, 90, 111, 116
Capitalism, 91, 109, 113, 149–50
    corporations and, 70–79
    land cases, 55–69
    Marshall Court and, 55–69, 70–79,
        146, 147
    states' right theorists and, 79–87
    Taney Court and, 94–101, 109, 113,
        116, 142, 148
    See also Commerce; Contract law
Cardozo, Benjamin, 14, cited, 16,
    quoted, 53
Carson, Hampton, quoted, 90
Case-controversy limitation, 7
Casto, William, cited, 24, 25
Catron, John, 93, 104, 111, 116, 131,
    139, 143
Certiorari procedure, 7
Chaffee, Calvin, 136
Charles River Bridge Company, 95–98
Charlestown convention (1860), 138
Chase, Samuel, 26–27, 28, 33–34, 144
Cherokee nation, 1, 6, 82, 85–86
"Chief Justice Taney: Prophet of Reform
    and Reaction" (Harris), 148
Citizenship, 12
    corporate law and, 74, 111–12
    Dred Scott case and, 132–33, 134, 135
Civil liberties, 146
Civil War, 1–2, 23, 137, 142–45, 147,
    150–51
Clay, Henry, 92, 108, 140
Clayton compromise bill (1848), 140–
    41
Clinton, Robert Lowry, 21

Coasting License Act (1793), 49, 51
Coke, Sir Edward, 5
Comity doctrine, 99, 102, 111, 120,
    126–27, 133
Commentaries on the Constitution
    (Story), 53
Commerce, 8, 11, 13
    corporations and, 59, 70–79, 94–101,
        109–14, 149–50
    expansion of, 40, 101–2, 109, 113–14
    federal powers and, 42–44, 49–52,
        54, 60–61, 77, 79, 83, 101–8, 111,
        114, 115, 122–23
    slavery and, 103, 104–5, 120, 123,
        142
    Taney Court and, 113, 117, 142
    See also Capitalism; Corporate law
*Commerce Clause under Marshall,
    Taney, and Waite, The* (Frankfurter),
    57
Common law, 5, 8–9, 12, 30, 38, 82,
    115
    constructive treason and, 35
    contract law and, 96
    corporate law and, 60, 73, 74, 75–76
    federal crimes and, 25
    property and, 62
    slavery and, 122
    stare decisis, 9, 12–13, 113, 117
Common Law (Holmes), 56
Commonwealth Bank of Kentucky, 100
Compromise of 1787, 119–22
Compromise of 1820. *See* Missouri
    Compromise (1820)
Concurrent power doctrine, 77–78, 103,
    106
Confederacy, 145
Congress (U. S.), 24, 60, 81, 105, 152
    constitutional interpretation by, 26,
        39
    constitutional powers of, 9–10, 11,
        15, 42–44, 50–52, 54, 62, 77, 78,
        102–8, 115, 133, 134, 136, 143, 144
    judicial review and, 2–10, 25, 26, 29–
        39, 54, 79, 136, 145

nature of legislation, 11–12
slavery and, 119, 122, 124, 128–30,
131, 133, 134–35, 136, 137, 140–
41, 142
Connecticut, 100, 124
Constitution (U. S.), 24, 36, 37, 108–9,
126–27, 140
Article I, Section 10 (bills of credit),
100–101
Article I, Section 10 (contract
clause), 11, 64–66, 67, 75, 76, 77–
78, 83–84, 95, 96, 97, 110, 114
Article I, Section 2, paragraph 3, 119
Article I, Section 3, 25
Article I, Section 8 (commerce
clause), 42–44, 49–51, 77, 83, 101–
8, 111, 115, 122–23
Article I, Section 9, 119
Article III, 2–3, 4, 9–10, 24, 29
Article III, Section 3 (treason clause),
34–35
Article IV (treaty clause), 3
Article IV, Section 1 (comity clause),
99, 102, 111, 127, 133
Article IV, Section 1, paragraph 3
(fugitive slave clause), 120, 125
Article IV, Section 3 (territorial
governance), 120, 128, 134
Article VI (supremacy clause), 3–5, 41
Bill of Rights, 26, 84
Civil War and, 90, 142–45
Dred Scott decision and, 131–38, 140
economic interest groups and, 58
Eleventh Amendment, 25, 26, 47–49,
63
Fifth Amendment, 84, 135, 136
First Amendment, 26
Fourteenth Amendment, 2, 136
intent of the framers, 13, 43, 55, 64–
65, 76, 119, 141, 146
interpretation of, 11, 26, 38–39, 52, 56
judicial review and, 2, 4, 79–80
limitations of Courts and, 7, 81
as living document, 42–43, 151–52
Marshal's view of, 54

nationalism and, 23–24, 41–44,
47–48
slavery and, 119–20, 121, 122–23,
125, 126, 127, 129–30, 134
Supreme Court authority and, 2, 4,
15–16, 30–31, 151–52
Tenth Amendment, 11, 43, 102
Thirteenth Amendment, 2
Constitutional Convention, 2–3, 4, 5, 7,
13, 24, 43, 64–65
contract clause and, 64, 65, 68
Constitutionalism, 4–5, 15, 23, 30–31,
42–43, 151–52
capitalism and, 57, 79, 149–50
Civil War and, 145
nationalism and, 38, 41–44, 53–54,
78, 104, 114–15, 117
slavery and, 141–42
Constitutional Problems Under Lincoln
(Randall), 145
"Constitutional Revolution of 1837 and
the Myth of Marshall's Monolith,
The" (Garvey), 86
*Construction Construed and Constitu-
tion Vindicated* (Taylor), 47
Continental Congress, 36
Contract Clause of the Constitution
(Wright), 57, 64
Contract clause, 11, 25, 107–8, 149
bankruptcy and, 77–78, 83–84
corporations and, 72, 75–76, 83–84,
95–98, 109, 111, 114
nationalism and, 62
public grants and, 64–70
Taney Court and, 110, 114
Corporate law, 149
Marshall Court and, 60, 70–79, 84
Taney Court and, 94–101, 109–11,
113, 114, 116, 117, 142
See also Capitalism; Commerce
Corwin, Edward, cited, 2, 31–32, 33, 56,
90, quoted, 62
Criminal law, 25, 65
Crosskey, William, 2
Currie, David P., 22, cited, 20, 93, 110

Curtis, Benjamin Robbins, 93, 106–7, 135–36, 139, 140, 147
Cushing, William, 27
Cutler, Manasseh, 69

Dane, Nathan, quoted, 54
Daniel, Peter, 90, 93, 98, 109
    slavery and, 125
    on states' authority, 104, 105, 106, 107, 108, 111, 116
Debtor relief laws, 110
Delaware, 83
Delaware Indians, 66
Democracy, 91, 114
    capitalism and, 60–61, 62–66, 114
    corporate threat to, 71, 99, 148
    judicial authority and, 2
    judicial review and, 5
    lawyers and, 8
    Marshall Court and, 19–20, 42, 50, 80, 84
    nationalism and, 19, 42, 91
    state government and, 60–61
    Taney Court and, 89–117, 149, 150
Democratic party, 130–31, 133, 137–38, 141, 142
Democratic Republican Party, 19, 25, 27–39
Department of Justice (U.S.), 8
Depression of 1819, 79
Depression of 1837, 110
Diversity of citizenship doctrine. See Citizenship
Documentary History of the Supreme Court, 1789–1800 (Marcus), 18–19
Dodd, E. M., cited, 72
Dorr Rebellion, 8, 108, 148
Douglas, Stephen A., 130–31, 137–38, 140
Dred Scott Case (Fehrenbacher), 138
"Dred Scott's Case—Reconsidered" (Mendelson), 140
Due process, 135, 150
Dutton, Warren, 95
Duvall, Gabriel, 67, 93

Economics. See Capitalism; Commerce; Contract law
Election of 1800, 26, 27, 34, 35
Election of 1828, 81, 91
Election of 1856, 140
Election of 1860, 143
Electoral reforms, 91
Eleventh Amendment, 25, 26, 47, 63
Ellis, Richard, cited, 35
Ellsworth, Oliver, 26, 27
Ellsworth Court, 24, 25, 46
Emancipation Proclamation, 142
Embargo of 1807, 36
Emerson, John, 131–32
Eminent domain doctrine, 72, 98–99
Exclusivism, 102, 103–4, 106–7, 115, 125
Executive powers. See President (U.S.)
Expansionism, 24, 40, 85, 120, 121, 127–31, 134–35, 136
    slavery and, 127–28

Farber, Daniel, cited, 142
Faulkner, Robert K., cited, 35
Federal courts, 6–15, 24–25, 28–29, 36, 77
    corporate cases and, 72–73, 74–75, 100, 111–12
    Dred Scott and, 132–33, 136
    establishment of, 26
    hierarchy of, 3
    jurisdiction of, 3, 27
    land cases in, 63–64, 69
    See also Ellsworth Court; Jay Court; Marshall Court; New Deal Court; Supreme Court (U.S.); Taney Court; Waite Court
Federalism, 13, 148
    economics and, 60–66
    Marshall Court and, 23, 25, 35–37, 42, 46–48, 79–87
    property cases and, 67
    Taney Court and, 92, 94, 115–16
Federalist (Hamilton, Madison, Jay), 5–6, 13, 15, 30, 46, 65

Federalists, 27–28, 34, 35, 40
    states' rights and, 19, 106
    Supreme Court and, 25
Federal law, 3–4, 11–12, 114–15
    corporate suits in, 111, 112
    Courts and, 59–60
    states' interpretation of, 36
Fehrenbacher, Don, 119, 138, cited,
    140, quoted, 126
Field, Roswell, 132
Fifth Amendment, 84, 135, 136
Finkelman, Paul, cited, 126
First Amendment, 26
Fletcher, Robert, 63–66
Florida, 69, 135
Formative Era of American Law, The
    (Pound), 72
Fourteenth Amendment, 2, 136
Frank, John P., cited, 90
Frankfurter, Felix, cited, 7, 9, 16, 42, 57,
    90, 101, quoted, 16, 116
Free enterprise, 61, 71, 73, 79, 113–14,
    149, 150
Fremont, John C., 69
Fries, John, 33
Fugitive Slave Act (1793), 104, 125,
    126, 127
Fugitive Slave Act (1850), 126, 139
Fulton-Livingston steamboat interest,
    49–50

Garrison, William Lloyd, 125–26
Garvey, Gerald, cited, 86
Georgia, 62–66, 85–86
Ghent, Treaty of, 18
Gibbons, Thomas, 49
Gibson, John Bannister, 73
Goebel, Julius, Jr., cited, 24
Government by the Judiciary (Boudin), 56
Greeley, Horace, quoted, 137
Greenleaf, Simon, 110
Grier, Robert, 104, 131, 139, 143

Habeas corpus, writ of, 142, 144
Haines, Charles Grove, cited, 90

Hall's Law Journal, 36
Hamilton, Alexander, 19, 53, 111, cited,
    30, 64, quoted, 5–6, 19
    implied powers and, 26, 42, 43, 45,
    46, 47
    national bank and, 26, 43
Handlin, Mary, cited, 78
Handlin, Oscar, cited, 78
Harris, Robert J., cited, 148
Hartz, Louis, cited, 58, 78
History of the Supreme Court (Myers),
    56
Hobson, Charles, 21, cited, 60
Holland Land Company, 68–69
Holmes, Oliver Wendell, cited, 16,
    quoted, 11, 17, 21, 22, 56
Huebner, Timothy S., cited, 147
Hughes, Charles Evans, 152, cited, 14,
    quoted, 1, 146
Hurst, Willard, cited, 10, 57, 149

Illinois, 131, 133, 134
Immigration, 102–3, 104–5, 122–23
Imperfect Union: Slavery, Federalism
    and Comity (Finkelman),126
Implied powers doctrine, 37, 42–44, 45,
    50, 52, 53, 78, 87
    corporate law and, 80, 96, 97, 108,
    109
    Marshall Court and, 26
    Taney Court and, 115
Incorporation, 42–44
Individualism, 91, 121
    capitalism and, 57, 58, 70, 71, 72, 74,
    149
    Civil War and, 143
Interest groups, 8
    capitalism and, 55, 56, 57, 58–59,
    60–62, 150
    states and, 60–61, 63, 77, 78, 80, 99,
    100, 114
Internal improvements, 40, 77, 114, 142
International law, 25, 124
Interstate commerce. See Commerce
Iredell, James, 26

Jackson, Andrew, 81, 82, 94
  Cherokee cases and, 1, 6, 85, 86
  Taney Court and, 92–94
Jackson, Robert, cited, 7
Jacksonianism, 91–93, 94, 95, 99–100,
  108, 114, 142, 148. *See also* states'
  rights
Jay, John, 2, 19, 27, quoted, 1, 38
Jay Court, 19, 24, 25, 46
Jefferson, Thomas, 81, quoted, 80
  Burr case and, 34, 39
  capitalism and, 55
  on Congressional powers, 43
  Marbury case and, 29, 30
  Marshall and, 24
  nationalism and, 39, 47
  Supreme Court and, 6, 19, 25, 26, 27,
    33–36, 37, 48, 68, 79–87
Jeffersonian Crisis (Ellis), 35
John Marshall (Thayer), 20, 21
*John Marshall and the Heroic Age of the
  Supreme Court* (Newmyer), 57
Johnson, Herbert, 21
Johnson, Reverdy, 139
Johnson, William, 36, 49, 53
  Jefferson and, 80, 82, 83
  property cases and, 65–66, 67, 68
  slavery cases, 123
Jones, Howard, cited, 124
Journal of the Convention, 13
"Judicial Behavior and the Sectional
  Crisis" (Schmidhauser), 141–42
Judicial opinions, 17, 28, 53, 80
  character of in Taney Court, 107
  function of, 14–15
  See also specific cases
Judicial Repeal Act (1802), 28, 31
Judicial review, 2–10, 25, 26, 30–39, 54,
  79, 136, 145
Judiciary Act (1789), 24, 26, 37
  corporate law and, 74
  Section 25, 4, 47–48, 81, 143
  Section 34, 112
Judiciary Act (1801), 27, 28, 29–32

Judiciary Act (1925), 7
Jurisdiction, 3, 4, 7, 10–12, 24–25, 27,
  28–33, 144
  appellate, 37, 48, 80–81
  Cohens case and, 47–48
  Congressional powers over, 10
  corporation cases and, 72, 73, 74,
    111–12, 117
  inland water disputes, 82, 113
  Marbury case and, 29, 30, 32
  Martin case and, 37
  political questions and, 108
  slavery cases and, 127, 132–33,
    134
  state politics and, 64
Justice Accused (Cover), 127
Justice Joseph Story (Newmyer), 22
Justices, 13–14, 16–17
  appointment process, 87
  factionalism of, 81–82, 103, 113,
    116, 117, 136, 141–42, 147
  impeachment, 9, 28, 33
  intent of the framers, 119, 141, 146
  interpretation of framers' intent, 13–
    14, 43, 55, 56, 64–65, 76
  justices of the peace appointments,
    28–33
  life tenure, 2, 80
  number of, 92–94
  requirements, 16–17, 26–27, 93
  sectionalism of, 36, 82–87
  stare decisis, 9, 12–13, 113, 115, 117
  style of opinions, 14
  unity of, 27–28, 78, 80, 81–82, 93–94
  See also specific justice
"Justices of the Supreme Court: A
  Collective Portrait, The"
  (Schmidhauser), 59
Justice William Johnson (Morgan), 22

Kansas-Nebraska Act (1854), 130, 131,
  135, 141
Kansas territory, 128, 130–31, 133, 136
Kent, James, 37, 73, 109, cited, 57–58

Kentucky, 38, 67–68, 86, 100–101, 127
Kentucky Resolution (1798), 26, 38, 45, 80
Klarman, Michael, cited, 87
Kutler, Stanley, 57, cited, 95, 97

Law, 22
  enforcement of, 9, 24–25, 36, 49, 66, 68, 86–87, 123
  hierarchical concept of, 9–10, 13, 24–25, 41, 44–45, 49, 51, 54–55, 102, 104, 106–7, 123
  society's impact on, 22–23, 40–41, 42–43, 44–45, 56, 57–58, 70–72, 79, 90–92, 101–2, 104–5, 106–7, 113–14, 117, 121, 124, 144, 145, 149–50, 151
  Supreme Court's legislation/ interpretation of, 9, 10–15, 21–22, 24–25, 28, 54–55, 58, 59–60, 70, 86–87, 96–97, 101–2, 103, 107–8, 112–14, 144, 145, 149–50
  See also Judicial review
Law and Social Process in United States History (Hurst), 149
Law and the Conditions of Freedom in the Nineteenth-Century United States (Hurst), 10, 57
Lawrence, Alexander A., cited, 90
Lawyers, 7–8, 52–53, 59, 79, 95, 109
Least Dangerous Branch, The (Bickel), 3, 6
Lee, Charles, 32
Legal Tender Act, 144
Lerner, Max, cited, 57
Liberal Tradition in America (Hartz), 58
Lieber, Francis, cited, 58
Life of John Marshall, The (Beveridge), 20
Limited national government doctrine, 31
Lincoln, Abraham, 137, 140, 142, 143–45
Lincoln's Constitution (Farber), 142
Livingston, Henry Brockholst, 36, 81

Locke, John, 62, cited, 57
Louisiana Purchase, 39, 69, 128, 130, 131, 134, 135

McClellan, James, cited, 90
McKinley, John, 93, 99
McLaughlin, Andrew, cited, 20
McLean, John, 82, 90, 93, 101, 104, 106, 107, 135, 140
  slavery and, 123
Madison, James, 26, 28–29, cited, 13, 15, 57, quoted, 40, 53, 65
  on slavery, quoted, 119
  Supreme Court and, 36
Magliocca, Gerald N., cited, 86
Magrath, C. Peter, cited, 57, 62, 63
Magruder, Allan, 20
Maine, Sir Henry, quoted, 149
Mann, Bruce, quoted, 77
Mansfield, Lord, 127
Marbury, William, 28 30
Marcus, Maeva, cited, 18–19
Maritime cases. See Admiralty and maritime law
Market Revolution (Sellers), 57
Marshall, John, 9, 31–32, 39, 40, 64–65, 82, cited, 58, quoted, 18, 53, 123, 146
  appointment of, 19, 26
  contract law and, 84
  corporate law and, 73–75, 76, 77–78, 79, 111
  currency issues and, 100–101
  framers' intent and, 13
  implied powers doctrine and, 42 44, 53
  Jefferson and, 19, 24, 29–39
  judicial review and, 2, 29–33
  legacy of, 14, 17, 108–13, 147
  myth of, 19–22, 147
  nationalism and, 18–54, 79–84
  property cases and, 63–65, 69, 83–84
  reforms of, 17, 27–28
  slavery and, 134–35
Marshall Court, 18, 21–22, 145

capitalism and, 54–87, 101
corporate law and, 114
internal procedures of, 27–28
judicial authority and, 25–26
legacy of, 146–47, 149–52
members of, 36–37, 81–82
nationalism and, 19, 22–54, 60, 78, 93, 114
slavery and, 122–23
stare decisis and, 9
Taney Court and, 108–17
unity of, 78, 80, 81–82, 94
See also Marshall, John
Marshall Court, The (White), 51
Martin, Luther, 34
Maryland, 15, 31, 32, 41–49, 50, 53, 60, 62, 77, 100, 124–25, 144
Massachusetts, 103, 104
Massachusetts Anti-Slavery Society, 126
Mendelson, Wallace, cited, 140
Mercantilism, 40–47, 58, 74, 78, 91, 94, 100, 114
state vs. national, 60–62
Mexican War, 129
Mexico, 69, 129
Mississippi, 123
Missouri, 46, 128, 131–33
Missouri Compromise (1820), 128–29, 130–32, 133, 134, 135, 136, 139, 141
Missouri Debates, 46, 79, 92, 121
Monopoly, 49, 53–54, 95–98, 109
Monroe, James, 37
Moore, Alfred, 27
Morgan, Donald, 22, cited, 53, 82
Morgan, Margaret, 124–25
Morris, Robert, 69
Murray, William Vans, quoted, 5
Mutiny on the Amistad (Jones), 124
Myers, Gustavus, cited, 56

National Association for the Advancement of Colored People (NAACP), 7–8

Nationalism, 13, 35–36, 78, 79, 106
capitalism and, 59–62, 114–15, 146–47, 149
Civil War and, 145
contract clause cases and, 83–84
federal power and, 19–54, 84–85, 93, 104, 106
individualism and, 81
judicial power and, 22–39, 81
Marshall Court and, 18–54, 87, 147
Taney Court and, 106, 114, 116, 148
National Republican Party, 53. See also Republicanism
National supremacy, 41–44, 47–50, 53–54
Natural law, 25, 56, 75, 115, 117
Natural rights doctrine, 62, 67
Nebraska, 130
Nedelsky, Jennifer J., cited, 23, 57
Nelson, Samuel, 104, 133, 139
New Deal Court, 57, 151
New England Mississippi Company, 63–66
New Hampshire, 75–77, 103
New Jersey, 66, 86, 110
New Mexico, 130, 140
Newmyer, R. Kent, 21, 22, 57, cited, 35, 90
New York, 49, 77, 83, 102–3, 104, 111–12, 123
New York Courier, 111
North, the, 23–24, 39, 40, 79–80
commerce and, 104–5
constitutional concessions to, 119–22
Dred Scott decision and, 137, 139
economy of, 121
fugitive slaves and, 125–26
mercantilism of, 40
nationalism and, 46
slavery and, 104–5, 119, 122, 124, 125–26, 127, 128, 129–30, 134, 136
state-based reform, 92, 101–2
Supreme Court and, 58–59, 81
Taney Court and, 93, 143

North American Review, 20, 60, 82–83
Northwest Ordinance (1787), 127, 128
Notes of the Debates (Madison), 13, 119
Nullification theory, 47

Obiter dicta, 37, 38, 85, 132
Ohio, 48–49, 86, 110
Oliver Wendell Holmes Devise History of the Supreme Court, The, 21, 91
Original Meanings (Rakove), 13
Original package rule, 52, 103, 104
"Origin and Scope of the American Doctrine of Constitutional Law, The" (Thayer), 56

Panic of 1819, 46, 79, 91–92, 121
Papers of John Marshall, The, 21
Paterson, William, 26, 54
Peck, John, 63–66
Pennsylvania, 24, 36, 38, 68, 105–7, 124–25. *See also* Constitutional Convention
People of the United States. *See* American people
Peters, Richard, 82, 93, 110
Philadelphia Convention. *See* Constitutional Convention
Pickering, John, 33
Pickering, Timothy, quoted, 81
Pierce, Franklin, 137, 140
Pinkney, William, 46, 52, quoted, 41
Police powers, 102–3, 104, 105, 115, 123
Popular sovereignty, 25, 38, 42, 46, 54, 130–31, 137, 141, 150
Pound, Roscoe, quoted, 72
Powell, Thomas Reed, quoted, 16
President (U.S.), 152
    Civil War and, 142, 143–44
    constitutional interpretation by, 39
    removal power of, 26
    slavery and, 128, 139
    Supreme Court and, 1, 6, 9, 10, 24–25, 35, 39

See also specific president
Prigg, Edward, 124–25
Private Property and the Limits of American Constitutionalism (Nedelsky), 57
Prize Cases, 144
Process Acts (1790s), 24
Property, 13, 23, 149, 150
    Civil War and, 143
    of corporations, 73–75, 109, 114
    eminent domain and, 98–99
    slaves as, 103, 122, 135
    state powers and, 57–69, 78, 83–84, 85–86, 96
    Taney Court and, 109, 142
Provincialism, 23

Racism, 90, 121, 126, 128
Radicalism, 23, 33, 99, 150, 151
Radicalism of the American Revolution (Wood), 23
Rakove, Jack, cited, 13
Randall, J. H., quoted, 145
Randolph, John, 80
Reconstruction, 145
Republicanism, 19, 22, 40
    judicial review and, 5
    Supreme Court and, 25–39, 79–87
Republican party, 131, 136, 137, 142, 143, 145
Republic of Debtors (Mann), 77
Reservation clause, 76–77, 86–87
Rhode Island, 103
Rhodes, Elisha Hunt, cited, 90
Richardson (judge in Dartmouth College case), 75
Richmond Enquirer, 47, 89, 115
Roane, Spencer, 47, 53, 80
Roger B. Taney (Swisher), 57
Role of the Supreme Court in American Government and Politics, 1835–1864 (Haines and Sherwood), cited, 90
Roosevelt, Theodore, 15
Roper, Donald, 22, cited, 78

Saltonstall, Nathaniel, 34
Sanford, John, 132–33
Saunders, Robert, cited, 90
Schmidhauser, John R., cited, 58, 141–42
Schouler, James, cited, 90
Scott, Dred (Sam), 7, 8, 118, 131–34, 136, 139
Secession, 34, 47, 143, 145
Sectionalism, 18, 40, 58–59, 79, 124, 147
  capitalism and, 59
  commerce and, 104–5
  economic stress and, 92
  slavery and, 120–22, 127
  Taney Court and, 141–42
Selective exclusiveness doctrine, 115
Self-determination, 130–31
Sellers, Charles G., cited, 57
Senate (U. S.), 9–10, 80–81, 128
Separation of powers, 15, 23, 26, 142, 148
Seward, William, 137
Shaw, Lemuel, 73
Sherwood, Foster H., cited, 90
Slavery, 42, 46, 79, 103, 117, 124
  antislavery movement, 104–05, 121–22, 128, 137, 139, 140, 142, 144, 145
  Civil War and, 142
  Constitution and, 119–20, 127
  Dred Scott decision and, 2, 3, 7, 14, 32, 89–90, 91, 108, 116, 117, 118–19, 126, 127, 128, 131–42, 143, 148, 150–51
  fugitive slaves, 123–27
  interstate commerce and, 102, 104, 123
  states' rights and, 116
  Supreme Court and, 122–23
  Taney Court and, 94, 148, 151
  in territories, 127–31
Smith, Jean Edward, 21
Snowiss, Sylvia, 21, cited, 60

Sosin, Jack, cited, 5
South, the, 23–24, 45
  agrarianism of, 40, 116
  capitalism and, 79
  commerce and, 101–2, 104–5
  constitutional concessions to, 119–22
  Dred Scott decision and, 137
  justices from, 93
  nationalism and, 46–48
  secession of, 143, 145
  slavery and, 104–5, 119, 120–21, 123, 124, 125, 126, 127–28, 129–30
  Supreme Court and, 58–59, 62, 79–80
Stare decisis, 9, 12–13, 113, 115, 117
State courts, 4, 5, 111, 112, 132
  Congressional power and, 41–52
  contract clause law and, 75, 110
  corporate cases and, 72, 73, 77, 111–12
  judicial review and, 4, 36–38, 39, 61–62, 114
  land titles and, 63
States, 75, 107, 148
  capitalism and, 60–61
  Civil War and, 143
  commerce and, 49–52, 83, 101–8, 114–15
  constitutional conventions, 110
  constitutional powers of, 11, 103, 104
  contract obligation and, 11, 62, 64–68, 77–78
  corporate law and, 60–61, 72, 75–77, 94–100
  doctrine of comity and, 99–100
  judicial review and, 24, 25, 26
  legislatures of, 61–62, 72, 80, 97
  police powers, 102–3, 104, 115, 123
  property and, 85–86, 98–99
  slavery and, 42, 119
  sovereignty limitations, 9, 25, 41–47, 60, 62–66, 75–76, 78, 86–87, 98–100, 146
  statutes of, 3–4, 77, 103

suits against, 25
Supreme Court's view of, 36, 77,
    107, 114, 148
taxation and, 44–45, 62, 66, 77, 84,
    110
States' rights, 13, 20, 35–36, 79, 86–87
commerce and, 41–52, 59, 60–61,
    106–7, 112–13
contract clause law and, 67–68
limitation of, 36–37
slavery and, 119–20
Supreme Court and, 25, 80, 82
Taney and, 94, 97, 107–8, 110, 115–
    16, 135, 148
Wilmot Proviso and, 135
See also Jacksonianism
Steamboat Monopoly, The (Baxter), 51
Story, Joseph, 12, 19, 20, 53, 60, 67, 79,
    81, 82, 110, cited, 58, quoted, 41, 89,
    99, 115
commerce and, 112–13, 115
corporate law and, 73, 74–75, 76,
    111–12
property cases and, 37, 45–46, 66, 84,
    86
slavery and, 122, 124, 125, 126
Taney Court and, 90, 93, 96, 101,
    103, 109, 147
Suffrage, 91
Sumner, Charles, 110
Supreme Court (U.S.), 1–2, 17, 24, 39,
    92–94
authority of, 2–6, 22–39, 47–49, 54,
    55, 60
capitalism and, 55–87
Civil War and, 1–2, 142–45
commerce and, 101–8
corporate law and, 60, 70–79
Dred Scott decision and, 131–42
formative years, 1–6, 23–27
functions of, 10–16
internal procedures of, 27–28, 117
judicial review, 2–10, 25, 26, 30–39,
    54, 79–80, 136, 145

jurisdiction of, 3, 4, 7, 10–12, 24, 47–
    48, 72, 74, 111
legacy of, 108–17, 138, 146–52
limitations, 1–2, 6–10, 12
majority ruling, 68
mercantilism and, 40–47, 58, 60–62,
    74
nationalism and, 18–54, 78, 81, 82–
    83, 87, 93
property and, 62–66
slavery and, 122–30, 133–38
states' sovereignty and, 41–47
unity of, 81–82, 93–94
See also Ellsworth Court; Jay Court;
    Jurisdiction; Justices; Marshall
    Court; New Deal Court; Taney
    Court; Waite Court
"Supreme Court and American
    Capitalism, The" (Lerner), 57
Supreme Court in United States History,
    The (Warren), 20, 56, 90
Supreme Court of the United States, The
    (Carson), 90
Swisher, Carl, cited, 57, 90, quoted, 116

Talmadge amendment, 46
Taney, Roger Brooke, 17, 84, 85, 87, 90,
    94, 143, quoted, 107–8
accomplishments of, 91–92, 107,
    116–17
appointment of, 93
Civil War and, 144
commerce and, 103, 109–10, 113
contract law and, 110–11
legacy of, 89, 118–19, 147–49
slavery and, 127, 132
Taney Court, 85, 87, 102–5, 152
capitalism and, 94–101
Civil War and, 1–2, 142–45
commerce clause and, 101–8, 142
contract clause and, 95–98
corporate law and, 94–101, 142
Dred Scott decision and, 125, 133–
    42, 148

eminent domain and, 98–99
factionalism and, 93–94, 113, 116,
  117, 136, 141–42, 147–48
historical view of, 89–90, 138, 146,
  147–52
internal procedures and, 117
Marshall Court doctrine and, 107–17
political climate and, 91–92
property titles and, 68
Reconstruction and, 145
scholarship on, 89–91
slavery and, 118–19, 122–29, 133–
  38, 142
stare decisis and, 9
*Taney Court: Justices, Rulings, and
  Legacy, The* (Huebner), 147
Taney Period, The (Swisher), 90–91
Tariffs. *See* Federalism
Tax immunity doctrine, 45
Taylor, John, 47, 55, 80, 84
"Tenants of the Log Cabin" (Gates), 68,
  cited, 68
Tenth Amendment, 11, 43, 102
Territories, 120, 127–31, 134–35, 136
Texas, 129
Thayer, James Bradley, 20, 21, cited, 56
Thirteenth Amendment, 2
Thompson, Smith, 52, 81, 93, 96–97,
  100, 123, 125
Tocqueville, Alexis de, 55, cited, 70, 71,
  150, quoted, 10, 55, 118
Todd, Thomas, 36, 81
Treason, 33, 34–35
Treaties, 3, 18, 26, 85–86
  of 1783, 25
  of 1794, 37, 66
  Adams-Onís, 45, 69
  of Ghent, 18
Trimble, Robert, 81–82

"Unanimity of the Marshall Court"
  (Roper), 78
Union. *See* Federalism; Nationalism

*United States Magazine and Democratic
  Review,* 37, 84
Utah, 130, 140

Van Buren, Martin, 93
Vermont, 99
Vested rights doctrine, 62, 64–66, 75
Virginia, 37, 38, 47–48, 79
  land cases, 36, 66–68
  property cases, 67
Virginia Resolution (1798), 45, 80
Von Holst, Hermann, cited, 90

Waite Court, 55
War of 1812, 23, 36, 39, 52, 61, 91
Warren, Charles, 20, cited, 56, 90
Washington (ship), 124
Washington, Bushrod, 27, 67, 76, 82
Washington, George, 9, 24, 25, 53, 69
Wayne, James Moore, 90, 93, 105, 106,
  107, 143
Webster, Daniel, 109, 115, 140, quoted,
  60, 104, 116
  Marshall Court and, 52, 69, 79, 106
  Taney Court and, 92, 96, 99, 100,
  106, 109, 140
Weisenburger, Francis, cited, 90
Welfare legislation, 103
West, the, 92, 121
  justices from, 93
  slavery and, 128, 129–30, 134
  Supreme Court and, 48, 58–59, 62
Whig party, 92, 93, 95, 99
White, G. Edward, 22, 51
Wiecek, William, cited, 121
Wilmot, David, 129
Wilmot Proviso (1846), 129, 135
Wilson, James, 24, 26, 61, 69
Wirt, William, 8, 52, 85
Wolfe, Christopher, cited, 145
Wood, Gordon, cited, 23
Woodbury, Levi, 104, 106, 107, cited,
  127, quoted, 114

Wright, Benjamin, cited, 57, 64, 90

Yates, Robert, cited, 13
Yazoo land grants, 62–66

The Supreme Court under Marhshall and Taney, Second Edition
Developmental editor: Andrew J. Davidson
Copy editor: Elizabeth Demers
Production editor: Lucy Herz
Proofreader: Claudia Siler
Indexer: Pat Rimmer
Printer: Versa Press, Inc.